WALKING IN DORSET

Path across the top of Lewesdon Hill (Walk 33)

WALKING IN DORSET

by
James Roberts

CICERONE PRESS
MILNTHORPE, CUMBRIA

*In affectionate memory of
Alice ("Caencame Hannah") -
the best of an excellent breed and a sparkling companion
over so many miles. Her death just as this book was started
was a very great loss.*

Acknowledgements

My thanks are due to my mother, Jane Roberts of Milborne Port, for her help, enabling me to research and write this book; also to my aunt, Ann Roberts of Puncknowle, near Abbotsbury. I owe a particular debt of thanks to Mark Fish and especially to Mike Grattan, without whom this book would never have reached the publishers. Thanks are owed again to Kev Reynolds and to Walt Unsworth. I am much indebted to Emma Fryer, for her wizardry in arranging matters during my frequent and lengthy sojourns in the Carpathians and the Himalaya. I would like to thank Rod Webb, Phil Drake, and all members of the Rights of Way section at County Hall in Dorchester. Not only have they been extremely helpful with the research for this book, but they are evidently doing an excellent job in caring for the county's footpaths and bridleways. Author and readers alike owe thanks to all who have been and are involved in the waymarking and maintenance of footpaths and bridleways in the county. Thanks are due to Gerald Pitman for his generous help; could anyone know more about the history of a given area than he? I owe a great debt of thanks to the Green family of Berry Farm at Kings Stag near Sturminster Newton. I would like to pay tribute to the unsung excellence of Britain's librarians - if only one were to find such dedication and thoroughness in every profession. Most of all I owe thanks to my wife Elena, for being a source of inspiration and for her help, understanding and support, without which none of my books would have got further than the planning stage.

By the same author
The Reivers Way
The Two Moors Way

Front cover: Corfe Castle from East Hill

CONTENTS

ADVICE TO READERS

Readers are advised that whilst every effort is taken by the author to ensure the accuracy of this guidebook, changes can occur which may affect the contents. A book of this nature with detailed descriptions and detailed maps is more prone to change than a more general guide. New fences and stiles appear, waymarking alters, there may be new buildings or eradication of old buildings. It is advisable to check locally on transport, accommodation, shops etc. Even rights of way can be altered, paths can be eradicated by landslip, forest clearances or changes of ownership. The publisher would welcome notes of any such changes.

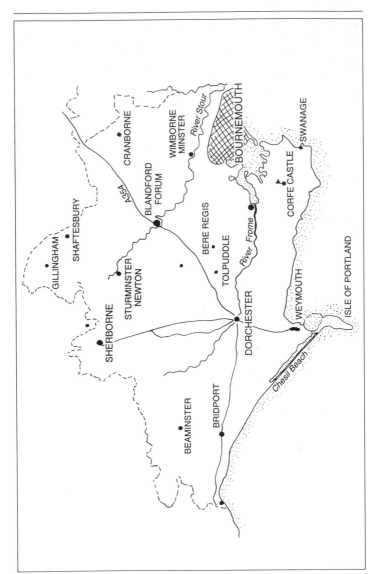

Notice threatening transportation to penal colonies in Australia on
Benville Bridge near Evershot. Such plaques can be found on a
number of bridges, the best known one over the Stour at
Sturminster Newton

CHAPTER ONE
Introduction to Walking in Dorset

So I am found on Ingpen Beacon or Wylls-Neck to the West
Or else on homely Bulbarrow, or Little Pilsdon Crest,
Where men have never cared to haunt, nor women have walked
with me,
And ghosts then keep their distance; and I know some liberty.

Thomas Hardy, *Wessex Heights* (1896)

There are some 3000 miles of public rights of way within the county boundaries of Dorset; I exclude, of course, roads, tarred or otherwise. To parcel these up into attractive and interesting walks has been at once both a challenge and an inspiration - it has been a labour of love.

Perhaps nowhere else offers the same combination of intensely varied and alluring landscapes, the same rich historical, and above all, literary connections as does the county of Dorset. It is walkers' country *par excellence*. Happily the inhabitants and local authorities encourage those whose delight it is to wander the footpaths. I do not know who in the county council originally came up with the idea of painting a grid reference on rural signposts, but it was an excellent one. This time-honoured benevolence from the county council has now been extended to footpath waymarking. Praise is due to those responsible for their admirable work. Many more miles have been covered in research than are described in this book. I can honestly say that I have never found a footpath to have been deliberately blocked. Almost everywhere farmers seem to go out of the way to point out the path across their land.

How to use this book

The key to the enjoyment of Dorset's charms is the Ordnance Survey's mapping. Before you set forth along the byways of the county learn at least the basics of using an OS map. None of the walks in this book should be attempted without a map. Buy the map, decide which walk or walks you want to do, and, using a highlighter pen, mark in the route on the sheet. There are two reasons why a section of mapping in a guidebook is inadequate for use on a walk. Firstly, covering only a limited area, it is quite possible even for experienced navigators to have a moment of inattention and become, let's not say lost, but at least "navigationally confused". In such a moment it is easy to walk clean off the section of map printed in a book, even if it is a reprint of

OS mapping itself. Secondly, almost every walk in this book includes a viewpoint, even if not all are as grand as Bulbarrow, with its glimpse of both English and Bristol Channels. The section of map for the particular walk cannot tell you what you are seeing from your viewpoint. Above all, navigation can be great fun; more than this, it can be immensely satisfying and, in extreme, an ability to navigate accurately can save your own and others' lives. I have seen what fun map reading can be for those to whom I have taught the rudiments.

There will always be debate as to which scale of map to use. All the research for this book was done with 1:50,000 mapping and any reference to "the map" is to this, not to the 1:25,000. I always walk with a 1:50,000 map because the relief is shown more clearly and it gives you more information about the layout of the landscape around you, rather than focusing your attention on hedge-by-hedge and stile-by-stile detail. However, the 1:25,000 series are quite excellent maps, with the advantage that every field boundary is shown. You may well prefer to use these.

I also recommend you take a compass. As a teenager I affected to scorn those I saw walking with a compass, with such comments as "we'll see them roped up on their way up Pilsdon Pen, next". However do not be misled into thinking that a compass is just for the misty moors and mountains. There are many occasions when you can cross a stile and see no sign of whether the path on the other side goes diagonally across the next field, or sticks to this hedge or that. At such times a Silva compass is invaluable.

I have consciously avoided creating a system of grading these walks as it is my experience that season has as much effect on the difficulty or otherwise of a walk in the county as does the terrain. If a walk does include notable ascents, or a number of them, this is mentioned within the first three sentences of the introduction. The walks are otherwise graded by their length. However I would ask the reader not to let the length of a walk be the overriding factor in deciding which of the walks to do. In many cases short cuts or extensions to the walks I have described suggest themselves and these are described in the text. It is also possible in many cases to combine two or more walks. If the text does not suggest a shortening or lengthening to what you require, take a look at the walk on the map and see if you can adapt the walk to your chosen length. In many cases you will find that it is perfectly possible.

The geology of Dorset

For those that would dismiss this subject as being the concern only of bearded weirdoes with hammers and sample-bags, I would make a plea to try and learn a very little of what lies beneath Dorset's greenery. For it is Dorset's rock that has dictated every aspect of the later development of the landscape.

The vague idea of the nature of Dorset's landscape held by outsiders is an elusive thing - for the simple fact that the landscapes of the county are remarkably varied and almost none of them unique. The largest single landscape type in the county is the chalk plateau. This is a flat layer of rock slightly tilted towards the south-east, which finishes abruptly in a long steep escarpment facing north-west. Thomas Hardy, in his *The Woodlanders*, used the image of the green sea of the Blackmore Vale to the north and west washing up against the chalk escarpment. I rather think he had in mind the view from High Stoy Hill (Walks 11 and 15). The north-west facing chalk escarpment provides some of the finest walking inland in the county, and it is no coincidence that a high proportion of my walks lie along and around it. The easternmost of these is Walk 4 - Compton and the Fontmell Downs. Between Durweston and Stourpaine the River Stour, whose course evidently preceded the uplift of the chalk, breaks through this escarpment. Walk 2 - Hambledon Hill and Hod Hill explores the chalk downs with their steep wooded escarpments and the fine Stour Valley. Geology may suddenly seem to be more relevant when you are clutching at trees, slithering down the steep path towards Shillingstone.

Further west this same chalk escarpment at Okeford Hill and Bell Hill overlooks the Stour Valley walk, exploring the productive Stour Valley below Sturminster Newton. Woolland Hill, the escarpment east of Bulbarrow, is perhaps the most dramatic part of the chalk escarpment and two of the walks explore the chalk uplands here: Milton Abbas and the Downs (Walk 8) and Rawlsbury Camp and Bulbarrow (Walk 14). The Dorset Gap is just that - a gap in the chalk escarpment formerly followed by a number of trackways, now rural rights of way. Two walks explore the chalk ridge here (12 and 13), approaching the lonely Gap from Plush and Ansty. The furthest extremity of the chalk south-west is Eggardon Hill (Walk 37). The gentle dip slope of the chalk to the south-east, gives rise to a number of roughly parallel valleys with convex sides, so that the habitation along the water courses is hidden from you when you are on the downs. This heightens the sense of emptiness in the landscape as you make your way across the downs around Milborne St Andrew (Walk 18) or across Toller Down (Walk 38); chalk landscapes are perhaps the most distinctive and recognisable to the layman of all.

Running parallel with the chalk on its north-western side are long outcrops of greensand and clay. Comparing a geological map with a general-purpose map it becomes obvious that the strip between the chalk and the clay has given rise to the great wealth of Dorset's villages. Perhaps the most important factor in siting settlements for our ancestors was the presence of water. The chalk, which as everyone knows is highly permeable, produced a number of reliable springs where the underlying less permeable greensand reaches the surface. The clay lands themselves were generally worked by villages lying on the greensand above. As you look across Blackmore Vale from Stour Hill above Kington Magna (Walk 17) you can see the villages sited on the outcrop of limestone - most noticeably Stalbridge and Henstridge.

The perfect illustration of the greensand overlying the clay is, of course, around Lyme Regis, including Golden Cap itself (Walk 26, 27, 28, 29). Notable too is the tendency of the sandstone, when capped with a more resistant rock, to give rise to conical hills, a number of which overlook the lower reaches of Marshwood Vale.

The study of the effect of geology on man's use of the landscape is fascinating; space precludes a more profound study here. I strongly recommend a perceptive summary of the geology and its effects in Ralph Wightman's chapter "The Shape of the Land" in his excellent *Portrait of Dorset.*

Dorset's early history

Dorset contains much of England's national early and pre-history within its boundaries; this is a subject which perhaps needs a little clarification for many walkers.

The first evidence of settlement in Dorset is from the Neolithic period, pointing to some 6000 years of man's impact on the landscape of the county. The oldest type of barrow to be found in Dorset is the long barrow, dating from around 2500BC. Perhaps the most remarkable of these is the Grey Mare and her Colts, one of several highlights of Walk 34 - Little Bredy and the Bride Valley. More remarkable perhaps is the Dorset Cursus, a mysterious dyke on the downs running south-west from the village of Pentridge, discovered on Walk 3. There is no connection with Bokerley Ditch nearby, which is dealt with below. In the past there were also long barrows on Hambledon Hill and Maiden Castle, but later Iron Age and Roman occupation removed much evidence of these.

Around 2000BC the Beaker Folk arrived in the south-west of England, and brought with them the Bronze Age. The most remarkable of their remains is Kingston Russell Stone Circle, also passed on Walk 34, an unsung miniature of Avebury or Stonehenge. Not passed by any footpath but in the area of Walk 6 are Knowlton Circles (sheet 195, GR 0210), in the east of the county. There is another stone circle on the top of the spur of Portesham Hill, north-west of the village; an extension of Walk 39 could be made to visit this. Just outside Winterbourne Abbas, on the A35 to the west of Dorchester, is another stone circle from this period. In the town of Dorchester itself is Maumbury Ring.

The other remains of this period are the round barrows of which a great number can be found right across the county. It is very sad that with the ploughing of Dorset's chalk, so many barrows that had lasted for thousands of years have been destroyed in such a short time. I can see no good reason why history and pre-history should be turned into a theme-park subject rather than something that is around us the whole time. So often one hears the specious argument put forward that because there is another example of this or that in the hands of the National Trust or English Heritage, any others may be destroyed.

The first historical records of the inhabitants of what is now Dorset refer to the Celtic tribes of the Belgic group, who settled in the area in the last five centuries before Christ. They spoke a language from which modern Welsh is derived and it was these people whom the Romans encountered in their invasion of the area in AD43 and AD44. At that time the density of human population was the reverse of what it is today in the county - it was denser on the uplands, whilst the forests of the low-lying areas were largely uninhabited. These forests were still post Ice Age climatic climax vegetation, largely of oak and ash with beech more common at higher elevations.

The Celtic tribe inhabiting this area, about which perhaps most can be learnt by walking around the ramparts of one of their hill forts, were called the Durotriges. The county is, of course, particularly rich in the hill forts they built, many of which are covered by the walks in this book. Mention should be made of Hod Hill, Hambledon Hill (Walk 2), Pilsdon Pen (Walk 33), Eggardon Hill (Walk 37), Flowers Barrow above Worbarrow Bay on the Ministry of Defence ranges at Lulworth, Poundbury Camp near Dorchester, Rawlsbury Camp by Bulbarrow (Walk 14), Woodbury near Bere Regis, and notably Cadbury Castle, across the boundary in Somerset (Walk 16).

The Durotriges were organised enough to offer effective resistance to the Roman invasion; the Second Legion, the Augusta (roughly equivalent in strength to a modern division) under the command of Vespasian, fought a number of actions to seize the area. He later became Emperor and set a precedent for military leaders of the Empire who used Britain as a springboard to their bids for the imperial laurels. The Roman army put small permanent detachments of troops on the captured forts of the Durotriges and two remains of these can be visited, on Hod Hill (Walk 2) and Waddon Hill (Walk 32). The result of the Roman occupation was the town of Dorchester (Durnovaria) and a network of famously arrow-straight roads, of which there was an important junction near Badbury Rings. A number of villas show increased use of low-lying areas during this time; there was even an aqueduct along the Frome Valley to Dorchester.

With the collapse of the Roman Empire the inhabitants of Britain were left to retreat before the onslaught of the Anglo-Saxons in the year 410 and following. Bokerley Ditch (Walk 3) was a highly effective defensive earthwork built by the Romanised Celtic population which had a tremendous effect on the English settlement of the area. I cannot recommend too highly a read of Christopher Taylor on this period (*The Making of the English Landscape - Dorset;* see bibliography). In 520 the Celtic leader Arthur won an important battle known as Mons Badonicus, which is generally accepted as being

Badbury Rings, near Kingston Lacy. Thereafter the county was settled by the Anglo-Saxons; examples of our ancestors' ecclesiastical art are to be seen at Melbury Bubb (Walk 36) and Winterbourne Steepleton, as well as Sherborne Abbey and St Martin's church at Wareham.

From this point on, Dorset took its share of great national and international events. There was a Viking landing at Charmouth in 833 and Alfred's navy defeated the Danes off Swanage in 877. Levies from Dorset fought under King Alfred, many links with whom can be found throughout the county. The vacillation of Ethelred Unraed, which to a great extent precipitated the Norman Conquest at his death in 1066, may be attributed to events at Corfe in 978, when his mother murdered his half brother King Edward the Martyr to allow her son to ascend the throne. The great Canute, creator of a Scandinavian-English empire, died at Shaftesbury in 1035. (The accommodation guide to the town, forbearing to mention this, or the fact that with Durham it is England's only hill-top town, or its monastic history, or links with Hardy, proudly boasts "once the scene of a Hovis bread TV advert".) The tower erected in his honour on Kingsettle Hill in Wiltshire overlooks much of the northern part of Dorset. An example of Saxon church architecture which is visited in one of the walks below is the well known font at Melbury Bubb (Walk 36).

The Norman Conquest of 1066 wiped away the pre-eminence of Wessex in England and incidentally caused the name of Wessex itself to fall into complete obscurity, so that Hardy when he revived the term, received letters asking where he had found the name. There are notable Norman churches to be seen still in the county, and not just in the great churches in Christchurch and Wimborne - the priory and the minster respectively. A Norman doorway remains at Sherborne Abbey (Walk 7); a short extension to the same walk takes you to the church of John the Evangelist in Milborne Port, within sight of which this book was written. In the crossing beneath the tower are two very fine Norman arches and pillar capitals. The churches at Worth Matravers (Walk 20) and Powerstock (Walk 37) have fine Norman chancel arches. The most impressive Norman church in the county is at Studland (Walk 22).

The greatest impact of the Normans on the landscape of Dorset was the building of castles; some of these remain as castles (for example Sherborne Old Castle - Walk 7 and Corfe - Walk 21). Others are just mounds marking the site of the former motte and bailey (for example Cranborne - Walk 6 and Powerstock - Walk 37). Dorset is not rich in the early Gothic "pointed arch" style of Early English, but two good examples are visited as part of the walks below. These are the church of the Holy Rood at Buckland Newton (Walk 11) and Whitchurch Canonicorum, with its shrine (Walk 31). The county is rich in churches built in the most developed style of English Gothic - Perpendicular. In particular, mention should be made of Sherborne Abbey's fan vaulting

(Walk 7), the church at Cerne Abbas (Walk 15), the rood screen and bench ends at Trent (Walk 10), and the misericords in Sherborne and Milton Abbeys. It was this same period - the late fourteenth and the fifteenth century - that saw the flourishing of the great monastic houses in England, and particularly in Dorset. As well as the great minsters of the county (for example Milton Abbey - Walk 8) there were the Benedictine Abbeys of Winterborne Came, just outside Dorchester, Abbotsbury (Walk 35), Cerne (Walk 15), and Shaftesbury. There were also three Cistercian Abbeys: Ford, Bindon (now completely ruined) and Tarrant Crawford.

In common with much of the rest of the country, the dissolution of the monasteries under the second monarch in the Tudor dynasty (Henry VIII) coincided with a period of building manor houses, indicating greater stability following the end of the Wars of the Roses. Examples are the now ruined Lulworth Castle, Wolfeton House near Charminster, Athelhampton Hall (near Walk 18), Sherborne Castle (Walk 7), Bingham's Melcombe (Walk 13), Cranborne Manor (Walk 6), Parnham and Strode (Walk 32). The one event that marked England's change of status from that of relative unimportance on the world stage to that of a European power was the defeat of the Spanish Armada in 1588. Spain, with its massive New World Empire, was then the superpower to the extent that the United States is today. Dorset, of course, played a great part in that battle, with ships from Dorset ports taking part in the naval engagement as it moved westwards up the channel, off the coast of the county. Sir Walter Raleigh, one of the most notable figures of the age, made his home in the county, at Sherborne; much of it and its environs has been preserved. As much as the county had flourished under the Tudor dynasty, it suffered under the Stuarts who followed.

Symbolic was the beheading of Raleigh owing to court intrigue in 1618; his estates at Sherborne, where he declared that he had been happiest in his life, passed to one of the new king's "favourites". A little over two decades later the Stuart attempt at Royal Absolutism resulted in the Civil War; there was a great deal of petty damage to churches in the county, which collectively amounted to a great deal. The most noticeable was perhaps at Nether Compton (Walk 10). Sherborne Old Castle and Corfe Castle were destroyed during the conflict. For a very brief period the fate of the country hung in the balance as the future King Charles II hid in the county and made his way across it in disguise, in peril of his life. This was following the Battle of Worcester in 1651; he stayed at Trent (Walk 10) and Broadwindsor (Walk 33) en route to try and flee the country at Lyme. The "what if?" school of history is a fool's game indeed, but certainly history would have followed a very different course had Charles been discovered at this time, as he very nearly was.

The Duke of Monmouth received much support in the county when he landed at Lyme in 1685; those who died in the one-sided Battle of Sedgemoor

15

and as a result of Judge Jeffries' Bloody Assize may be seen as martyrs to the cause of removing the unpopular James II. The tragedy was heightened by the fact that three years later he fled the country during the Glorious Revolution. William of Orange stayed in Sherborne en route to London from his landing at Torbay. The eighteenth century saw a continuation of the forest clearance that had been progressing steadily throughout Dorset's history. In this century the changes in the landscape were particularly marked, with the increase in landscaped parks (in some cases in the medieval deer parks - see Walk 7) and the enclosure movement, which saw a move away from the great fields around the villages. Much of the view from Dorset's hilltops is of hedged fields dating from this time.

Whilst France embroiled itself in its revolution King George III was persuaded to come to Weymouth by his brother the Duke of Gloucester; he continued to visit until 1805 and his presence brought large numbers of visitors. The Napoleonic Wars that followed the French Revolution meant that the nobility were prevented from making their grand tours; Constable had his honeymoon at Osmington (Walk 24) and Jane Austen stayed at Lyme (Walks 29 and 30). Dorset's agriculture, which had always been the pre-eminent concern of its population, began to be joined by what we now call "tourism". As the nineteenth century progressed, the industrial revolution produced an urban population who desired seaside holidays in the summer and the railways provided the means of their getting there. The importance of tourism in the county grew and grew until it reached the enormous scale it has today. Thus the footpaths which were means of communication in the county came to be used as recreation, as they are largely now.

Literary Dorset

Dorset has been the home and inspiration of some of England's most notable writers. By far the most famous both as a poet and author and a man of Dorset is, of course, Thomas Hardy. This book has no pretensions to be a guide to Hardy country. However Thomas Hardy is a unique phenomenon; with Kipling perhaps the last author who drew admiration from academe and vast numbers of ordinary readers alike. His inspiration was the landscape of his native county and the rustic characters he listened to as a child; it is salutary to remember that his Dorset novels were set as far back as the Napoleonic Wars and yet the final revision of his novels was made well into the twentieth century. His characters give the lie to the concept, so beloved of the modern entertainment media, of West Country men of the soil being merely lumpen turnip-heads.

Thomas Hardy was an author of worldwide renown, who knew Dorset intimately and was inspired by it; he should not therefore be ignored by a writer of a guide to walks in the county. Anyone who delights in lengthy walks in Dorset is privileged to have a special window into Hardy's inspiration because, as he makes clear in his novels, walking was then the standard way of moving from village to village and indeed a good deal of Hardy's early exploration of his native county was on foot. Those readers who are Hardy-phobes should simply skip past those passages about him or his work. Numbers of people do, of course, visit the county to discover the locations of his novels. For such people, Hardy's writing is their introduction to the beautiful landscapes of the county. There is no reason, however, if you have not read any Hardy, why the landscape in which he grew up and which to an extent was his inspiration should not be your introduction to his work. Above all, it makes highly enjoyable reading. I would recommend a start with *The Woodlanders* or *Under the Greenwood Tree*.

Large numbers of people involve themselves in the game of identifying this or that farm or village that Hardy wrote about in a particular episode and usually renamed. However, in many cases the actual buildings or hamlets he wrote about have been altered, developed, or indeed visited so much that a great deal of the spirit of place is now lost. A visit, therefore, to a farm or hamlet hidden away, similar in situation to what he wrote about but transferred in location, can take you closer to his work than the actual spot which he adapted. For example, the forests between Dorchester and Sherborne that he evokes so beautifully in *The Woodlanders* have now almost completely disappeared; I believe that the walk through the extensive coppices of Cranborne Chase will take you far closer to the environs of "Little Hintock" than poking around Hermitage. Ideally it should be combined with the Evershot and the Melburys walk. Bear in mind that Hardy was not averse to making subtle alterations to the topography of the county to suit his world of Wessex.

If you want to discover a similar landscape still peopled with peasants of a very comparable culture, who work their very similar land in much the same way still, you should take a walking holiday (I recommend Waymark Holidays) in the hidden world of rural Romania, where the horse and cart is still the principal transport and the scythe the principal tool. Life here goes on at much the same pace as nineteenth century Dorset and at a state of material development little removed; the essential quality of picturesque charm is to be found there too, in equal quantity to Dorset.

There is, of course, much more to Dorset's literary connections than Hardy. T.E.Lawrence scarcely needs introduction. The landscape where he made his home in deliberately created obscurity is not the best in the county. However there are good views across the now wooded lowland drained by the parallel river-courses of the Piddle and the Frome, on the Tolpuddle and the Downs walk (18) and from the top of Chaldon Down (Walk 23). The literary wealth of Lyme Regis is well known - a superb setting for John Fowles' excellent *The French Lieutenant's Woman*. This is only the latest in a history of distinguished literary connections; Jane Austen stayed there and the town to an extent inspired *Persuasion*. In the latter part of the nineteenth century the town was the home of F.T.Palgrave, a poet himself but more famous for his compilation *The Golden Treasury*. County-wide there is a wealth of literary connections waiting to be discovered: Henry Fielding (Walk 17), Alexander Pope (Walk 7), John Keats (Walk 23), the Powys brothers - the list goes on and on. If you do become addicted to hunting these out, I very much recommend Rodney Legg's excellent *Literary Dorset* (see bibliography).

Equipment

If any reader is planning to come to Dorset on a first visit and walk with this book as a guide you should be aware of something that affects all these walks to a greater or lesser extent in almost any season except at times of extreme drought - mud. You had better make up your mind that you like mud before you start. In fact, for many of the walks the route near the start can be the muddiest stretch, as the path takes you from the road, later to convey you along the well drained chalk ridges, ridges which nevertheless contain pockets of wonderfully glutinous clay along their flanks. There is a great variety of mud in the county, reflecting its distillation of much of southern England's geology. In one walk you can move from the cattle-pocked manure-rich and puddled dark brown morass of the lowland pastures to the pasty whitish concoction of the downs, rather like wet marzipan. I have little time for those who moan about mud; it is simply a fact of life in Dorset as well as most of rural Europe away from the Mediterranean. Within living memory mud has in fact become much less of a factor in rural lives. All our ancestors had to contend with the entire rural road system being made of it, and did so without wellington boots or walking boots of rubber soles and hydrobloc uppers. I can see no reason why adults should not enjoy walking in mud as much as small children do.

My experience of growing up in the county and of extensive walking elsewhere is that there are three ways of equipping your feet and legs for the mud. I adopt any of these three, depending on my needs at the time. The first is the best - a high-tech and expensive method: good quality, all-leather walking boots and high gaiters. The apogee of this system is the almost perfect Gore-tex Berghaus Yeti gaiter mated to the Italian Scarpa boot. If you are walking all day in wet mud, foliage, peat or deep snow, camping wild in damp or frost all night and walking on next day and for days to come, then this system will permit you to keep going with dry feet where otherwise you would be forced to stop and dry out feet and boots. If you have to depend on boots and gaiters for doing this, as I have frequently had to, then Scarpa boots and Gore-tex Yeti gaiters are excellent value for money. However the walks here described are day walks, and it is supposed that you will be in shelter at night, be it a room at Plumber Manor or a tent in a field. With the capacity to change your footwear at the end of the walk you may consider that this method of protecting yourself from Dorset's mud is something of a sledgehammer to crack a nut.

The other end of the spectrum of ways to tackle muddy lanes is to wear running shoes. This method is particularly appropriate in summer, although I have worn them through wet mud all through the winter. The key is that you should keep moving in the cold, although in summer months this does not apply. Having wet feet for most of a day does no-one any harm as long as your shoes and socks are a good fit. As long as you dry your feet out in the evening and through the night there is no problem. The advantage of running shoes is that they tend to lace tightly to the foot and therefore resist being sucked off your foot when crossing mud. They also dry easily and suffer no lasting damage from immersion in mud as leather shoes tend to do. Changing into dry shoes and socks when you get back to the car is a delightful sensation. Running shoes generally, of course, are light and comfortable to walk in and minimise fatigue, on soft or smooth ground at least. Notice that I avoid writing of "trainers", the fashion born in the Negro ghettos of North America. The trainers beloved of teenagers are mostly of little use for walking and are very overpriced.

The third method of tackling mud is the one I grew up with - the humble wellie. Generally, in wellington boots as in walking boots, the price is a good indication of quality. The Hunter type are very comfortable and well designed, though they are expensive. However you should not walk in new wellingtons all day long unless you have tested them for a good few miles beforehand. Wellies are despised by those who consider themselves to be "serious" walkers - in fact they can be a great boon. Many of these walks have been researched in wellies and I have had good reason to be thankful for them.

One item of equipment can help a great deal with walks, but relatively few walkers seem to use it - a map case. It is a fallacy to think that you only need a map case in the rain, though after a few consultations of an uncased map outside in the rain you may as well throw it away. A map case will prevent your map from getting worn even in dry weather, and I defy any walker to visit a pub without wanting to put his or her map on the table with the resulting likelihood of testing its beer-absorbency. As important as this is the fact that the map is folded, so that when you pick it up you see the walk you are doing, rather than fishing the map out of your pocket and unfolding it this way and that until you find where you want. A self-locking polythene bag for freezing food makes a very good map case, or you could buy a purpose-made one. By far the best is the most expensive - the German Ortlieb case. It never cracks, lasts seemingly forever, and its excellent design means that a map thus encased can be immersed in a river for some time and remain dry.

A word of warning

Most people who walk these routes will arrive at the start point by car. You will notice that I have endeavoured to avoid start points where you need to park on a wide verge - a valuable embellishment to many of the county's minor roads. I have seen too many instances recently where a guidebook has made the fatal comment "plenty of room to park on the side of the green lane" or something similar. Such a phrase in a guidebook can be a death sentence for a sizeable strip of rough grass, now an ever more precious flower habitat with the pressures of intensive farming. Sad to say, even in Dorset theft from cars parked in rural spots is rife. It is vitally important you take the normal precautions of removing or at least concealing all valuables, including if possible the radio. The more you make yourself known to those around when you park your car, the more you tend to minimise the risk from thieves. Most thieves in the county seem to be of the car-window smashing disposition (rather than adopting any more elaborate methods); I have to say that my car (never the most attractive vehicle even in its youth), now a battered and rusty wreck though well maintained and reliable, seems to fare best with the doors obviously unlocked and nothing inside. It is the kind of car that makes a thief assume he would do the owner a favour were he to steal it - and so it's left well alone!

A great number of these walks start and finish at a pub. It goes without saying that you should not park in a pub car park unless you are going in. If you are parking in the morning before the pub opens, you should endeavour to see someone to explain what you are doing. If you visit for a pre-walk drink or lunch it is both polite and sensible to explain to the landlord that you are going for an afternoon walk and ask to leave your car in his car park for the afternoon. The pubs of Dorset are one of its glories - they are great receptacles of local culture. The more contact you have with the local population, in general the more interesting your walk will be - and pubs are perhaps the best place for this contact.

A word of advice

I have consciously avoided quoting the Country Code. It is too easy for committees to come up with a fancy-sounding, catch-all rubric. What I ask of those who walk in the county is that there should be no sign of their passing when they go home. The one exception that I make to this when walking is the occasional judicious snapping or bending back of bramble sprays that threaten to block the path. A great deal of antagonism is engendered by those who write so vehemently of the "rights" of this or that group of individuals. If those who use rights of way across land which does not belong to them treat this facility as a privilege then they are welcomed in the fields and byways. The simple fact is that farmers have to earn their living from the land and their produce feeds the nation. We are lucky indeed to be able to use that land for our recreation as well and we should never forget it. What may seem a remote spot indeed to the town-bred walker is known intimately to a surprisingly large number of people in the villages round about. That same town-bred walker may have come to that spot in search of a supposed sense of timelessness - he will frequently be rewarded in Dorset. The fact is, however, that the countryside is no more a static entity than the town. For that reason you may well find minor inaccuracies in this book, as footpaths have sections diverted, new barns go up and so on. The earliest research for this book was made in the spring of 1994. It was checked using the County Council Public Rights of Way Definitive Map available for reference in Sherborne Library in July 1994 in accordance with the Wildlife and Countryside Act 1981.

It only remains for me to express a hope that you will have some of the pleasure that I have enjoyed walking in the county where I grew up.

CHAPTER TWO
Long-Distance Paths in Dorset

I believe Dorset contains within its boundaries a greater number of long-distance paths than any other county. This chapter contains instructions as to how to mark all of them on your map and thus follow them, with the exception of the Dorset Coast Path. This is marked on the OS map and in any case is covered by Volume Two of Martin Collins' guide *The South West Way* (also published by Cicerone Press), which I recommend. If you are an avid walker of long-distance paths rather than circuits from a fixed point - usually a parked car - then you can have a superb review of much of the county by combining several paths. An example would be the combination of the Dorset Ridgeway to Lyme, followed by the Coast Path to Ballard Down, continuing onto the Wessex Way, which takes you north across the eastern part of Dorset, crossing the boundary into Hampshire at Bokerley Ditch, thence into Wiltshire to finish at Avebury.

The Dorset Ridgeway: Ashmore to Lyme Regis - 62 miles

The Dorset section of the Wessex Ridgeway has lately been waymarked as a long-distance path running for 62 miles from the village of Ashmore, in Cranborne Chase on the border with Wiltshire, to Lyme Regis, on the coast and the border with Devon. Whilst its waymarking as a continuous long-distance path is relatively recent, it has long been known about as a continuous route for walkers; its origins as a route of communication are, of course, prehistoric. A guide to the complete Wessex Ridgeway is available from the Ramblers' Association (see bibliography); in fact you can walk it using the directions given below to mark the route on your map.

The dedicated long-distance walker who wants to explore Dorset has the opportunity to walk the Ridgeway, finishing at Lyme, thence to turn east and follow the Coast Path to Studland. The resulting walk is a superb long-distance route and a fine introduction to walking in the county. The combined route is a worthy rival to my *Reivers Way* (Cicerone Press, 1993) a walk of roughly similar length exploring the county of Northumberland. A further extension to this would be to head north from Swanage on the unofficial Wessex Way, taking you north across the eastern part of Dorset, reaching the beginning of the Ridgeway Path at Avebury after 103 miles.

The combined Dorset Ridgeway and Coast Path (total 130 miles, assuming the shorter inland route above Weymouth) may conveniently be walked in the space of a week's holiday, using the weekends at each end.

Given this amount of time, it is possible to travel from almost any point in the country and return home at the end of the week. Unlike many long-distance routes the enjoyable walking can start from a main line station. My route for the combined Dorset Ridgeway and Coast Path starts at the town of Tisbury (map sheet 184 GR 9429), lying just to the north of Cranborne Chase in Wiltshire. It is reached by direct train from Waterloo in around two hours.

In common with the Dorset Coast Path, the Dorset section of the Wessex Ridgeway can be walked in the space of two long weekends from London (or elsewhere, train connections permitting), arriving and departing by rail. In this way the combined route may be walked in the space of four long weekends. The first weekend of the Dorset Ridgeway (you should allow three days) takes you from Tisbury to start the route at Ashmore, walking to Maiden Newton, just north of Dorchester. From Tisbury to Maiden Newton there are 41 miles of walking. From Maiden Newton you can return to Waterloo; trains also run to Castle Cary where you can change to catch the train to Paddington up the main line from Plymouth and Exeter. There are also connections to Bristol and the Midlands from Castle Cary. For the second weekend you should return to Maiden Newton by train and walk the 31 miles to Lyme Regis, which is a 5 mile bus ride from Axminster, on the Exeter-Waterloo line.

Walking the Dorset Ridgeway

The directions below enable you to mark the Dorset Ridgeway on the relevant 1:50,000 map sheets (in order of walking - 184, 194 and 193) and walk the route.

From Tisbury to the start of the junction with the Ridgeway path in Ashmore you have 9 miles of fine walking up on to the chalk ridge, westwards along it and then descending on its south side. From Tisbury station turn left on the Shaftesbury road, walk under the railway bridge, turn right after 300 yards and then immediately left into Wallmead Farm (GR 944284). Follow the bridleway south-west for two-thirds of a mile to the public road where you turn left and then left again at spot height 157m to walk south-east to meet the main A30 road at spot height 156m. Cross over the road here and keep heading south-east towards the escarpment of White Sheet Hill. When you reach the barn by the copse at the foot of the escarpment turn right to follow the bridleway over the ridge, crossing it at Cross Dyke (GR 950232). The bridleway crosses the ridge top track and descends southward to Woodlands from where you take the farm lane to Berwick St John. The dedicated student of hill forts may want to walk over the ramparts of Winkelbury, just east of the village, joining the Ox Drove route along the top of the hill. The shorter route is to leave the village down the farm lane (GR 943218) and take the bridleway south-west to climb the escarpment of the western end of Monk's Down. You turn right off the road at the top of the hill and follow the ridge top track over

23

Win Green to reach the old Roman Road (GR 918203). Turn left on the road and cross over the main road heading south-west along the minor road over Ashmore Down. After a quarter of a mile turn left onto a track leading to the road taking you down to Ashmore.

The Ridgeway takes you south from Ashmore on the farm lane, past spot height 193m and into Ashmore Wood. You turn right at the end of the wood (GR 914925) and follow its edge south-west, into the dip of Stubhampton Bottom to the public road (map sheet 195 GR 899145), west for half a mile until you turn left to head south into Haddock's Bottom and west along the southern edge of the wood (GR 894137). This footpath now takes you west to Iwerne Courtney and then straight up the eastern escarpment of Hambledon Hill, following the bridleway to Shillingstone via Handford.

From the south edge of Shillingstone (GR 831102) the path takes you up the spur in Eastcombe wood, south-east past the trig point (spot height 223m) to cross the Turnworth Down road at the picnic site. Maintaining its course south-west along the crest of the escarpment, joining the public road (GR 795077), the path takes you across the southern edge of Rawlsbury Camp on Bulbarrow Hill to Crockers Farm and on to the Dorset Gap via the eastern end of Breach Wood. From here you climb Nettlecombe Tout (GR 738028) and head west to Folly, over Ball Hill and Church Hill to cross the Piddle Valley road (GR 698033) en route to the Giants Head Farm campsite and so down to Minterne Parva.

From Minterne Parva you follow the minor public road to Up Cerne, then north-west up towards the head of the Cerne Valley, turning left (GR 653035) to head west out of it to the farm lane on Gore Hill (GR 637033), where you turn left to head south along the ridge to Higher City Farm (GR 646000), descending to Sydling St Nicholas over Eastfield Hill. From Sydling the Ridgeway takes you over Break Heart Hill to Maiden Newton, and from the church in the centre of the village north up the river to Chilfrome from where you head west along the road past Lancombe Farm to meet the main A356 (GR 564991). The bridleway to Lower Kingcombe continues west from the main road, taking you north into Kingcombe Coppice and west over Rampisham Down to cross the River Hooke (GR 534005). From Hooke Court there is a footpath up to the public road (GR 524004) which you follow to Toller Whelme, heading west to the B3163 to Dirty Gate (GR 509013) and the ridge-top route north-west to the Beaminster Down road (map sheet 193, GR 491035). Here you follow the public road west to the picnic site (GR 485035) and turn left to head south into Beaminster along the dead-end lane.

You leave Beaminster along Church Street and follow the footpath from the western end of the town (GR 473015) due west over Gerrard's Hill (trig point spot height 174m) and onwards over Waddon Hill, crossing the B3162 (GR 445015) and keeping west across the northern edge of the National Trust property of Lewesdon Hill, descending to meet the B3164. There is a slightly circuitous route to the summit of Pilsdon Pen (north along the farm lane to turn left at GR 422025, thence south-west to the summit). From the top of the highest hill in Dorset you descend westwards to meet the B3165 (GR 396020) where you head north to Cole's Cross and along the path over the summit of Blackdown Hill, then west from Venn along the public road through Synderford and south past Yewtree Farm (GR 383030).

From here your course is almost due south to Wootton Fitzpaine, via Grighay Farm (GR 380015) and Gashay Farm (GR 376006), crossing the infant River Blackwater (GR 374003), west up to the road and due south over the top of Lambert's Castle to Fishpond Bottom, whence you follow the Morcombelake road, turning right after a mile (GR 372968) along the footpath to Wootton Fitzpaine.

You head west out of the village and turn left off the Monkton Wyld road (GR 361958) to descend into the valley and follow the river upstream for most of a mile, then turn left (GR 347961) to head south-west out of the valley to Penn, where you cross the main A35 to descend south-west into the valley of the River Lim to Rhode Barton. From here a bridleway takes you south-west through Sleech Wood and a footpath south-east down the valley to the centre of Lyme Regis.

The Dorset Coast Path: Lyme Regis to Studland - 66 or 73 miles

The Dorset section of the South West Coast Path runs for 73 miles from Hengistbury Head to Lyme Regis; it scarcely needs an introduction. The Dorset section is well worth walking in its own right. Of course, several of the walks in this book take you along sections of what we used to know as the Dorset Coast Path. The advantage of walking it all from end to end is that proportionately you spend more time in the less visited spots. Necessarily, day walks such as are described here start and finish at a point accessible by road. Walking the coastline end to end across the county allows you to spend more time "far from the madding crowd's ignoble strife" as Gray so succinctly expressed it.

There is an inland section of the Dorset Coast Path which shortens the route by 7 miles, reducing the total to 66 miles. Walking eastwards, it diverts from the coast itself at West Bexington and rejoins the route after 16 miles of walking at Osmington Mills. Although the route takes you several miles inland it is much to be preferred to the alternative of the shore of the Fleet and the suburbs of Weymouth. The inland route follows part of the Dorset Ridgeway and has superb views southwards across Lyme Bay, the Isle of Portland and Weymouth Bay for much of its length. The best viewpoint of all is the Hardy Monument. The inland route also takes you past a number of prehistoric remains along the chalk downs.

What may not generally be realised is that for walkers based in London it is possible to walk the Dorset Coast Path within two long weekends. Start the walk by taking the train direct to Axminster (Exeter-bound) from Waterloo, where you connect with the bus to Lyme Regis. On Sunday evening, having walked 34 miles to Weymouth, take the direct train back to Waterloo. On the second weekend of walking return to Weymouth by train and walk the 30 miles to Shell Bay and either walk to the ferry across the mouth of Poole Harbour from Studland or, probably preferable, take the bus from Studland to Bournemouth and return to London by train. Monday morning will find you at your desk feeling as if you have spent the weekend in a remote part of a foreign country.

There is an excellent two-volume guide by Martin Collins, also published by Cicerone Press. The advantage of these over the glossy production from the Ordnance Survey (a slightly unhappy blend of a coffee-table book and true walking guide) is that you have to carry the OS sheet mapping anyway - sections printed in books are inadequate. Far better, therefore, to put the smaller, less expensive Cicerone guide in your pocket for occasional consultation and walk on the route highlighted on the map. I would give one final word of advice to those walking along the Dorset coast. It is that you should walk from Lyme to Christchurch rather than vice versa. It is a windy coast and the prevailing wind is from the south-west. At the end of a day's walking, much of it on exposed cliff-top, the difference between the amount of effort made battling against the wind rather than being blown with it is huge.

The Liberty Trail: Ham Hill (Somerset) to Lyme Regis - 28 miles

The Liberty Trail is a 28 mile walk from Ham Hill, 6 miles north of Dorset's boundary with Somerset to Lyme Regis, the greater part of the walk being in Dorset. In fact the last 9 miles follow the same route as the Dorset Ridgeway. If you have not walked a long-distance path before, there can be no finer introduction than this path; it can easily be completed in a weekend. It is a pleasing combination of superb landscapes, delightful villages, and a dramatic finale on the coast at Lyme Regis. It was created as an attractive walking route retracing the steps of a number of inhabitants of the Yeovil area who, in June 1685, made their way to Lyme Regis to join the ill-fated Duke of Monmouth. He was the illegitimate son of Charles II and a focus of protestant activity on the accession of the Catholic James II. The rebellion ended in defeat at the nocturnal slaughter on Sedgemoor and a grisly end for some 300 folk at the subsequent Bloody Assize under Judge Jefferies. The courtroom where so many were condemned can still be seen in Dorchester. Three times this number were transported for life to the West Indies. The vicious repression of the would-be absolutist Stuart monarch James II was in vain, for three years later he fled the country as the West Country rose en masse a second time to support a protestant claimant to the throne. This was William of Orange and his wife Mary who landed at Torbay to ascend the throne as the country's first constitutional heads of state.

There is a guide package to the Liberty Trail available in bookshops and tourist offices in the area and also by post from Dorset County Council Surveyor's Department (price 1994 £4.65, cheques payable to Dorset County Council - see appendix for address). Following the success of Somerset County Council's guide to the Leland Trail, this is a series of laminated cards in a wallet, rather than a guidebook. Each card shows a one-colour reprint of a section of the OS 1:25,000 map with the route highlighted; there are walking directions and historical background linking each stage of the walk to one of the rebels. It is well researched and attractively laid out, although it contains less print and fewer colour photographs than would a book of similar price.

The Liberty Trail can conveniently be walked in the space of a weekend by a walker travelling to the region by train by taking a taxi or bus from Yeovil Junction station to Montacute and climbing St Michael's Hill, linked by a mile of fine hilltop footpath to Ham Hill, just to the west. At the end of the walk a bus journey from Lyme Regis to Axminster enables you to return by train.

The Avon Valley Path: Salisbury to Christchurch - 34 miles

The Avon Valley Path runs for 34 miles from Salisbury along the Hampshire and Wiltshire Avon to its mouth at Christchurch Harbour. For 16 miles, from Fordingbridge to the village of Sopley, it follows the the Hampshire-Dorset border but remaining within Hampshire. The final 3½ miles only lie in Dorset, and this only due to the still controversial 1974 boundary changes. It is waymarked with a green arrow on a beige ground with an emblem of a stone arched bridge in the arrow. A leaflet on the walk is available from Hampshire County Council, Countryside and Community Department (01962 846002). This contains enough information to mark the route on OS map sheets 184 and 195.

The Stour Valley Path: Christchurch to Stourhead - 61 miles

There is a particular pleasure in walking the course of a river, particularly one as fine as the Dorset and Wiltshire Stour. It was no doubt inevitable that someone would create a guide to this route and call it the Stour Valley Path. Thanks to modern boundary changes the Stour now flows entirely through Dorset, from a point close to its source in Wiltshire. It used to be that it crossed into Hampshire at a point half way between Wimborne and Christchurch.

There is a guide available to the Stour Valley Path, by Edward R.Griffiths (see bibliography). The author has gone to a great deal of trouble to detail the public transport that is available for those that wish to walk this route by parking their car, catching a bus ahead and walking back to their car. This is admirable and something that by no means all guides to long-distance Paths do. The guide is, of course, of use to those who wish to walk the whole path from end to end and the author divides the path into five easy day stages, one of 7 miles, one of 16 and the rest of 12 miles. The author intends that you should dispense with OS mapping for this walk and use the maps that he includes in the text. Whilst his maps are excellent, clearly laid out and with a wealth of annotation, no-one should set off for a walk in the area without the latest OS map. The Stour Valley Path, like my *Reivers Way* in Northumberland, is not an official path and is therefore not waymarked in any way to distinguish it from other footpaths. However the route outlined lies all along rights of way and the very small amount of road walking is limited to quiet country lanes. One can only feel sorry for the author that, after what was evidently a great deal of research and writing, he "... a few days before the first printing of this guide, found that Dorset County Council had been preparing 'The Stour Valley Way'". This, being a local authority created path, seems destined to take over entirely from the author's route.

The Wessex Way: Swanage to Avebury (Wilts) - 103 miles

The Wessex Way is an unofficial link path from the western end of the Ridgeway Path at Avebury in Wiltshire to Swanage in the Isle of Purbeck; you will not find it marked on any map. As far as I can ascertain, it was devised by Alan Proctor and the guide to it was published by Thornhill Press (Moorend Road, Cheltenham, Gloucestershire). In comparison to the Coast Path or the Ridgeway it must be said that it is unremarkable; with the exception of its very beginning, along the central ridge of Purbeck and its exit from the county, across Bokerley Ditch, the landscapes it crosses are not the most spectacular in Dorset. What it does offer is a good weekend's walking across the often overlooked scenery of the eastern part of the county.

The original guide to it was written assuming a start near Avebury, at the end of the Ridgeway Path. This being a book on Dorset, rather than Wiltshire, I am assuming a start at the end of the Dorset Coast Path, in Purbeck.

From Swanage the Wessex Way follows the Coast Path northwards to Ballard Point. From here it follows the crest of the central Purbeck ridge to Corfe and then continuing west along the ridge, over Knowle Hill. Descending on the northern side of the ridge via spot height 145m it runs along the road, northwards, past the eastern end of East Creech and thus along the road except for a short diversion, all the way into Wareham. From the hospital at the western end of Wareham it leads, along a footpath at last, under the bypass and over the River Piddle beneath the railway. At Carey it joins a track which joins the public road (GR 904885), goes north-west along this for half a mile and then turns right (GR 898887) onto a bridleway and heads due north for 3 miles through Wareham Forest before crossing the main A35 Dorchester-Poole road (GR 893938). There follow 2 miles of road walking, heading just west of due north via East Bloxworth to the Red Post crossroads at Anderson, then northwards along a bridleway from Anderson Manor via Goschen and so up onto the downs and across Combs Ditch at spot height 124m. From Combs Ditch (GR 875008) it heads north-east along a farm track, down to the Stour Valley by Spetisbury church and, continuing north-east, over the various flows of the Stour by footbridges into Tarrant Crawford.

From Tarrant Crawford it heads south-east, steeply up onto the downs before dropping into a chalk dry valley where it turns left along a track (GR 929033) to head steadily up onto the plateau, crossing the B3082 Blandford-Wimborne road (GR 942040) and continuing north-east. Reaching a track junction half a mile from the main road it turns right (GR 958047) and heads south-east to the edge of the wood before continuing east along its northern edge and onwards down to the public road (GR 976058). From this point its course may be followed by the line of the Roman road of Ackling Dyke, one of a number of Roman roads that radiate across the land from Badbury Rings. Avoiding any village, it takes you north-north-east and off the Bournemouth and Purbeck map (sheet 195, GR 010150).

Following Ackling Dyke, the Wessex Way brings you on to Oakley Down, to a point just short of where the Roman road is overlain by the modern A354 Salisbury-Blandford road (GR 020175). Here it turns east and follows a bridleway over the downs, crossing the Dorset Cursus and reaching the upper end of Water Lake Bottom, just below the village of Pentridge (GR 032172). Heading north through Pentridge (see the Bokerley Ditch and Martin Down walk) it follows a track up to the county boundary with Hampshire on Bokerley Ditch (GR 044190). At which point, strictly, it leaves the scope of this book. Its alignment may be followed, through the village of Martin and the hamlet of Tidpit (GR 077190) and north-east over Toyd Down, from where it follows the Hants-Wilts boundary northwards over Little Toyd Down and Toyd Clump to cross the A354 at Jervoise Farm (GR 090235). Continuing north over Throope Hill, it crosses the Ebble Valley at Stratford Tony and rejoins Ackling Dyke for a mile, before heading east off it to descend into Salisbury, past the old quarry at Harnham (GR 128288). There is the picturesque walk across the Avon meadows and half a mile of Salisbury city centre before joining the footpath along the valley past the school (GR 140310) and up over Old Sarum.

From Old Sarum the Wessex Way keeps to the east side of the Avon Valley, past Little Durnford and Salterton, heading north on a variety of tracks and footpaths to reach Great Durnford, from where you may divert to visit Stonehenge, crossing the Avon on a footbridge and heading north via Springbottom Farm (GR 122400) from where it is suggested that you follow the main A303 east to Amesbury - unpleasant and dangerous madness. From Great Durnford village the Wessex Way takes you direct north-east to Amesbury, crossing the meander of the Avon by a footbridge (GR 148410) and again by the church and leaving the town over the A303 by the footbridge at Ratfyn to follow the bridleway to Bulford and then the A3028 back on to the A303 (is this really a long-distance path?) to the top of Beacon Hill (GR 192425). Leaving the A303 it follows the top of the escarpment of Beacon

Hill, heading north-east to cross the boundary into Hants at Devil's Ditch (GR 215449) and so through Shipton Bellinger where it crosses the A338 and heads east, up onto the downs to Pickford Hill (GR 266466) and then north along a track past Newdown Copse (GR 268483) to Perham Down and the footpath north-north-east to Ludgershall.

From Ludgershall Castle it follows a footpath north over Blackmore Down and into Collingbourne Wood, following a track along its edge to reach the Shears pub (GR 254537) and down through Collingbourne Ducis and along the A338, north out of the village to turn left after a mile (GR 239554) and follows a track west over the downs for 2 miles to the edge of the army ranges (GR 210553). Here it follows a well used track north over Aughton Down to the north-facing escarpment of Easton Hill (GR 200593) and follows the public road steeply down, through Milton Lilbourne to cross the Kennet and Avon Canal at New Mill (GR 183620). There follow nearly 2 miles more of road walking until the woods by Clench Common (GR 184645) where the path turns left off the road to head west over Martinsell Hill and along a track down Oare Hill to cross the A345, continuing west up Huish Hill to Gopher Wood and over the summit of Golden Ball Hill (GR 131639), crossing the road by Knap Hill to head north along the Ridgeway past Furze Hill to the village of East Kennet to finish by the Ridgeway Cafe on the main A4 (GR 119680). Thus ends the Wessex Way - in concept an interesting route but marred by too much road walking, some of it quite inexcusably on fast, busy main roads.

A miscellany

There is no reason why any individual should not devise his or her own long-distance walk from the map and set off to walk it; several suggest themselves in the county.

A walk which I have enjoyed is to follow the longest river that lies entirely within Dorset, the Frome. This rises in the delightful village of Evershot (see the Evershot and the Melburys walks) and flows south-east, through some fine chalk scenery, through meadows by the county town of Dorchester, and then meanders its way east, past Wool and Wareham, to reach Poole Harbour. There is particular pleasure in planning your own route on the map (for this you need just two 1:50,000 sheets, 194 and 195); I recommend this walk to anyone who is so inclined.

A walk has been devised by Rodney Legg, from Sherborne to the coast; the issue of this from his Dorset Publishing Company (see bibliography) is awaited. The Kingcombe Centre (see Walk 38) has its own Raven's Way. This is a walk planned by Mike Bisset in 1993 and takes you across 60 miles of varied Dorset scenery from the Kingcombe Centre to the coast. It is operated as a complete package from the Kingcombe Centre (see Useful Addresses and Telephone Numbers).

CHAPTER THREE

Walks in East Dorset

This section covers all that part of Dorset lying east of the River Stour. It is something of a land of unsung delights, for the walking on the downs of the Wiltshire and Hampshire border, along the chalk escarpment south of Shaftesbury, or the downs near Blandford is as delightful as any in the county. Hardy's great Egdon Heath has all but a few remnants disappeared under bricks and mortar and foreign coniferous trees. However, even in these areas towards the coast it is still possible to enjoy good walking, although not perhaps of a quality that you would travel great distances for. North-east Dorset is a quiet area where you can walk in solitude and contemplate the landscapes around you.

1) The Forests and Downs of Cranborne Chase

Distance: 12 miles
Start: Garston Wood, Sixpenny Handley
Map: sheet 184, GR 003195

> *...one of the few remaining woodlands in England of undoubted primeval date, wherein Druidical mistletoe is still found on aged oaks, and where enormous yew trees, not planted by the hand of man, grew as they had grown when they were pollarded for bows.*
> Thomas Hardy

This is one of the few walks in the county that takes you through extensive woodlands for mile after mile - though by no means the whole walk. These are superb woods, mainly of native species, much of it coppiced still (or at least until recently). There is a magnificent avenue of beech and scattered ancient oaks; for much of the way the path is along wide grassy rides with enticing tracks leading through the trees on either side. It is a poignant reminder of the richness of the forests we have lost in this country, gone to build "the wooden walls of England" and to build the merchant ships, too, that built the biggest empire the world has seen. On few other walks in Britain have I felt myself almost transported to the mighty woods of central Germany or of Moldavia or Transylvania, as I have on this one. This walk is certainly not all arboreal; it takes in a stretch of lofty downland, along a wide chalk ridge with views of the surrounding downs of Wiltshire to the north and east, all the

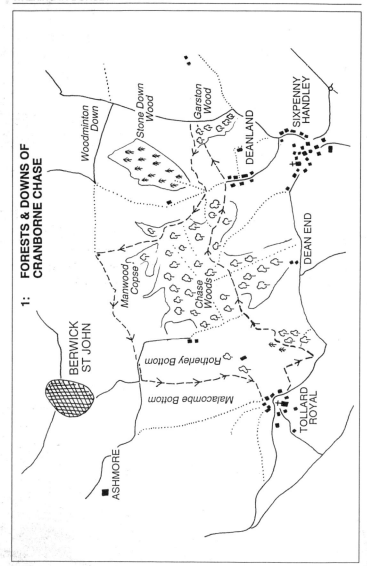

1: FORESTS & DOWNS OF CRANBORNE CHASE

Above: View looking east, across Child Okeford from the top of Hambledon Hill *(Walk 2)* *Below:* The high ramparts of Bokerley Ditch *(Walk 3)*

Milton Abbas *(Walk 8)*
Milton Abbey *(Walk 8)*

way to the sea to the south.

The route takes you to the King John Inn in Tollard Royal, two-thirds of the way through the walk. There are two pubs in Sixpenny Handley (the Roebuck and the Star), 2 miles from the start, as well as a village shop. The walk starts in Garston Wood, a small nature reserve on the southern flanks of the chalk downs a mile and a half north of Sixpenny Handley on the Bowerchalke road. It is described more fully in Walk 3 Bokerley Ditch and Martin Down.

From the car park turn left along the road and turn left to follow the footpath due west along the north end of the wood. After a third of a mile you reach the ramparts of the fort hidden among the trees of Mistleberry Wood. The path continues west to descend to the chalk valley of Deanland with a field almost of parkland on your left. Turn right at the road (you are now at Shermel Gate - GR 989192) and make your way north-west along the track beneath the trees departing to the left of the bungalow.

The byway running north-west up the valley below West Chase Farm brings you up the valley to a long clearing beneath the trees. You exit from the woods after a mile (GR 979202) and head north up a chalk spur along an ancient hedged-in byway; Manwood Copse is on the far side of the chalk gully to your left. It brings you to Bigley Buildings, an old farm, now used as a barn on top of the ridge (GR 975 215). Turn left here along the Ox Drove byway, an ancient route, muddy and now tree-lined. You meet the tarred public road above Berwick St John (GR 953207) and continue west for 500 yards before turning left where the road down to Berwick (GR 948206) turns off to the right. You head south, off the ridge, initially on a track which immediately becomes a path across the middle of a large arable field with views all the way to the sprawl of Bournemouth and the sea beyond. The arable fields run for a mile and a half of gentle descent off Dorset's chalk ridge, with an ancient wood on your left, clinging to the western side of Rotherley Bottom.

You reach a gate in a fence marking the end of the arable and descend along a twisting track across the greensward to Mundays Pond (GR 950184), at the junction of two chalk valleys - Malacombe Bottom and Rotherley Bottom. Here you have to decide whether or not you are going to make the pilgrimage to the King John Inn in Tollard Royal; I recommend it, not least because the village itself is a delight. If, however, you are forsaking the pleasures of the village then simply go through the gate and head down the dry valley of Tinkley Bottom amongst parkland with woods on your left for a further mile. Now omit the next paragraph and read on from*.

To reach Tollard Royal go through the gate leading down the valley and bear right, up the steep side to the dry valley towards a clump of Scots pine, following a line of overhead cables. You come to a steel hunting gate which

33

leads into an arable field; you are following what appears to be the line of an old hedge across the chalk spur. To the left are a number of scattered clumps of beech trees. The path descends steeply, leads you into some trees and brings you to a stile by the pond in the centre of Tollard Royal. Turn right, up the hill for the King John Inn and the village stores. To continue, turn left out of the pub and walk down past the pond and then for a further 200 yards, past an old well on the right. You reach the back of two warning road signs on the left ("oncoming vehicles in middle of road"); immediately after them a track leads up to the left, through a gate diagonally up the valley side. Bear left at the top to keep the red brick cottage to your right, descending steeply into the dry valley. Go through a gate at the bottom of the valley and bear right, heading down Tinkley Bottom.

*At the end of the valley you arrive at a very short avenue of ancient beech trees to the right, running north-east from the main road (GR 954169). Cross over this avenue and bear left up the hill through a gate into a field of grazing. Go straight up the hill towards a long avenue on the top; make for a stile in the fence, heading north-east, and go obliquely across the avenue to the left to make your way to a second stile on the tarred drive in front of the wood. Go into the wood and follow the path through it marked with discreet yellow arrows painted on the tree trunks (so much more pleasant than white plastic discs).

You are following an old fence on the left, now collapsed, marking the boundary between coniferous plantation (Uddens Coppice) to the left and the more natural wood on the right (Brookes Coppice), largely coppiced or formerly so. Notice the contrast in ground covering, especially if you are walking in March or April before the full leaf growth on the deciduous trees. On the right is a healthy carpet of dog's mercury and bluebells with a scattering of more unusual species here and there; to the left, beneath the alien, light-blocking conifers merely a sterile carpet of needles - nothing. The miraculous thing is that a quite fantastic array of species are lying dormant in the soil beneath the conifers and when they are felled there will be a display of this latent beauty.

You turn sharply to the right among the trees, just as the map shows (GR 957178) and head east to the edge of the wood. Turn left out of the trees and notice the now disused ornamental brick park gate at the corner of the field (GR 960183). Make for this and go through the galvanised steel farm gate just to its right to follow the edge of the woods gently downhill, bringing you to Badgers Glory - something of a dream cottage hidden on the edge of the woods, flint and thatch with a pink-painted extension. I suspect there has been a diversion of the path here for I seem to remember as a child that the path ran along the drive through the trees behind the cottage. In any event you cross over a track exiting from the wood and heading south-east down a narrow gully to follow the path along the boundary of the Chase Woods.

The path follows the southern edge of the woods, turning sharp right (GR 964185) before descending again to a track running along the base of a chalk valley. For this stretch your route is marked with arrows painted yellow on the tree trunks. A steep climb brings you to a small plateau in the forests where you meet Bridmore Ride, a magnificent beech avenue leading straight through the forests (GR 971187). Cross over this avenue, the path then swinging to the left to head almost north through Shire Rack before dropping to another lane along the valley. Cross this to follow the county boundary path through the forests with Chase Woods on the left and Great Shaftesbury Coppice on the right to the fifth dene, a mile and a half after the pink cottage in the woods. Turn right here and follow the lane down to the collection of cottages at New Town by Dean Land.

The name is derived from "dene lane" - the road along the valley. "Dene" is a term I am more familiar with from Northumberland than Dorset. Chase Woods are, of course, full of dene lanes - predictably enough, on the southern edge of the woods is Deanend (dene end) a mile and a half west of Sixpenny Handley.

Cross over the road in Deanland and head up a chalk track just to the left of a pair of fine small cottages of flint and brick. You pass three dilapidated sheds on the right; the lane turns right here and you head straight on through a gate, north-west across a field, following a hedge on your left. This becomes a track across the flinty arable fields as you reach the top of the downs and runs straight and true to meet the western edge of Garston Wood at a stile (GR 999193). Follow the path through the woods, past some traditional hurdle fencing on the right down, and so down to your car.

2) Hambledon Hill, Hod Hill and Blandford Forest

Distance: 9 miles
Start: Child Okeford
Map: sheet 194, GR 8312

In the lowlands I have no comrade, not even the lone man's friend -
Her who suffereth long and is kind: accepts what he is too weak to mend:
Down there they are dubious and askance; there nobody thinks as I.
But mind-chains do not clank where one's next neighbour is the sky.
                                        Thomas Hardy, *Wessex Heights*

Starting in the delightful village of Child Okeford, this walk is an almost perfect balance of generous amounts of physical challenge, history, pre-history and superb views of the chalk downs of central Dorset and the pasture lands of the north of the county. There are steep ascents of 400 feet to Hambledon Hill and (slightly less) to Hod Hill and an equally abrupt descent of 600 feet through Eastcombe Wood to Shillingstone. The walk starts at the Baker Arms in Child Okeford (there is also the Saxon Inn, just round the corner, on the Manston road) and passes very close to the White Horse in Stourpaine and the Old Ox in Shillingstone. Durweston has a well stocked village shop but no pub. Child Okeford has a village store and a butcher.

From the centre of Child Okeford leave the village on the road to Fontmell Magna and Shaftesbury. Four hundred yards after the junction you see the entrance to Hambledon Cottage on the left. Turn right, at the end of the last cottage in the village and make your way east along a fenced-in footpath to the right of an arable field, leading you straight towards the ramparts of Hambledon Hill. Make your way up the hill over the ramparts and south-east for half a mile across the top. Rightly, Hambledon Hill is one of the most famous viewpoints in the county; to the north lie the chalk downs of Wiltshire, their western extremity indicated by the landmark of King Alfred's Tower, exactly 15 miles away as the crow flies. The immediate vicinity are the western slopes of the downs of Cranborne Chase and the villages clinging to the base of the escarpment.

As you approach the trig point you find the bridleway hemmed in between two fences; keep this to your left, so that as you reach the trig point it lies behind the fence. From the trig point on the summit of Hambledon Hill you are walking for a brief stretch along the Dorset Ridgeway, this route having reached the top via the spur from Shroton. Make your way south-east towards the end of the wood along the south side of the chalk dry valley of Coombe Bottom. As you approach the end of the wood you see two tracks either side of a wire fence. You should be on the right-hand of these two - the one further away from the wood. Along the top of the wood is a narrow arable field sloping down to it; keep this field to your left as you approach the Dutch barn (GR 855116). Turn right in front of the barn to make your way down to a stile at the corner of a copse (Hambledon Plantation); cross this stile to continue very steeply down the hill to Keepers Cottage. As you reach the road there is a gate directly opposite you with a badge informing you that farmers welcome careful walkers; strictly this is not your right of way here. Turn right on the road and turn through the first gate on your left to make your way steeply up the northern slope of Hod Hill, following the chalky track. This finishes just before a fence at the ramparts on Hod Hill by the National Trust information board. From the gate your route lies exactly south-east across the tight springy turf of Hod Hill and the obvious remains of the Roman fort in the north-eastern corner.

At the far corner of Hod Hill your path is a cutting through the ramparts, leading you into a hedged in track heading steeply down the hill to the sparkling River Iwerne (pronounced "yew-urn") running bright over gravel beds. You cross the stream at a culvert and make your way south down past

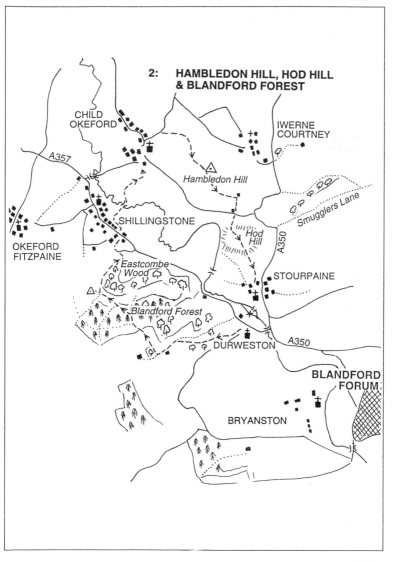

2: **HAMBLEDON HILL, HOD HILL & BLANDFORD FOREST**

CHILD OKEFORD

IWERNE COURTNEY

A357

Hambledon Hill

Smugglers Lane

SHILLINGSTONE

Hod Hill

A350

OKEFORD FITZPAINE

Eastcombe Wood

STOURPAINE

Blandford Forest

DURWESTON

A350

BLANDFORD FORUM

BRYANSTON

the cottages in Stourpaine. The White Horse pub, should you be in need of what it provides, is on the main road up to your left. Make your way past the church; at the end of the lane follow the path heading to the left, past a Dutch barn on your left, bringing you to a stile at the corner of a track. Turn right down the track, beneath the bridge under the old Somerset and Dorset (S & D) railway and along a brief stretch of concrete path to the river.

Cross the river by the concrete footbridge with its high railings and make your way across the field to the mill, where you turn right and follow the drive up to Durweston village. Turn left along the main road and then immediately right off it along a street with overhanging conifer trees on the right. (If you are in need of a snack at the village shop, you can find it 100 yards east along the main road.) It turns sharp left; 50 yards later turn right, opposite number 31 in a row of white-painted thatched cottages, to head south-west past a farmyard on your right up the dry valley to enter the woods (GR 851083). The bridleway through these open-floored woods does become muddy; there is plenty of opportunity to walk on the mossy ground on either side. Leaving the woods at a gate into an area of scattered trees and pasture, you continue up the gully to a second gate and a broad field before the flint and brick barn and barn conversion at Folly. Take your time to turn and look behind you as you climb away from the trees to see the view of Stourpaine Down unfold.

Turn left at Folly to follow the tarred farm lane south-west, past cottages on either side of the road, to a right-hand turning and the end of a plantation of young beech. Turn right here, along a hard stony track to enter Bonsley Woods by a hut on the right. Bear right at the fork in the woods and follow the track through the open woods for 400 yards to a second fork (GR 833089) where a rougher track (shown on the map as a bridleway) turns left. Follow this, heading north-west, out of the woods to make your way across the arable fields with a hedge on the left. Five hundred yards after the end of the woods you meet a grassy track leading from a pond on the corner of the wood over to the left. A post here has a Dorset Ridgeway waymark, indicating the way to the Ridgeway, rather than along it.

Turn right at the Ridgeway Path marker post, the path across the arable marked by tractor ruts to the corner of the field, where you enter conifer plantation and cross over a track traversing around the top of the hill. Initially your path is along a forest ride; it steepens and becomes a very steep muddy rut pocked with hoof marks. You reach the tarred lane along the south side of Shillingstone; follow this for 400 yards until you see a bridleway to the right with a Ridgeway waymark. Turn right here along a grassy track along the back of a small housing estate to cross a small field before the main road. Turn left along the main road and then right after the telephone box along Hine Town Lane. (If you reach the Old Ox pub, you have gone too far.) After 100 yards this turns sharp left by the entrance to the playing field. Cross the playing field to the disused railway line on the far side - not a public right of

Path and River Iwerne at Stourpaine

way but a path nonetheless. Turn left on the railway and after 200 yards right off it, following a hedge on your right towards the narrow steel footbridge across the Stour. Turn left over the footbridge and head north using Child Okeford church as your landmark, across two fields, to reach a green lane.

The paths for this stretch are at the time of writing in the process of change. You should be able to cross the green lane and make straight for the old stone barn (GR 833118). The older path, which I found still to be in existence in the spring of 1994, is to turn right along the green lane; where it finishes turn left to follow the left-hand side of field round to the old barn. From the barn follow the similar track to reach a T-junction of tracks by Melway Farm. Keep straight ahead here to follow the footpath which leads you northwards across a field with some antiquated railway wagons to a white cottage at the beginning of the village. Ciimb a stile to the left of the white cottage and follow the road into Child Okeford to your car.

3) Bokerley Ditch and Martin Down

Distance: 10 miles
Start: Garston Wood, Sixpenny Handley
Map: sheet 184, GR 003195

This is a walk across the largely uninhabited downland landscape on the boundary of three counties - Dorset, Hampshire and Wiltshire. The one village it passes through is somnolent in the extreme; in all this walk there is little to distract you from your contemplation of the great wealth of history that is around you, most especially, of course, at Bokerley Ditch.

The walk starts at the car park for Garston Wood nature reserve, a mile and a half north of Sixpenny Handley on the road to Bowerchalke.

The wood belongs to the Royal Society for the Protection of Birds and was established as a nature reserve in 1985. Its importance is due to the fact that the majority of its area is coppiced. Coppicing is, or rather was, the cutting of trees at their base to encourage them to grow a number of trunks from the same rootstock. Thus cut repeatedly a wood became a very productive source of hurdle fences, fence poles and thatching spars. There can be no finer description of such woodland economy than that in the pages of Hardy's The Woodlanders; *Marty South's cutting of thatching spars assumes heroic status. Among the coppiced trees some mature oak and ash trees were grown to provide more substantial timber for building and fuel. In my childhood hurdle fences could still be seen in use on sheep farms on the downs, their place now taken by electric fences. Curiously, the coppiced species in this wood, as in other coppices, are around three centuries older than the mature trees (oak) that stand above the short and slender coppices. The species coppiced in Garston are maple, ash and hazel. Coppicing produced a habitat which a number of species of plants, birds and animals adapted to; the loss of this habitat was catastrophic to the population of, amongst other species, the dormouse.*

Although the wood is an RSPB reserve, it is, of course, not just bird species that benefit. On the woodland floor grow bluebells, primroses, early purple and bird's nest orchids, toothwort, Solomon's seal and butcher's broom. A number of butterfly species can be found, including pearl-bordered and silver-washed fritillary, white admiral, grizzled skipper and purple hairstreak. Notable among the bird species is the nightingale, which likes to sing from the cover close to the ground that coppiced woodland provides. Garston Wood is an island of this richness surrounded on all sides by arable. And yet nearby are great areas of former coppice; the Forest and Downs of Cranborne Chase walk explores them in detail.

From the car park turn left along the road and then right at the end of the wood to head east, with a hedge on your left, up the hill to a copse. Follow its southern edge along to reach a farm lane (GR 009196) and follow this east, across the arable fields to West Woodyates Farm. Keep the farm on your right - notice a sign, partly hidden in a laurel hedge, pointing the way to "Cobley ³⁄₄". This seems a very generous estimation of the distance. Make your way north-east along the good farm lane to a wood on your right. At the end of the wood the track turns left; turn right here and follow the hedge on

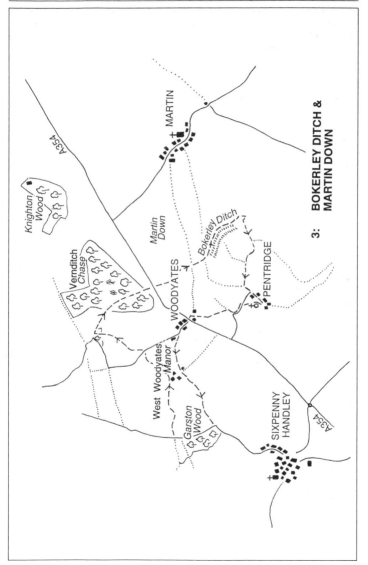

**3: BOKERLEY DITCH &
MARTIN DOWN**

your left along to the road just south of Cobley (GR 022003).

Cross the road at Cobley and go through a metal hunting gate to head north, keeping the beech copse on your left; bear right at the end of the trees to follow a hedged in track north-east, across the dry valley to a water tank on the site of an old barn (GR 025209). Turn left here and follow the hedge on your right to reach the wood - Chettle Mead Copse. Go into the wood at a stile and head north to the far side, where you turn right to head south-east along a lane, downhill to Kitty's Grave and into the woods of Vernditch Chase. A badge nailed to the walker's signpost informs you that you are on the boundary with Hampshire. Follow the line of the old oak trees through the wood of younger trees along the edge of the Forestry Commission (now renamed Forest Enterprise) land. As you exit from the woods into an area of gorse and bramble you should follow the most prominent of a number of tracks; this brings you after two thirds of a mile to a memorial plaque at the edge of the wood on the old Roman road (GR 035203). Turn right here to head south to cross the A354, main Salisbury-Blandford road into a car park.

Leave the car park heading south on a well used vehicle track heading towards a prominent level-topped bank. This has nothing to do with Bokerley Ditch but is a backstop from an old military rifle range. The track takes you past the end of the bank; turn right and make your way to the top to enjoy a magnificent view across Martin Down and a large swathe of three counties - Dorset, Hampshire and Wiltshire. Walk to the far end of the bank and descend it to find yourself on a grassy path following the eastern side of Bokerley Ditch.

Bokerley Ditch takes its English name from "Buck Ditch" - its Celtic name is unknown. It was originally built around the year 370 expressly to block the principal line of advance of the English-speaking Saxons into the territory of the remaining Romano-British population. Bearing in mind the heavily wooded lowlands, the open chalk downs offered more or less the only routes (cf the Hare path on Exmoor - see my Two Moors Way). The Saxon invasion of the West Country to create Wessex - the Kingdom of the West Saxons - was from the north and east. The area of what was to become Dorset was well protected by limestone escarpments in the north (a fact which becomes clear by walking the Trent and the Comptons and Corton Ridge walks) and by impenetrable forests in the clay vales. The coast line, with the exception of Poole Harbour with its unattractive hinterland, was too hostile for landings. The Celtic population had therefore correctly identified the Roman road running south-west from Old Sarum as the line of advance they had to block if they were to resist the Saxon incursions. The result was the cutting of the Roman road in the vicinity of the car park you have just left and the building of the 6 mile long Bokerley Ditch, clear across the chalk ridge. All over Dorset you can find "Cross Dykes" earthworks built to block ridges - Bokerley Ditch is the largest and most important of these.

It is still an impressive feature and its design still has military relevance today. It consists of a deep dyke (probably twice as deep as it now is when new) with a high bank made of spoil behind. In the period of military build-up prior to the UN invasion of Iraq and Kuwait in 1991 the "berm" was talked of - a very similar feature built on the Saudi border for exactly the same reason. Bokerley Ditch was, however, rather more successful than its latterday Iraqi counterpart; it lasted for some two centuries, being broken, it is thought, in the second half of the sixth century. The successful resistance of Saxon invasion for so long completely changed the English settlement of the county in comparison to neighbouring Somerset, Hampshire and Wiltshire, which were in English hands more than two centuries before Dorset.

Follow the Ditch along on its "enemy" side; you cannot help but be impressed by its scale. A mile after the car park a track cuts through the ditch (GR 042193) offering the first of several short cuts before you reach Blagdon Hill (GR 056180). Notice how the ditch keeps to the forward side of the hilltop. Just before you reach the summit of Blagdon Hill turn right, along a well used chalk track past a horse paddock on the left. This brings you after 150 yards to a track junction.

Turn sharp right at the track junction, reaching a wood on your left after a further 100 yards. Now turn left along a well marked (and rather muddy) bridleway along the edge of the small wood. You exit from the trees, heading west, up the hill to pass the southern end of conifer plantation (GR 046179), and follow the grassy track which becomes a farm lane going steeply down to the dairy unit at Whitey Top. Turn left at the bottom of the hill and walk down into Pentridge village to turn right up the lane to the church.

Pentridge is first recorded from a document of 762; at first it seems to be one of those Celtic-English tautologous names which mean the same, such as the numerous Pen Hill. In fact the second element may be derived from tyrch, meaning wild boar, so that the name has a wholly Celtic origin.

With the road south down the valley towards Cranborne now disused, Pentridge has seen few alterations to its buildings since Hardy used it as his "Trantridge" in Tess of the d'Urbervilles, *perhaps the most geographically wide-ranging of his Wessex novels. In fact, whilst in its other locations* Tess *is the most findable of his novels, for the area around "Trantridge" his fictional topography is a little vague. Nevertheless a read of* Tess *prior to doing this walk gives it added pleasure.*

Inside the church is a plaque commemorating "Robert Browning of Woodyates... the first known forefather of Robert Browning the poet". Woodyates is the next settlement reached on the walk. The lane past the church becomes a bridleway leading up the hill across two fields to the road, where you turn left to go down the hill.

Turn right off the road where it turns sharply to the left at an old junction (Peaked Post - GR 031184) and head up a green track to turn left at a track junction among some bushes. This leads you straight across the arable fields, north to Woodyates where you turn left cross back over the A354.

Fleeing from the nocturnal slaughter of Sedgemoor in 1685 the ill-fated Duke of Monmouth abandoned his horse here and headed south on foot in disguise as a shepherd, no doubt making for Poole in the hope of a boat to France. He was captured at Horton, to the north of Wimborne, and was beheaded on Tower Hill. The Bloody Assize which followed was remembered in Dorset for generations.

Leave Woodyates heading north-west along the Bowerchalke road; after 500 yards turn left immediately before a row of houses to follow the path behind the gardens, bringing you to an obvious track which takes you to West Woodyates Manor. Cross over the main drive and head south-west down the tarred private road to the Sixpenny Handley road at a cattle grid (GR 006187) on the eastern corner of Garston Wood. Follow the road along the dry valley to a gate at the end with a sign asking you to park in the car park. Turn right through the gate to follow the track up the western side of the wood for half a mile to a T-junction of paths between two high hurdle fences. Turn right on the path to return to your car.

4) Compton and Fontmell Downs and Melbury Hill

Distance: 5 miles
Start: Fontmell Down car park
Map: sheet 193, GR 885187

Travelling west from Salisbury along the time-honoured route of the A30 main road you see the high rolling chalk downs to your left as you approach Shaftesbury. At Fovant are the famous regimental badges cut into the chalk during the First World War. These high chalk downs finish in a series of dramatic west-facing spurs to the south of Shaftesbury, overlooking the largely clay lowlands of Blackmoor Vale stretching to the west. This walk takes you over two of those chalk spurs, both of them now nature reserves and part of what has latterly been designated the South Wessex Downs Environmentally Sensitive Area. This is the shortest walk in the book, however the fact that it takes in two excellent viewpoints, a hefty climb of 400 feet onto Fontmell Down and a variety of walking makes it seem longer than it is and may well take you longer than you imagine. It passes no pub or shop; there is a restaurant near the start, at the clubhouse of the delightful Compton Abbas airfield less than half a mile south-east.

Park your car in the National Trust car park (GR 885187) giving access to Melbury Hill and Fontmell Down. This can be found by turning south off the A30 just east of the large roundabout by the Grosvenor House Hotel. Keep straight on through Cann Common where the B3081 turns left to go up over
44

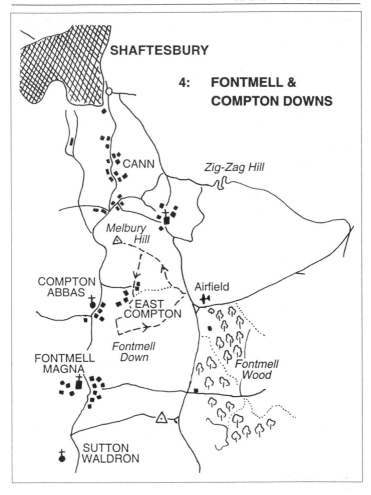

SHAFTESBURY

4: FONTMELL & COMPTON DOWNS

CANN

Zig-Zag Hill

Melbury Hill

COMPTON ABBAS

Airfield

EAST COMPTON

Fontmell Down

Fontmell Wood

FONTMELL MAGNA

SUTTON WALDRON

the downs towards Zig Zag Hill on its way to Tollard Royal and Sixpenny Handley. You are now on the "high road" from Shaftesbury to Blandford which offers a better road than the main A350 which keeps parallel to it at the base of the downs to the west. There is a curious similarity to the two routes from Sherborne to Dorchester, the one (better) unclassified across the

45

downs just to the east, the other twisting through the vale below. The road twists sharply through Melbury Abbas and climbs steeply up Spread Eagle Hill onto Compton Down; you will find the car park a mile after Melbury Abbas on your right. If you reach the turning for the airfield on your left, you have gone too far.

From the car park a chalk track marked "unsuitable for motors" heads down the hill towards East Compton. Rather like the signs at the head of elevators leading down to London Underground stations which state "dogs must be carried" - much to the confusion of foreigners - the "unsuitable for motors" notice means in fact that you are allowed to drive your car down it. Perfidious Albion indeed. Set off down this track to find a chalk pit dug out on your right after a few hundred yards. One hundred yards after this a well used but concealed path takes you up the steep bank on your right to a stile hidden in the bushes by a National Trust sign. Climb this stile and set off up the steep hill in front of you. This path is a permissive path created by the National Trust. It is not a designated right of way and so is not marked on the map.

Once over the stile bear up the hillside to your left. You come to the corner of the hill and find yourself contouring along the escarpment, heading north. To your right the top of Compton Down has been ploughed; your course lies parallel to the fence on your right. There is not much of a path, but the walking is easy across the sheep grazed turf. This is a superb stretch of downland, in April studded with cowslips, which are later followed by the early purple orchids. To your left is a view down the chalk re-entrant, looking south-west to the hamlet of East Compton and the village of Compton Abbas beyond, with the spire of its church reaching above the trees. Ahead, the hill top town of Shaftesbury comes into view, a town with a great wealth of pre-Norman Conquest historic links.

You reach the rounded chalk saddle between Melbury Hill and Compton Down. A hunting gate in the fence (GR 879197) across the saddle marks the course of the bridleway heading north down to Melbury Abbas. This ancient route over the downs from Compton Abbas to Melbury Abbas will soon take you south, off the chalk. For the moment, however, Melbury Beacon is our goal. Follow the path along the broad spur heading west up to the trig point. From here there is a quite superb view to the west, across the low-lying land of south Somerset and north Dorset.

To your left, looking along the edge of the chalk escarpment, you see the table-top mass of Hambledon Hill. A similar distance away to the right you can see King Alfred's Tower on the top of Kingsettle Hill, also a west-facing chalk spur. Four miles away to the north-west is the flattened conical mound of Duncliffe Hill, mantled in woods which have now become a nature reserve. Beyond Hambledon Hill the north-facing chalk ridge runs away to the horizon - Dorset's central spine.

Melbury Beacon dates from the preparations for an anticipated invasion

East Compton Church

by Napoleon's forces in 1804. This acted as a communications node, passing on the signal of the sighting of an invasion fleet towards London. Dorset had seven signal stations on the coast - Golden Cap, Abbotsbury Castle, Portland, White Nothe, St Aldhelm's Head, Durlston Head and Ballard Down. The western of these sent their signal via Shipton Hill and Black Down (now the site of Hardy's Monument) and Puddletown Heath; the eastern ones via Lytchett Heath and Badbury Rings - Puddletown and Badbury both being visible from Melbury. From Melbury it was sent via the Wiltshire Downs to London. In daytime it was planned that the signal would be sent by shutters set up for the purpose, with a kind of prototype Morse code. At night beacon fires would have been lit.

When you have had your fill of the view, retrace your steps to the saddle. Turn right at the gate in the fence to descend the hill, joining a well defined chalk track leading to a wooden five-bar gate (GR 877194). This marks the end of the National Trust property. You could, if you wanted, head south-east from the top of Melbury Beacon to join the bridleway as it leaves the National Trust land, but this involves some tricky walking across steep escarpment.

At the bottom of the hill you find yourself in a field of pasture; make your way to the far left corner of this and follow the obvious chalk track south with a fence on your left which brings you to the road by a litter of farm implements. Turn left on the road beneath the stand of beech and horse chestnut trees

47

and ignore the turning left taking you along the "unsuitable for motors" track back up to the car park. You pass the remains of St Mary's church on the right, now just a tower in a vast sea of nettles and cow parsley; walk down the hill and turn left, off the road as it goes round a right hand bend with a wall on the right. Having turned left you find yourself on a track which takes you downhill to a patch of mud beneath a stand of poplars. Turn right here through the gate and follow a slightly overgrown old track along with a high hedge on the left and a fence on the right. The track appears to end as you look down a tiny valley towards Compton Abbas to your right. It soon starts again, now with hedges on both sides - it is all a great contrast to the free and easy walking across the downs above and good illustration of why our ancestors used these routes for their ancient trackways.

Over some fine non-man-made earthworks you follow the track along, hidden from the surrounding fields by the high hedges. The track finishes abruptly. Formerly the route turned sharp right from the end of the hedge, making for what is now a lone ash tree. This hedge has now been removed and the bridleway diverted; keep straight ahead along the headland and turn right at the end of the field, to head south-west with an arable field on the right. You come to a stile at the end of the field; turn left over this and walk up to the copse clinging to the side of the down.

Turn left at the end of the copse to follow the fence and overgrown hedge along on your right, angling up the hill. You enter a stand of trees and find a gate; go through this to find yourself on the National Trust property of Fontmell Down. It would be pleasant to turn sharp right here and climb the spur of Fontmell Down, bearing in mind that this is National Trust land with open access; however you will find a field fence blocking your way, so continue along the well defined track angling up the hill to find a stile on your right near the corner of a small sycamore wood. Ahead you can see your car and a well used permissive path heading north-east across Clubmans Down leads you straight to a stile in the corner of the car park. However you are free to extend your walk across the top of Fontmell Down. The National Trust have constructed a footpath along the west side of the road south from where you parked your car and this offers an alternative route back.

It would be pleasant to extend this walk to the south, to include views down into the dramatic bowl of Longcombe Bottom and over Fontmell Hill to Littlecombe Bottom. At the time of writing this is being opened up for walkers by E.S. and J.E.Gardiner. Immediately before the Second World War Littlecombe Bottom was planted with conifers which, at the time of writing (summer 1994), are being felled as part of a wider chalk downland restoration scheme. A car park has been created in the old chalk pit on the south side of the road down Littlecombe Bottom (GR 885168), slightly hidden from the road. The ancient bridleway which runs north from near this point, the Gallops, is being augmented by a number of permissive paths which enable the walk described above to be extended to the south to enjoy the landscape above Fontmell Magna.

There could be no more dramatic way of finishing a walk over the downs south of Shaftesbury than by having an aerial view of what you have just walked over. The airfield for light aircraft and microlights, just behind the chalk escarpment, offers trial lessons - why not put your OS map in your pocket (or have a pose and strap it to your thigh) and have a spin in a Cessna?

5) The Stour Valley and Forest Trail, Ferndown

Distance: 10 miles
Start: Stapehill
Map: sheet 195, GR 052017

Among the walks in this book, this is unique in that it is a waymarked trail laid out by Dorset County Council and Ferndown Town Council, rather than having been researched by the author. I am grateful to both these organisations for being able to include this walk here. The walk takes you past (or close to) no less than three pubs and one hotel. In the order passed, these are the Angel Inn at Holmwood, the Bridge House Hotel on the main road by the Stour, very close to the Kings Arms at Longham and the Old Thatch at Stapehill. It makes a good introduction to the idea of day walks for those who are new to the pursuit, lying as it does so close to the huge swathe of the Poole-Bournemouth conurbation, and is therefore highly accessible to the many inhabitants of the south-east corner of the county. Moreover, being continuously waymarked so as to distinguish it from other footpaths it meets, it is easy to follow and lies across gentle terrain. A leaflet is available free of charge from Dorset County Council (see useful addresses) although it gives less information than does the text below.

Lying as close as it does to the Poole-Bournemouth conurbation, the presence of suburbia (something from which I regard the walks in this book as an escape) is never far away. Even when the sprawl of housing is out of sight its hinterland pervades, with weedy paddocks full of old baths and tyres, overgrazed by teenage girls' nags. Overhead the air is full of the sound of airliners landing and taking off at Hurn and you seem never to be far from the unnerving hum of overhead high tension cables. Sad to say, a faint whiff of sewage hangs over the Stour on still days, mingling in macabre way with the smell of lunch being cooked at the Bridge House Hotel. Alas, this is the fate of Hardy's Egdon Heath. Nevertheless this is a worthwhile walk, with glimpses of fine old remnants of the heath, oakwoods and hedged-in lanes.

Your landmark to find the start is the Old Thatch pub, beside the old Wimborne-Ringwood road on the western outskirts of Ferndown. Turn north

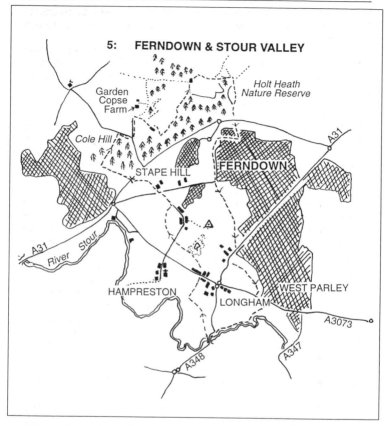

5: FERNDOWN & STOUR VALLEY

off the main road at the Old Thatch into the dead end road of Uddens Drive. The third entrance on the left (somewhat concealed between rhododendron bushes) is the car park for the start. From the car park head west, along the "Castleman Trailway", for 400 yards to bring you to the footbridge over the A30 Ferndown by-pass in its cutting. Keep straight ahead from the footbridge, taking you into the woods. You turn right in the trees (GR 041011) to walk up the slope of Cannon Hill, bringing you to the tarred lane (GR 045018). Turn right on the road and after 300 yards turn left along the dead-end road (GR 047018) to head north. After a similar distance the road bends to the right whilst the drive to Garden Copse Farm keeps straight on. Turn right off the road through a gate and follow the track through the trees south-east to Bedborough Farm, continuing past the farm, over the stream into Uddens Plantation.

Once inside the plantation turn left onto the wide track, cross back over Uddens Water and turn immediately left (GR 057022). You emerge from the pines, cross the other arm of Uddens Water and reach the houses at Clayford (not named on the map - GR 060030). Walk through the timber yard and bear right to follow the bridleway along the southern edge of White Sheet Plantation. Beyond the eastern end of the conifer plantation you are walking along the edge of Holt Heath nature reserve - important as one of the very few remnants of the Dorset Heath. It was bequeathed to the National Trust as part of the Kingston Lacy estate by the late Ralph Bankes in 1981. The track improves and then turns sharp right (GR 070030) to leave the trees and cross over Uddens Water by the tarred road leading from the roundabout leading to Ferndown industrial estate.

Head south on this tarred road, through the tunnel past the bollards to find yourself momentarily in a housing estate, on Ameysford Road. Take your second turning on the right after the tunnel, into Kingsway (GR 071018). At the end of the road you find yourself at a T-junction; cross the road to a sign telling you you are in Leeson Drive and follow the path through tall gorse bushes beneath the pylons to rejoin a road heading south through the new bungalows. You emerge onto the main road a mile east of the start, at the end of Bracken Road, adjacent to a Jet petrol station (directions are beginning to sound less and less like those for a get-away-from-it-all country walk).

Cross over the old A31 main road through Stapehill to find yourself in a gravel car park and head south along the bridleway signed to the Great Barrow (GR 065098). Immediately after the electricity sub-station turn left onto a narrow path heading south-east, past some playing fields on the left. The path winds its way through the bracken, rough grass, gorse and birch trees of the southern end of what remains of the once extensive Ferndown Heath, eventually bringing you to the main road (GR 070993). Turn right along the main road and cross over to arrive at the Angel Inn, a Hall and Woodhouse establishment (GR 069991). Continue south-west along the main road and turn left immediately before a set of recycling bins in a lay-by (GR 069990). You find yourself on a track leading to number 180. This ends at two gates; go through the left-hand one to follow the track south-east. Initially you are walking through ancient mixed deciduous woodland, followed by mature Scots pine - altogether woodland walking for half a mile. At the end of the wood a fenced-in path leads you down the left-hand side of a paddock to the main B3073 (GR 074982).

Turn left along the road and follow it east for 300 yards to turn right down a tarred lane to Dudsbury Guide Camp. Follow the drive south-west to a gate; 100 yards after the gate turn right at a holly bush against a tree trunk and take the riverside path. Follow the path west, upstream along the north bank of the Stour, to leave the river along a narrow, fenced-in path by a car park to meet the main A348 just east of the bridge (GR 066975); the Kings Arms pub is just to your right. You are adjacent to the Bridge House Hotel, which is more than a pub, but if you are not too muddied from your exertions I am sure they would be pleased to serve you lunch. Turn left along the road and then immediately right along a grassy lane at the end of a row of houses; it is marked with a footpath sign to Hampreston Church. Turn right off the lane at a narrow stile and head north across the flat fields, making for the left of a new bungalow. Cross over the stile and follow the path across the flat fields of the alluvial valley floor. It swings to the left to reach a sunken green lane under a pylon line (GR 060983). Turn right along the track to bring you back to the B3073 (GR 063987).

Cross over the road and follow the path between iron railings adjacent to an ornamental weeping willow tree; it takes you through a small copse with a good deal of undergrowth and into a flat field with oak trees on the right. On the southern edge of a small wood of oak you join a track and follow this to the road, which you cross to find yourself on a gravel track heading north-west to a fork with a copse overgrown with rhododendrons facing you. Turn right; the track becomes a footpath at a stile and leads you back to the road. Turn left on the road to reach the Old Thatch pub and your car.

6) The Woods and Lanes of the Crane Valley

Distance: 11 miles
Start: car park in Cranborne
Map: sheet 195, GR 056133

Lying close to Wimborne and Ringwood, and highly accessible to the inhabitants of Poole and Bournemouth, this walk gives a glimpse of an older Dorset - an intricate landscape of ancient woods, high hedges, narrow tracks and small fields of pasture and plough. It takes you across an area just north of the extensive modern development of Verwood and west of the swathe of close-packed conifers of Ringwood Forest. There is a tearoom in Woodlands; sadly the former shop adjoining closed whilst I was writing this book. The gardens to Edmondsham House are open on Wednesday and Sunday afternoons from April to October. The house itself is open on Easter Sunday and all bank holiday Mondays. I originally designed this walk as being suitable for those staying at the youth hostel in Cranborne. This has now closed, but the walk is a very pleasant one nonetheless. There are village shops and two pubs - the Fleur de Lys and the Sheaf of Arrows - in Cranborne. Cranborne became "Chaseborough" in Hardy's most controversial novel, *Tess of the D'Urbervilles*. In a well known passage, Tess waits for her friends after a Saturday evening at the "Flower-de-Luce Inn". The Fleur de

Lys is still recognisably the same pub photographed by Hermann Lea with the connivance of Hardy. There is also a connection with the war poets, for Rupert Brooke, already a poet before the outbreak of the First World War, was moved to write:

> *We somewhere missed the faces bright,*
> *The lips and eyes we longed to see;*
> *And Love and Laughter and Delight*
> *These things are at the Fleur de Lys.*

The experience of the First World War from afar also moved Hardy to poetry as an old man. In the year following the armistice Robert Graves, who had survived the entire war as an officer in the Royal Welch Fusiliers, spent his honeymoon in Dorset and visited the grand old man of letters, as he was by then. Such delights were not permitted most of the other war poets, who died during the conflict; among them Rupert Brooke, who died en route to the carnage of the Dardanelles in 1915.

From the car park turn right on the main road, heading up the hill towards Fordingbridge. Turn first right along a road past the sports field and follow this after it ends, keeping a hedge on the right. Cross obliquely over the road in front of Holwell Farm (GR 065132) and head up the lane through the farm. You are following a track between an established hedge on the right and a newly planted one on the left. You reach a gateway adorned with no less than three yellow footpath arrows; bear left, heading up the slope of Jordan Hill (normally fairly wet underfoot here) and follow the edge of the conifer plantation along on your left. Turn left into the trees over a stile and turn right to join the drive to an isolated house in the trees (GR 075130). The drive becomes a particularly muddy track descending through the trees. After half a mile you meet a T-junction of gravel tracks; turn right and go up to the road by Hare Lane Farm, where you turn right to take you past the pottery.

At the end of the pottery garden turn left over a stile and go down a path along the edge of the garden to join a damp, hedged-in green lane at the bottom. It goes down the hill and gets wetter, ending as a difficult steep gully bringing you to a gravel track beneath trees. (If you wish to visit the Heavy Horse Centre - GR 079109 - to find out about the world of Suffolk Punches and Percherons, then head south down the track and turn left on the road to bring you to the beginning of the drive to Tweseldown Farm.) On your left here, at the top of a bank, is a stile; cross this and head south-east across an arable field to a stream in a bramble and gorse-filled gully. Cross the stile, go over the stream at a footbridge and continue up the hill in the same direction, crossing underneath the pylon lines, to bring you to the end of a farm lane. There is rather more to this than the map shows, but it does eventually bring you on to the public road (GR 084112).

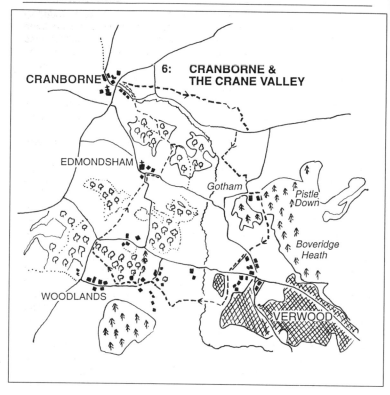

Turn right on the road for 400 yards and where it turns sharp right, turn left off the road so that your are heading east, down the drive to Tweseldown Farm. Follow it over the old railway bridge and round to the right, through the farm buildings. It brings you along the edge of the conifer plantation to your left, south to Burrows Farm, which leads you to another potholed farm access drive towards Verwood. You reach a T-junction of semi-suburban unsurfaced roads (GR 989097) where you turn left, then immediately right, to follow a post and rail fence on your left through the trees, walking on a little-used track. This returns to being a gravel access road as you continue and brings you, after 500 yards to the Royal British Legion club and the playing fields.

Turn right on the main B3081 and follow it west for 600 yards (if you come to the pub you have gone too far) to turn left, down Dewlands Road. This takes you south for half a mile, at which point, by a noticeboard about

Dewlands Common, you turn right into a narrow lane - Roe Lane. Suddenly the uniform late twentieth-century bungalows, of no style that has anything to do with Dorset, give way to a few tiny cottages, reminding you that once (though it were hard to believe now) Verwood was real Dorset. The lane becomes a footpath in the trees at a stile and takes you over the old railway line and the River Crane at a footbridge, across flat fields, past Ninney Coach Wood on the right to Mount Pleasant Farm at Woodlands. Keep Mount Pleasant Farm on your left; immediately afterwards turn right at a junction of lanes (GR 067085) to head north-west to meet the public road (GR 063091) through Woodlands; turn left here and walk west for half a mile.

Immediately after the village hall turn right into a drive to two modern bungalows. You reach the edge of the wood at a gate; take the right-hand of the two paths that fork inside the wood and head north-west through Boys Wood. The path leaves the trees to follow its western edge to the road (GR 051099), where you turn right to bring you to a T-junction with the B3081. Cross over the road and head north-east along the footpath signed "Edmondsham 1 mile". You descend to a stream-ditch and join an old track on the far side to keep Maldry Woods to your left as you cross a number of small fields. Bear right as you reach the north-east corner of Maldry Wood (GR 059109) and keep the long copse on your left as you approach the village. Turn right on the track at the end, then left on the road to walk in to Edmondsham. At the T-junction in the middle of Edmondsham turn right and walk to the end of the village, where you turn left to head north-east along a gravel track for half a mile to a T-junction. Turn left here, up a slope, to enter Castle Hill Wood. Immediately inside the wood a track turns right, muddy, to head north-west through the trees and then descends to meet a sunken lane running along its northern edge; turn left here (GR 065125). A third of a mile along the northern edge of Castle Hill Wood turn right, over a stile, to follow a footpath diagonally across the arable, north-west to the road junction at the end of Cranborne. Follow the road into Cranborne for 300 yards and turn right into Curtis Close. Cross the stream, running clear over its bed of bright gravel, and follow it upstream to your car.

CHAPTER FOUR

Between the Stour and the Frome

7) The Hinterland of Sherborne: In Raleigh's Domain

Distance: 6 miles
Start: Sherborne station
Map: sheet 183, GR 640182

The walk starts at Sherborne station car park. No pub or shop is passed on the walk, although afternoon tea can be enjoyed at Sherborne Castle when it is open - see below. Sherborne itself has pubs, cafes, shops and restaurants galore. Almost alone of walks in this book, it can be covered as a day return from London or indeed anywhere on the London-Salisbury-Exeter main (and very scenic) line. The journey to Sherborne - the walk starts at the station - takes a little over two hours from Waterloo.

The major feature encountered on the walk is the beautiful deer park at the heart of Sherborne Castle Estate. The advent of the deer park following the Norman Conquest had considerable impact on the landscape of Dorset; at one point there were more than ninety such enclosures in the county and many of these walks pass their remains. Some of these were held directly by the crown but most were the creations of the nobility. Sherborne Park was laid out adjacent to the castle (now Sherborne Old Castle) by the Norman Bishop of Salisbury. The deer which were thus protected from predation (unsanctioned human and otherwise) provided sport when released to be hunted with hounds across the unenclosed fields and through the then much more extensive forests. Perhaps more importantly they were (and are) able to graze and browse right through the winter months, unlike the humbler domestic beasts, and so could provide fresh meat during the cold months of the year. Sherborne Park has happily been preserved, together with its herd of fallow deer; this walk takes you along the only public right of way through it. Visitors to Sherborne Castle are not permitted to wander at will in the park east of the castle.

This walk can ideally be combined with a visit to Sherborne Castle; it is open in the afternoon on Thursdays and at weekends from Easter Saturday to the end of September. Built by Sir Walter Raleigh following his unsuccessful attempt to make a dwelling out of what is now known as the Old Castle, Sherborne Castle is well worth visiting to discover the home of a man who must be considered as one of England's premier heroes. Raleigh was a determined explorer and far-sighted coloniser; he was a poet and an accomplished seaman. The Digby family, to whom the estate passed upon Raleigh's death on the scaffold, a martyr to the cause of his own greatness, have preserved his home and its estate almost perfectly. Sherborne Castle should be more famous than it is; it is an exquisite rural seat and a monument to a great man.

There are literary as well as historical aspects to this walk; the poet Alexander Pope, translator of the *Odyssey* and the *Iliad*, was a frequent visitor to the house and walker in the park in the early part of the eighteenth century. (The county seems to have a special affinity for notable classicists; T.E.Lawrence would have been famous for his translation of Homer were it not for his other exploits "in a foreign field".) The famous diarist Parson Woodford eschews his usual obsession with everyday life at Ansford by Castle Cary to recount his watching (among a large crowd) King George III visiting Henry, the Seventh Lord Digby - shortly afterwards elevated to Earl Digby - on Tuesday 4th August 1789. The characters in Hardy's *The Woodlanders* make several journeys to "Sherton Abbas"; the Dorchester ("Casterbridge") road then passed much closer to the castle entrance than it does today.

Start the walk at the car park adjacent to the station at the south end of the town. Leave the car park past the front of the station and turn right over the level crossing to bring you after 100 yards to a T-junction. Cross the road here and pick up the path which heads diagonally up the grassy slope in front of you to your left. At the top of the hill you bear right through an old iron park gate and are presented with a fine view of Sherborne Castle and Park in front of you. If you are leaving your car at the castle, simply retrace your steps down the drive to the entrance and turn left through the iron turnstile gate to walk steeply up the slope with the tall iron fence on your left. Looking from the gate at the top of the hill (GR 645163), the wooded hill directly in front of you due east is known as Jerusalem Hill (it is not named on the map).

Set off down the hill along a grass path following the line of an old hedge latterly ploughed out. After a little over a quarter of a mile you reach a stony farm lane at a fork. The footpath is signed along the lane heading due east, marked merely as a footpath on the map. Until a few years ago there was a deep ha-ha ditch on the left. The lane turns to grass as you start to ascend the hill until you reach a tall wooden park gate adjacent to a rustic thatched lodge at the base of a steep slope. The lane is now tarred again as it climbs steeply up Jerusalem Hill, some venerable oaks on your left. This is a delightful stretch of the walk; here, one feels, has been achieved what Capability Brown was aiming at in his landscaping. The rough grass and anthills are a favoured feeding ground for the green woodpecker and the park

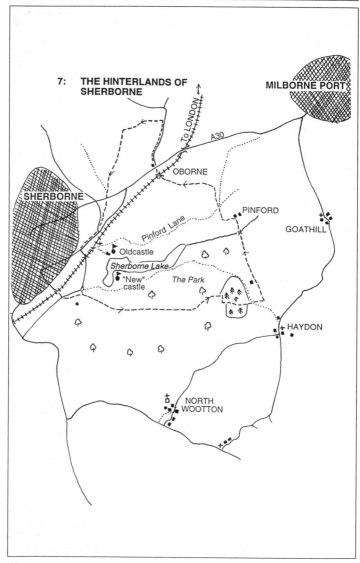

7: **THE HINTERLANDS OF SHERBORNE**

deer can often be found among the bracken. At the top of the hill you see a high gate in the park fence; make for this and bear right among the trees. The path swings to the left beneath the trees, past an old Nissen hut and a brick water tower on the right. Follow the path through the plantation - the site of a Second World War Polish refugee camp - east to a collection of modern barns in the woods. The path takes you, past a weighbridge on the left, to a junction with the drive at a red brick shed on the left, part of the old camp. Here the path has been sensibly diverted for a short stretch from what the map shows.

Turn left at the brick shed (GR 666161) and 30 yards later, right, off the drive onto a green track with a broad hedge on your left. After 150 yards turn left through a gate at a tiny brook. Follow the path beneath the trees with the fence on your right. Fifty yards east of the gamekeeper's cottage you return to the deer park through a pedestrian gate. Follow the path down the hill through the clearing, Pinford Farm lying straight ahead. As you descend the hill, crossing a hard stone track, you have a view of the ornamental balustrade and stone arches of Pinford Bridge to the left. Pinford is first recorded in 1160. The name obviously refers to a crossing of the Yeo here - the first element may refer to a personal name or perhaps a pine tree. You leave the deer park through a gate in the high wall and descend to cross the River Yeo at a wooden footbridge. Make your way up to the stile just to the left of Pinford Farm and turn left along the drive. Turn right to make your way up to the ornamental gates in the park wall (GR 662174).

At this point you are standing on the old London-Exeter main road. In Raleigh's day it headed south-west from here, the deer park wall on the left, to reach Castleton and the entrance to the Old Castle. With the diversion of the route north the nature of the road has changed but little in centuries. Make your way to the far side of the slightly strange arboreal roundabout and pick up the yellow disc waymarks indicating the path through the wood. As a child I always found this almost impossibly overgrown; happily now it is well signed and regularly used. The path takes you twisting through the trees on the little escarpment to leave the wood at a stile. Pause at the stile and look for the bridge through the railway embankment ahead. The path takes you on a very slight dog-leg to reach across three fields to reach it. Its route is marked by stiles in the hedge.

Immediately before the bridge under the railway you join a farm lane. As you walk under the bridge you will see in front of you a stone stile at the back of a cottage garden. Cross this and make your way to the main road by St Cuthbert's Chancel - not marked on the map.

I used to pass this every day on the way to school and for much of my childhood I was under the impression that a "chancel" was a kind of church - a sort of half way measure between a chapel and parish church. The chancel of old St Cuthbert's church is maintained as a redundant church, worship being carried on in the new St Cuthbert's church half a mile to the north.

Cross over the main road here and make your way north to Oborne. Half a mile after the A30 road turn left at the old school house.

On days when I spurned the bus to walk into school I would generally walk past the then Oborne school just as the morning hymn was being sung, reminding me that I was going to be too late for my own school assembly - never a cause for much lament on my part.

Make your way up the hill past St Cuthbert's church, the farm lane becoming rougher as you go. At the top of the hill it turns left at a gully and takes you south-west along Underdown Lane, following the top of the escarpment with a fine view of Sherborne Park, Jerusalem Hill and the Old Castle ahead and to the left. You meet the A30 again at Dodge Cross (not named on the map); cross the road here and make your way down the hedgebound bridleway to the riding stables on Oborne Road. Turn right at the T-junction with Oborne Road and make your way south-west to two turnings off to the left. If you still have the time and the energy you can turn first left here, up to Castleton Church, and the Old Castle. The old main road to London departs east behind the tiny Castleton church.

To reach your car, turn second left, over the railway and the River Yeo. A hundred and fifty yards after the bridge turn right through a gate in the iron fence to follow a footpath parallel with the railway line to bring you to the level crossing and the station. Alternatively you could follow Long Street west and turn left at the end to reach the station. Sherborne itself richly repays time spent in exploration.

8) Milton Abbas, Hilton and the Downs

Distance: 5 or 8 miles
Start: Milton Abbas
Map: sheet 194, GR 806017

This walk is an exploration of the empty downland landscape that lies around the well-known village of Milton Abbas. An extension of 3 miles of fine hill-top walking may be made to this walk; see below. The village of Milton Abbas has a good pub, the Hambro Arms, towards the top of the street, just above St James' church and the village shop. There is also a tea room in the village, open the year round; several houses also offer bed and breakfast. No other pub or shop is passed on this walk. Milton Abbas can be found by turning north off the A354 Blandford-Dorchester road in Milborne St Andrew, 8 miles out of Dorchester. Milton Abbas is one of the most visited villages in Dorset; this walk through beechwoods, pasture and along farm tracks, gives good views of the great abbey and the fine buildings of Milton Abbey School. The walk lies entirely along bridleways which, unlike some in the county, I have not found to be excessively muddy; with its extension, therefore, north-west to the top of Bulbarrow, it would make a pleasant excursion on a mountain bike.

Legend has it that King Athelstan, king of Wessex and of all England, camped at Milton on his way to do battle with the Danes. Here he dreamt of victory; when his dream came true he founded Milton Abbey (in 933) as an act of penance. The actual site where he camped is supposedly occupied by St Catherine's Chapel, a twelfth-century Norman building now replacing the Saxon original. The eleventh-century abbey was burnt in 1309, apparently following a lightning strike; the structure you see now (there is no nave) dates from the early fifteenth century. What you see now is simply the church building and Milton Abbey house, which has become a boarding school. The monks' refectory is the sole survivor of the monastic buildings, incorporated into Milton Abbey house. In 1752 the first Earl of Dorchester bought the abbey; with it was sold Milton Abbas town, its buildings clustering around the old abbey. He had the whole lot removed and built the replacement village out of sight from the abbey; the result is the double row of thatched houses marching down the street, St James' church fitted in with them, and the Hambro Arms pub at the top. I have seen photographs of this scene in Europe, North America and Australia, purporting to be a "typical Dorset" or, even more bizarre, a "typical English" village. It is, of course, no more typical than Hyde Park is typical English countryside; it is one of the earliest examples of town planning and one that I cannot see has ever been bettered.

The wide village street has ample room for parking, although it can become very busy on summer weekends, especially bank holidays. At the bottom of the street the road forks; turn right, following the road signed to Hilton. After a few yards you come to a lodge and a drive turning off to the left. Follow this drive towards the lake and then up the valley towards the abbey and school buildings. Strictly speaking the right of way ends at the abbey's west door. However the gravel path that turns right in front of the abbey may be used, and customarily is by those walking down to visit the abbey from the road. Bear left, following the signs leading you to the exit and bear left when you reach the road to follow it across the dry valley leading up to Broadfield to your right. There is a superb view of the north front of Milton Abbey House to your left. In front of you is the beechwood clinging to the escarpment; turn right as you reach the wood to head up the hill, north along a bridle path; you are now walking through Thomas's Hill Plantation.

Typical of beechwoods everywhere, there is no undergrowth on the woodland floor; in the early spring wild onion, celandine and dog's mercury give the ground a rich, verdant (not to mention pungent) carpet.

The path twists in detail through the trees, taking you from Thomas's Hill

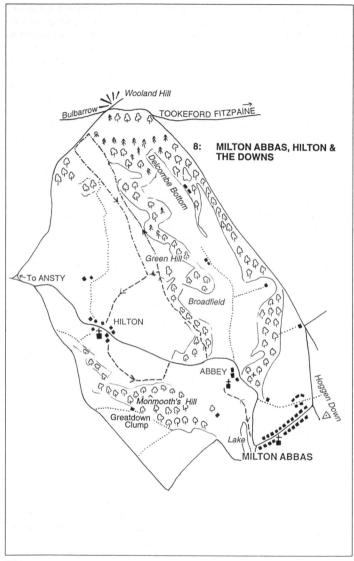

Wooland Hill

Bulbarrow

TOOKEFORD FITZPAINE

8: MILTON ABBAS, HILTON & THE DOWNS

Delcombe Bottom

Green Hill

←To ANSTY

Broadfield

HILTON

ABBEY

Monmooth's Hill

Greatdown Clump

Hoggen Down

Lake

MILTON ABBAS

plantation into Horse Park Plantation and finally exits at the top of the hill with fine views of Houghton Downs away to your right. It takes you across two hill-top fields of rather rough grazing and past a sign informing you that you are entering Dorset Naturalists Trust's Green Hill Nature Reserve. Just as you are about to enter the woods again (GR 789038) you see a farm gate on your left beneath some ancient trees taking you into a farm lane through a small copse. This is the shorter return route, taking you south-west past Hilton Hill buildings and steeply down the chalk escarpment to Hilton. Miss out the following paragraph and read on at the following one.

Should you wish to take the extension then keep straight ahead here. The longer route is well worthwhile if you have the time and the energy; there is a special pleasure in ridge walking and Bulbarrow, a mile and a half north-west of Green Hill, is one of the best viewpoints in the county. To follow the extension route keep straight ahead on Green Hill and follow the bridle way north-west past Hill Barn, eventually to join Bulbarrow Farm Lane, along the western edge of Delcombe Wood (the viewpoint lies across to the right). Turn left when you meet the public road and after 400 yards turn left through a farm gate to follow the bridleway, known locally as Ice Drove, on an almost exactly parallel route to rejoin the lane up to Green Hill from Hilton (GR 787037).

As it descends towards Hilton the farm lane becomes a hard flinty track - very welcome in wet weather after the soft going through the woods. There are picturesque views of Hilton church against the background of the woods on the escarpment of Combe Hill ahead; you reach the road through the village almost opposite the church. Turn left here and almost immediately right, down Duck Street. The village street, accompanied by the tiny stream that gives rise to its name, becomes a green lane and takes you down the broad rounded valley towards Milton Abbey. Two-thirds of a mile after leaving the village (GR 790023) you reach a beautiful chalk track running along an avenue of ancient, once pollarded trees. Turn left here to head up to the road, where you turn right to retrace your steps to Milton Abbas, rather than turning right back down to the abbey to follow the footpath down the valley.

9) The Vale of the Stour

Distance: 8 miles
Start: The Fiddleford Inn, near Sturminster Newton
Map: sheet 194, GR 804132

This walk takes in a fine stretch of the Stour Valley and the slopes on the south side of the valley with their tight-knit fields of pasture bordered by thick hedges and tall trees. It finishes with a walk among the delightful oaks of Piddles Wood. The walk passes a village store and pub in Okeford Fitzpaine, as well as starting and finishing at a pub. It is a walk which I feel gives some

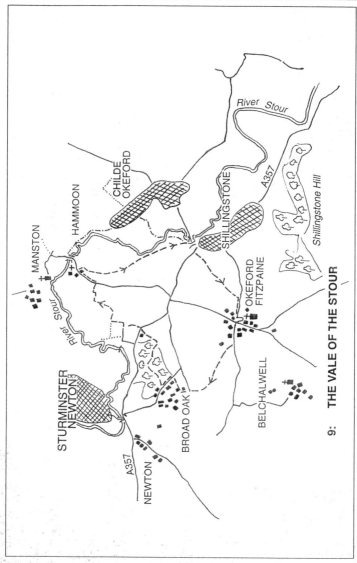

9:   THE VALE OF THE STOUR

Looking north-east from Bladeley Hill, above Buckland Newton *(Walk 11)*
Melcombe Horsey Parish Church at Binghams Melcombe *(Walk 13)*

Looking across the arable downs above Tolpuddle *(Walk 18)*
Houns Tout, Swyre Head and westwards along the coast from the
top of Emmetts Hill *(Walk 19, 21)*

of the flavour of Hardy's "Valley of the Little Dairies". It can be combined with a visit to Sturminster Newton and indeed can be started from there by taking the path from Penny Street along the banks of the river to Fiddleford Manor and thence to the Fiddleford Inn. If you are on a Hardy pilgrimage you will want to see "Riverside" (GR 785144), the northern half of a semi-detached Victorian villa in which he spent the first two years of married life and wrote *The Return of the Native.* The Fiddleford Inn is a mile and a half out of Sturminster Newton on the A357 towards Durweston and Blandford (if travelling from Blandford turn right at Durweston Bridge).

Park your car in the road outside the Fiddleford Inn (GR 804132) and walk north up the lane through the hamlet of Fiddleford. Four hundred yards from the main road the road turns sharp left and you turn right through a wide gap in the hedge. Head due east for 100 yards on the bridleway and follow it round to the left to reach the old Somerset and Dorset railway line. Turn right on the old S & D track (alternatively known to its passengers as the "slow and dirty" or the "swift and delightful", depending on their experience of it). After 200 yards you meet a bridleway signpost and turn left off the old track to head north east across some flat hedge-bound fields of pasture until you meet a hard farm lane, where you turn right to reach the road to Hammoon. Turn left along the road and walk into Hammoon.

In the Domesday Book this was just plain Ham, occupying a site by the Stour very similar to that of Ham near Richmond on Thames. Very shortly afterwards the manor was granted to one of William the Conqueror's henchmen and in the following century it is recorded as Ham Galfridi de Moiun - a reference to the town of Moyon in Normandy.

From Hammoon you may wish to extend the walk by rather less than a mile by turning right on the far side of the bridge just after the hamlet to follow the footpath along the east bank of the Stour, taking you into Childe Okeford village, recrossing the Stour at the footbridge just east of Bere Marsh Farm (GR 824125) and rejoining the route below by Hayward Bridge.

Turn right in the hamlet by the post box in the wall in Hammoon (GR 817145). The metalled lane turns to grass by a red brick cottage and finishes by a sign beseeching you to "Please keep to footpath" - in fact a bridleway. A mile and a half away to your left the grassy ramparts of Hambledon Hill rise above Childe Okeford. The bridleway follows a broad thorn hedge on your right to bring you to the district council-owned woods (GR 819133). There is a small vineyard on your right; you are now walking along the top of the tiniest of escarpments with fine views across the intricate field networks of the alluvial valley floor of the Stour to your left. You reach a fine cottage of stone and brick set off the track on the right. Now the ancient route from Hammoon to Shillingstone becomes a hedged-in farm lane, its surface steadily improving as you approach Bere Marsh Farm. At the farm you see the iron span of

Hayward Bridge, carrying the Childe Okeford road over the Stour. Properly this should be Hayford Bridge - the modern bridge replacing the much more ancient ford "by the hayfield". Turn right on the road here to pass under the railway bridge; keep right at the fork and cross over the main A357 by Hambledon Farm (GR 821120).

A muddy farm lane runs south-west from the left-hand side of the farm. Follow this for a mile until you reach Mill Farm and the road running into Okeford Fitzpaine (GR 812 110). Turn right on the road and follow it into the village, past the church on your left. The road forks at a warning sign for the school; keep right here and make for the Royal Oak pub ahead across the main street to your right.

The gathering of moss from the north-facing slopes of Okeford Hill and Belchalwell Hill was once a moderately lucrative trade in the village, being raked from the grass or gathered by hand and taken to Shillingstone Station for despatch to Covent Garden.

From the Royal Oak the Fifehead Neville road takes you west out of the village. Ignore the delightful cast iron sign pointing right down Darknoll Lane indicating the "Halter path to Sturminster". A hundred and fifty yards later turn right immediately after a very modern red brick bungalow, up a drive and over a tiny brook. The drive brings you to a house standing amid a wide expanse of gravel (GR 800112) and a large grassy garden. Keep the hedge on your right and make your way north-west across two arable fields to a tiny brook which follows a hedge punctuated by gnarled ash trees. The path up the gentle slope of Banbury Hill is waymarked with the usual Dorset county council white disc waymarks; you may find binoculars useful on this stretch for spotting the gateways thus marked.

The ramparts of the hill top fort are hidden behind a hedge on the left. You join a green lane at a hunting gate with some scruffy sheds on the right (GR 791119) and follow this down the hill joining the public road. Directly in front is the tall modern house replacing an old cottage with the most delightful of names - Dirty Gate (GR 791124). The road turns sharp left and you turn right, past the front of the house and the covered swimming pool on the far side of it. The path takes you along the slope with a delightful old thick hedge on your left, bringing you to the road running uphill into Piddles Wood. Turn left on the road (GR 794124) and follow it to the top of the rise, where you find a woodland track turning off to your right. Follow this, heading north-east, until it forks at a clearing. Turn right here (GR 796130), following the path indicated due east to Angiers Farm.

Piddles Wood is first recorded as Puttekwurth in 1244. A worth is an enclosed area, whilst the first element seems likely to refer to a hawk or a kite.

The next path junction is very slightly at variance with what the map shows. You reach a T-junction of woodland tracks; turn right, following the path downhill, signed to Angiers Lane. You exit from the wood and turn left to follow the edge of the wood along on your left, heading north-east. Very soon the Fiddleford Inn comes into view; the path reaches the main road by a telephone box and a red brick stable, almost opposite the pub.

10) Trent and the Comptons

Distance: 6 miles
Start: the Rose and Crown, Trent
Map: sheet 183, GR 590184

Just east of the growing sprawl of Yeovil a small salient of Dorset's hills overlooks the flat lands of south Somerset, with views all the way to Glastonbury Tor and the Mendip Hills to the north. This area, lying to the north of the main A30, is particularly rich in sunken lanes. Some of these are now followed by tarred public roads; many are followed only by footpaths and bridleways. The walk has as its start point a particularly delightful pub, the locally renowned Rose and Crown. There is a particular delight in an ancient village pub whose windows open over fields; the Rose and Crown is as "real" a pub as you could wish for - moreover it serves very good beer. Many of the houses in Trent (the walk finishes along the main street of the village) were in existence when Charles II spent three weeks in the village in hiding following the Battle of Worcester in 1651. An unusual attraction of this walk is that it takes you past the butterfly farm in Over Compton; this would make an attractive start point when open. This walk starts at a fine pub and passes another along the way. There is also a village shop in Trent.

To reach the start, turn north off the A30 at the junction just east of the top of Babylon Hill, climbing out of Yeovil on its way to Sherborne. After a mile and a half the road forks; turn right and find the pub after 400 yards on the right. As you look at the L-shaped front of the pub you will see a stile on the left-hand end of the building. Climb this and set off across the middle of this field (occasionally arable, latterly seeded grazing). The path takes you south-east, the small sewage works partly screened by trees away to your right. You cross a tarred farm lane and descend to cross a tributary of the Trent Brook at a small wooden footbridge (GR 596181). Cross over the stream (the map marginally inaccurate here) and turn right to see a stile in a hedge. A large oak tree stands just to the left of a wooden electricity pole in the field in front of you. Make for the tree and as you reach it you will see a row of new houses in front of you. Make for the left-hand end of these (again the map very slightly inaccurate) and find a stile by a holly bush. Turn right over the stile to walk south with the new houses on your right; turn left when you come to the road to reach the Griffin's Head pub. Turn right here and, after 150 yards, right at the telephone box to leave the village on the Stallen

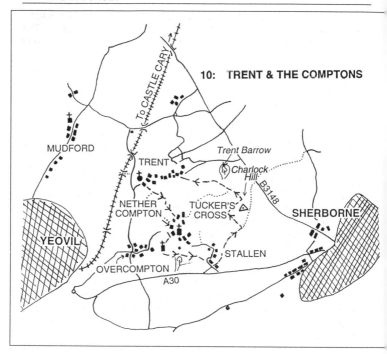

10: TRENT & THE COMPTONS

road. After a little over 200 yards you reach a wide modern drive turning right opposite the entrance to the rectory. Follow the drive as it turns left into the chicken farm by an old twisted beech tree, turn right to head up the gentle slope to a recent "set-aside" plantation, apparently all of oak.

You exit from the new plantation at Over Compton church and Compton House, the home of Conservation Worldwide (formerly Worldwide Butterflies). Turn left down the drive, through a fine old wooden gate with an intriguing latch. You reach the bottom of a dip with a new pond on the left, not yet shown on the map. The drive reaches a fork in the trees; bear right up the hill through the trees, heading east. You exit from the trees and walk straight ahead with a hedge on your right; when you reach the corner of the wood again, turn right to follow an old lane inside the edge of the wood - this not being marked on the map. The lane becomes sunken, marked as a black pecked line on the map; a similar sunken lane comes in from the left and then immediately turns right at the top of a short rise. Keep straight ahead to turn right on the road in Stallen. After 300 yards a narrow lane turns left between two cottages. Follow this through its cutting up the hill in the conifer plantation. The entrance to the walk's second chicken farm turns left. A third of a mile later (GR 614174) you reach a track junction.

Turn left at the track junction to follow the level track to the dutch barn at Tucker's Cross.

Robert Tucker was a suicide, a "notorious bad character" buried here in 1820; at that time few incumbents would have suicides buried in consecrated ground, hence his lonely resting place.

Turn right off the track here to follow the green lane north-east. You enter a miniature arboreal tunnel and find a track junction hidden below the level of the surrounding fields. Turn left at this bucolic traffic triangle and follow the sunken lane, now somewhat eroded by gullying despite the efforts of the farmer to prevent it by installing land drains. The sunken lane ends with a view of the spire of Trent church just over a mile to the west; beyond stretches the expanse of the Somerset levels to the north-west.

The west-facing escarpment of Charlock Hill is much in favour with kestrels, buzzards and the occasional sparrowhawk taking advantage of the lift given by the prevailing wind.

The bridleway continues down the small grassy valley, past a series of hydraulic rams, and brings you to an elegant old iron five-bar gate, where you turn right to join a hedged-in farm lane taking you down to Trent. The final part of the walk gives a glimpse of some of the sturdy houses in the villages, largely now the homes of well-heeled exiles from Yeovil. Turn left at the T-junction at the end of the village by the almshouses to walk down the road to the church and your car.

Trent church and its environs are well worth a little exploration. The tall stone house between the church and the road is the chantry house, built by John Frank, Henry VI's Lord Keeper. Behind the church is Church Farm, hiding its beauty from the road. In the church are memorials to the Windham family - the fugitive King Charles II was the guest of Frank Windham whom he described as "my old acquaintance and a very honest man" - as well as to one Roger Wyke, a knight in the reign of King Edward III. The ancient stones of Trent church and much of the village are perfectly preserved, but the way of life that created them has gone for ever.

11)   Dogbury Gate and Minterne Hill

Distance: 6 miles
Start: the Gaggle of Geese, Buckland Newton
Map: sheet 194, GR 688050

The walk has been laid out to give the widest views possible; across the Stour Valley from Bladelely Hill all the way to the Wiltshire Downs, from Little

The Church of the Holy Rood, Buckland Newton

Minterne Hill south along the Cerne Valley as it slices through the chalk downs towards Dorchester and north across the clay lowlands of Blackmore Vale from Dogbury Hill. This is one of several walks that explores the landscape of Hardy's *The Woodlanders*; the glorious native forest cover of his novel survives only in tiny remnants. In fact the woods he portrays so well were not as extensive as he describes in his lifetime - he is harking back to a slightly anachronistic Arcadia. The walk takes us through a fragment of such natural wood tucked beneath the north-facing escarpment of the chalk. Buckland Newton is a pleasantly straggling village whose real centre is hard to divine; it is beautifully sited against the chalk spurs. Little visited, it makes a fine start point for a walk. This walk starts and ends at a pub but passes no other; there is a shop on the main road in Buckland Newton.

Park your car at the Gaggle of Geese pub (GR 688050) just west of the B3143 Sturminster Newton to Dorchester road. Turn left out of the pub and left again immediately after the telephone box to head up the dead-end road towards Court Farm. You reach a double gate across the farm road; go through this and turn right, a wooden bridleway sign indicating the route for Watts Hill. The lane is muddy at first then becomes drier as you leave the clay and ascend the chalk spur of Bladeley Hill with the chalk bowl of Whitcombe Bottom down to your right. Take the time to turn round occasionally as you

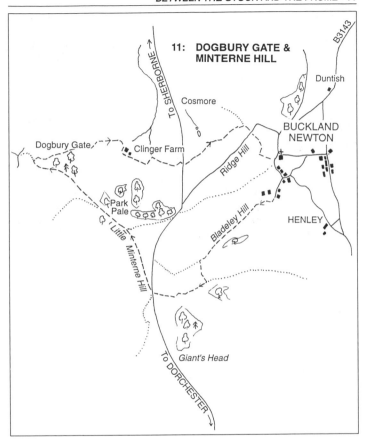

11: DOGBURY GATE & MINTERNE HILL

climb; there are superb views to the north-east across the valley of the Stour to the line of the Wiltshire chalk downs. A mile from the pub brings you to a metal-clad barn (GR 678040). Turn left here on the hedged green lane and after 300 yards right at a T-junction of tracks. This farm lane brings you to the Giants Head road running north from Dorchester (GR 673036). Despite its lack of any identifying number it is busier and faster than a number of A-roads I can think of in the county; take care when crossing it. Bear right once over the road to head just west of north, through a field of grazing making for a gate in the far corner.

There are good views south down the valley of the Cerne; Little Minterne Hill is a fine escarpment with scattered trees and gorse. Ahead is Dogbury gate, effectively a miniature pass at the head of the Cerne Valley taking the main A352 over to the clay lowlands of Blackmore Vale. Make your way along the escarpment with a fence on your left until you reach a T-junction with the unsurfaced road from Gales Hill to Dogbury Gate (GR 669044). Turn left here, following the old embankment enclosing the medieval deer park - the "Park Pale" as named on the map. Follow this road for almost a mile along the top of the escarpment of Little Minterne Hill, with good views of Minterne Magna house, the seat of Lord Digby, of a branch of the Digby family that owns Sherborne Castle. During the Second World War it was a Royal Navy hospital and for a time my mother was stationed there as a naval nursing sister.

You walk through the earthworks of Dogbury camp among the beech trees and then descend Dogbury Hill with fine views of High Stoy Hill in front of you, sadly without a footpath to its summit. You are now overlooking what some believe to be the location of the opening scene of Hardy's *The Woodlanders*, where Barber Percomb enquires the way to "Little Hintock", approximating to Hermitage. (More recent research seems to point to a location on the Yeovil-Dorchester road, now the A37.) A few yards after you leave the trees a path turns right off the track (GR 658052), a fence gap and a makeshift gate (looking as though its origin was a bed-frame) marking the spot. For the next stretch of the walk as far as the Giants Head road care is needed in navigation.

The path sets off across rough turf and bends to the right. You come to an old quarry on the right and then descend steeply to cross the field below the trees clinging to the steep chalk escarpment to your right. You enter Dogbury Plantation at a hunting gate and leave it by a similar gate. Bear slighty to the right up a bank and then keep the wood boundary on your left as you follow the hedge around the left-hand side of a sheep-grazed field. Three hundred yards after leaving the wood you turn left through a farm gate through a hedge so thick it is really more of an elongated thicket. Ahead of you are two mature oaks in a hedge; 15 yards to their right is a gate in the same hedge. Go through this gate and bear right, making for Clinger Farm. At the end of the field you join a hedged-in bridleway and descend to cross a tiny stream in front of the farmhouse. Turn right on the track past the farm buildings and left at the end, steeply up, through a farmyard gate. Through this gate you head south-east along the farm lane, passing a row of old red brick pigsties on your left (used as pheasant pens when I last walked through), followed by a modern barn on the right and lastly a red brick farm cottage. The bridleway descends to a confluence of two tiny streams. Turn left as you cross the stream to follow an old track for 40 yards, the tiny brook on your left, a row of trees in a hedge on your right.

This green lane ends with a gate directly ahead and one on the right. Go through the gate on the right and head up the hill with the twisting hedge on your left-hand side. Below you is Cosmore and the former Revels Inn, now Revels Farm, or as Hardy had it in *The Woodlanders*, "The Revellers Inn". Cross over the Giants Head road and head north-east down the drive to Vale View Farm, which soon turns to a grassy track. You see the recent fishing ponds below you to the left and the track climbing the hill from them appearing on the ground as a grey stripe on the grassy hillside. Follow this track up the hill, crossing the Ridge Hill road at a manure dump. On the north side of the road the path runs along with the wood on your left; you enter it and descend on a good path, turning left as you leave it. You bear left through a gate and resume your former course now very steeply down the escarpment to the penultimate gate of the walk by the corner of the copse behind the Manor. Continue down the hill with this copse on your left and find a narrow track at the corner of the field taking you to the road by a magnificent thatched double garage at Manor Cottage. Turn right on the road, keep left at the village pound with the bridleway leading up Gales Hill to the right and follow the road around to the Gaggle of Geese and your car.

When you join the road, take a few minutes to enjoy the church of the Holy Rood. Inside is a brass, dated 1624, to Thomas Barnes, a kinsman of the Dorset Poet.

12) Plush and the Dorset Gap

Distance: 8 miles
Start: The Brace of Pheasants, Plush
Map: sheet 194, GR 714021

This walk starts and ends at a notable pub; it passes no shop nor any other pub on its way. However it can of course be combined with the Melcombe Bingham and the Dorset Gap walk, to make a real day of it, and giving you the chance to pause half way at the Fox. It is a little-walked route which straddles the chalk ridge north of Dorchester, giving fine views both south as far as Hardy's Monument and the Purbeck Hills and, later, northwards clear across Blackmore Vale as far as Duncliffe Hill, just west of Shaftesbury and the Wiltshire Downs beyond. Much of the walking is along the top of chalk escarpments, giving easy and exhiliarating walking. The start point is the Brace of Pheasants pub in the hamlet of Plush. To look at the pub now, snug beneath its thatch, it is hard to believe that it burnt down in 1979. I shall forgo giving directions to Plush, for however you reach it you will have a certain amount of twisting along very minor roads. It can be reached from Hazelbury Bryan, or more usually by following the sign pointing the way up East Hill from Piddletrenthide. The hamlet of Plush is the strongest candidate for Hardy's

"Flintcomb Ash" of *Tess of the D'Urbervilles*. However, like "Hintock House" in *The Woodlanders*, the part it plays in his narrative means that Hardy purposely makes it hard to identify with a real house or village.

The pub lies at a T-junction; walk away from the pub down the stem of the "T" and follow the Hazelbury Bryan road as it swings to the left and goes up a short rise towards the chapel, hidden away from the road on the left.

Until 1936 Plush was part of the parish of Buckland Newton, which meant that any death in the hamlet required burial at Buckland Newton. The journey over to Buckland was doubly difficult if carrying a corpse.

Immediately before the chapel is an entrance to a house set back from the road on the left; turn right opposite the entrance, the gate marked with a footpath arrow. The path follows a chalky track, south, diagonally up the hillside to a fence where you climb a stile into an arable field. The path swings left here to head west across the top of Plush Hill; I have found that the farmer marks its route with tractor wheel ruts. You reach a second fence and keep heading west, following the border between plough and pasture. You reach a circular concrete platform immediately before a gate in a fence (GR 720018).

From the top of Plush Hill there are very fine views across a sizeable area of south Dorset. Ahead of you is a small copse; keep straight ahead towards the corner of it to see a bridleway waymark on a fencepost (GR 722018). Turn left to follow the edge of the copse along on your right. When you reach the end of the copse look ahead to see the fence you have just crossed. Ahead of you that fence reaches a clump of hawthorn; make for the left-hand end of the hawthorns and find a hunting gate in the fence. Turn right on the far side of the fence and follow it along the top of the escarpment; the trig point lies back from the path on the right. Three hundred yards after the end of the wood the path crosses a prominent dyke running down the hillside to your left.

You are now walking with the hedge on your left. Keep along the top of the ridge here to follow the crest of Lyscombe Hill around as it swings to the right. You meet the prominent earthwork of Cross Dyke, surmounted by squat oak trees; two hunting gates mark the path. From the dyke make your way due east with views to the right down the dry chalk valley of Lyscombe Bottom. You reach a patch of gorse as you look to the right along the escarpment of Bowdens and make your way across the grassy hilltop to the left-hand (western) end of the prominent earthwork built across the ridge (GR 741025). From here there are views south-east all the way to Poole, Poole Harbour and out into the Channel. Corfe Castle can be made out in its gap in the Purbeck Hills, not silhouetted as it has the line of the ridge stretching east of Smedmore Hill behind it. This is one of my favourite viewpoints in the county.

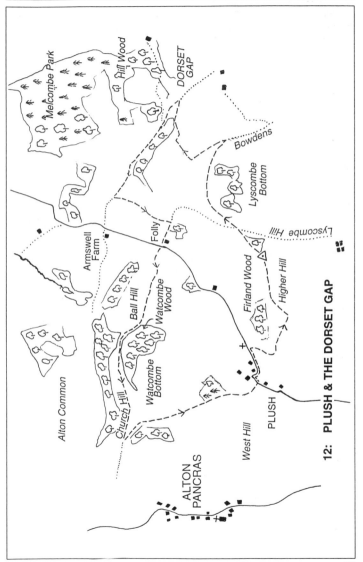

12: **PLUSH & THE DORSET GAP**

Now double back to your left, climbing gently, following the bridleway climbing gently north-west with a hedge and thicket on your right. At the end of the hedge at the top of the hill you see an iron tank atop a breeze block stand built just where one might site a viewing platform. On the north side of this platform are the bridleway waymarks. Turn right here when you have had your fill of the view and head north-east, gently downhill. There is a fence on your left; bear slightly away from this to see the waymarks on a post as you approach a gap in the trees on the east-facing escarpment of the hill. The path (a bridleway) goes steeply downhill as a sunken lane. A footpath bears off it to the left and a private track to a gate turns right at the same point. Keep heading down the hill on the sunken lane and turn left at the track junction at the bottom (GR 744031). This is the point where, if you wish, you can make more of a full day's walk and turn right to combine the Melcombe Bingham and the Dorset Gap walk.

You walk north-west for a few yards to the four way signpost at the Dorset Gap. Keep straight ahead here, following the sign for Armswell Farm and follow the track through the a wood of fine mature ash. As you exit from the wood below Nettlecombe Tout bear left, making for the gateway in the hedge on the skyline immediately in front of you. Keep the wood on your left; the path is marked with bridleway signs as you pass through two hedges en route for the three new barns east of Armswell Farm. The map is now a little inacurrate for this stage. A concrete road runs west from the new barns and bungalow down to Armswell Farm. The footpath shown on the map as running just west of south from a point half way between the barn and the road (GR 733038) in fact heads southwards from the barns themselves.

The route over the top of Ball Hill is an improvement on the one running at the foot of its north-facing escarpment simply because of the views it offers. Turn left here; you are walking with a thorn hedge on your right, making for a point just to the right of a small chalk scrape on the little spur to the west from Nettlecombe Tout. The path is indicated with several waymarked stiles before you reach the hedged-in bridleway taking you down to Folly. Cross over the road at Folly (named after the old Folly pub, commemorated in the name of the house by the road) and make your way west, steeply up through a copse and on to the top of Ball Hill. Turn round and you can see directly behind you the steel water tank that gave such fine views above the Dorset Gap. The path takes you along the northern side of Watcombe Wood - Watcombe Bottom originally meant "the combe where wheat was grown". Along the top of Church Hill the pasture fields with their earthworks have been declared to be part of the Countryside Stewardship scheme. The point you should make for is the right-hand corner of the conifer plantation above Plush (GR 712026). From here a chalky track takes you steeply downhill; turn left on the road at the bottom to the Brace of Pheasants and your car.

13) Melcombe Bingham and the Dorset Gap

Distance: 7 miles
Start: the Fox, Ansty
Map: sheet 194, GR 766033

This walk starts and finishes at a pub, now developed almost more into a hotel; it passes no other pub nor any shop along its route, although it is perfectly possible to walk on to the Brace of Pheasants at Plush from the Dorset Gap. There are very varied views - for its relatively modest elevation the narrow ridge of Nordon Hill, just east of the Dorset Gap offers a remarkable view both north and south. Bingham's Melcombe House and church are very beautiful, almost more so for the former not being open to the public. You are free to gaze at its exterior in solitude from the footpath through the grounds and absorb the spirit of the place. Reaching the Ansty Fox involves, if anything, even more rural lane driving than reaching the Brace of Pheasants. If you are travelling from the direction of Blandford or Dorchester, I suggest you turn north off the A354 main road at Milborne St Andrew, 8 miles from Dorchester. A mile and a half from the village turn left at Hewish, a row of cottages tight on the road on the left; follow this unclassified road north-east for 3 miles, up the chalk valley and along the top of Combe Hill to the dip at Ansty Cross; turn left here to find the pub on your left.

Head down the hill from the Ansty Fox, past a row of burnt out cottages on the right. At the end of these turn right, keeping Brewery Cottage, a red brick bungalow set back from the road, on your right. The path brings you to a gate leading to a small field. Make for the gate at the far side of this, crossing the tiny brook at a culvert. Make your way up the hill to the right-hand corner of the field and cross the road (Cothayes Drove) here to find yourself in an arable field where the right of way is usually marked by a tractor driving through the winter barley. The path brings you to a stile. Cross this and keep straight ahead. On the hillside in front of you is a prominent small conifer plantation, shaped on the map like a meat cleaver (Fern Wood - GR 755032). Keep this to your left as you make your way gently uphill following the prominent track to bring you to the left-hand side of the Melcombe Park Farm (GR 751034) - slightly at variance with the map. A surfeit of waymarks greets your arrival at the back of the farm.

Turn left through the gate and bear right, keeping the wood below you to your right; this is Cony-gar Copse - the name may well refer to its use in the Middle Ages as a purpose-built rabbit colony for food supply. You pass through a hunting gate and find yourself walking along a narrow ridge with very fine views. To your right you are looking over the top of Hill Wood and Melcombe Park, tiny fragments remaining in situ of the once extensive forest

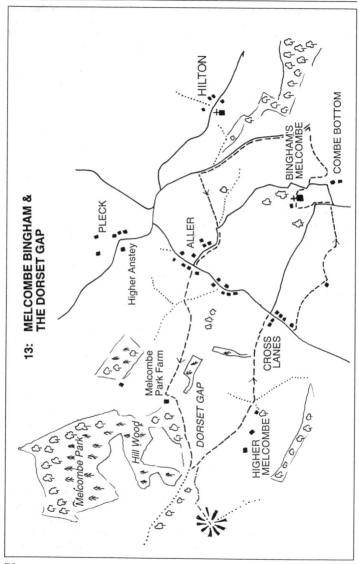

**13: MELCOMBE BINGHAM &
THE DORSET GAP**

HILTON

PLECK

Higher Anstey

ALLER

BINGHAM'S
MELCOMBE

COMBE BOTTOM

Melcombe Park Farm

DORSET GAP

CROSS
LANES

Melcombe Park

Hill Wood

HIGHER
MELCOMBE

of the clay lowlands north of the Dorset chalk. The inhabitants of this now forgotten world peopled one of Hardy's most enjoyable novels, *The Woodlanders*. To your left you are looking down the chalk valley to Higher Melcombe and beyond. The path dips and suddenly brings you to the Dorset Gap, a pass in the central chalk spine of Dorset where the ancient ridgeway along the ridge met slightly less ancient routes from Blackmore Vale to the lower Frome Valley. Nowadays a walkers' signpost marks the spot. Turn left here to head south-east along the sunken green lane. (After 100 yards a sunken lane turns right up the hill through the trees. A half mile side track from your route gives you one of the best views in the county.) The sunken lane leaves the trees and follows the edge of an arable field with a hedge on your right, making for the left-hand side of the houses at Higher Melcombe.

As you pass Higher Melcombe, notice the chapel attached to the house. This dates from 1610 although there has been a chapel here since 1302. You pass through two farm gates, then bear left as you join the private drive taking you from Higher Melcombe to meet the public road at Cross Lanes (GR 761024). Turn right at the crossroads and walk down the Cheselbourne road. After the last house on the right (Badger Sett does bed and breakfast - see accommodation guide) turn left off the road at a footpath sign into a field. A chalk track then swings to the left and takes you diagonally up the side of Henning Hill, almost to the flint barn by its summit. Turn left at the track junction. There are fine views here down to Bingham's Melcombe. Follow the track down the hill and turn left on the public road (GR 772017).

As the road turns left, keep straight ahead down the drive to Bingham's Melcombe (it is a right of way although it is not waymarked) and turn right as you reach the house to walk down to the church - well worth a visit.

Bingham's Melcombe House, though not open to the public, is one of the oldest and most interesting manor houses in Dorset. It was the seat of the Bingham family for no less than 600 years; one Sir Richard Bingham fought at the turning point Battle of Lepanto in 1571 when the naval power of the Ottoman Empire in the Mediterranean was broken for ever. The beautiful buttressed gatehouse dates from the reign of Edward II or III.

The church is well worth a visit; on the far side cross the tiny stream flowing along the edge of the garden and bear right, following the stream along to reach a gate where you turn right onto the public road (GR 774021). Turn right and, after little more than a hundred yards, left at a right-hand bend, a bridleway taking you across a small field with a hedge on your right.

Bear right on the far side of the hedge and follow the path, stepped into the abrupt hillside as it makes its way up the spur of Combe Hill. There is a fine view down into Combe Bottom and west across Melcombe Bingham. Follow the path up to the road and turn left to follow it as it heads just west of north along the escarpment. You pass the track coming up from the left from Binghams Melcombe, then the bridleway from the right, although the copse does not reach the road, as the map shows. Two hundred yards after the track joins the road the road bends to the right and a bridleway turns off right. One hundred yards after the bridleway turning right you see a hedge leading off the road to the left. Turn left through a hunting gate on the north side of this hedge and follow the bridleway steeply down the escarpment to Aller. I noticed some severe gullying as I descended, apparently caused by ploughing up and down the slope rather than across it. Keep straight ahead when you reach the road to follow it through Aller to the T-junction below the Fox. Turn right here to reach your car.

14) Rawlsbury Camp and Bulbarrow

Distance: 7 miles
Start: the Fox, Ansty
Map: sheet 194, GR 766033

Bulbarrow is simply one of the finest viewpoints in the county; most of north Dorset can be seen from its summit and the view on a clear day extends well into Wiltshire and Somerset. This walk combines the summit with a walk along the fine chalk ridge of Hilton Hill and the village of Hilton itself; it can be extended to visit Milton Abbas if you wish. The walk begins with an ascent of just over 500 feet in 2 miles, latterly quite steeply - just the thing to set you up for a meal later at the well-known Ansty Fox. To reach the start, turn north off the A354 Blandford-Dorchester road at Milborne St Andrew, 8 miles from Dorchester. A mile and a half from the village turn left at Hewish, a row of cottages tight on the road on the left; follow this unclassified road north-east for 3 miles, up the chalk valley and along the top of Combe Hill to the dip at Ansty Cross; turn left here to find the pub on your left. If you are driving to Ansty from any point to its north I recommend you mapread your way there.

Turn right out of the Fox towards Higher Ansty. Three hundred yards after the pub you see a thick-set oak tree in the hedge on the left (GR 767034); turn left after this and cross the field of pasture, making for a prominent stile with a farm visible beyond it. Keep the farm to your right and cross the road to head into the yard of Hollybrook Farm. Turn left as you approach the yard to head diagonally across an L-shaped field full of discarded farm machinery. On the far side of the field a stile brings you into a narrow lane; look down to the left to see a fine thatched cottage, half hidden down the lane. Turn right on the lane and immediately left at the T-junction to head up Pleck Lane, through the farm buildings. A quarter of a mile after the farm you come to a pond on the right (GR 765040) and the track ends at two gates. Go through the left-hand gate and head up the hill to another gate, following a fence which becomes a hedge 50 yards to your right. You reach the remains of an old farm on your right; this is Rawlsbury Farm which earlier this century had a good

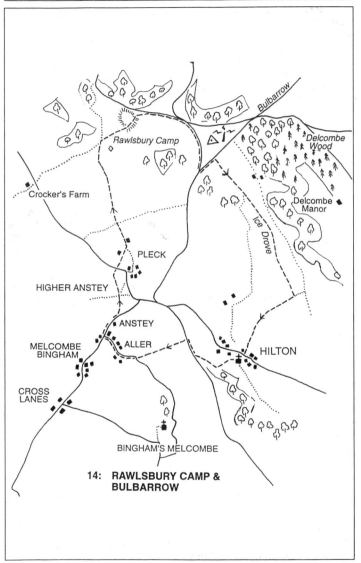

Bulbarrow

Delcombe Wood

Rawlsbury Camp

Crocker's Farm

Delcombe Manor

Ice Drove

PLECK

HIGHER ANSTEY

ANSTEY

ALLER

MELCOMBE BINGHAM

HILTON

CROSS LANES

BINGHAM'S MELCOMBE

14: RAWLSBURY CAMP & BULBARROW

reputation in the village for the cider made here. Ahead of you is a prominent ash tree at the top of the slope with a signpost beneath it. Turn right when you reach it to head north-east, steeply up the hill past a chalk pit; you are now walking along the Dorset Ridgeway. You arrive at a gate and the first of the impressive ramparts of Rawlsbury Camp.

How it came by its English name is not clear. It does, of course, pre-date the Anglo-Saxon settlement of Dorset by some time, being an Iron Age hill fort.

Follow the green track across the turf of the hill fort and keep left at a fine fork just after the fort to join the road to the summit of Bulbarrow.

Until soon after the Second World War, the summit of Bulbarrow and the roads across the grassy plateau on the summit were unfenced. You reach the end of the hedge on your left; it now continues as a simple wire fence. At this point the road was gated as were all the roads leading from the summit. Keep left at the fork on the summit (GR 774058) to take in the views north from the top of the escarpment of Woolland Hill, across Wiltshire and much of Somerset. There is a plaque with an explanation of what you are seeing (GR 785059). From the viewpoint head back the way you came and turn left at the fork so that you are heading south-west with Delcombe Wood on your left; a third of a mile later you see a wooden sign on the left with a blue waymark indicating the bridleway to Milton Abbas and Hilton, taking you along the hill-top track known as Ice Drove. Turn left here to head south-east, along the escarpment above Hilton Bottom.

After a mile and a half you reach a T-junction of tracks and turn right to head steeply down the hill on a hard flinty track. There are picturesque views of Hilton church against the background of the woods on the escarpment of Combe Hill ahead; you reach the road through the village almost opposite the church. Cross the road by the church and make your way through the churchyard to the lane behind it. A signpost points the way ahead to "Aller 1 mile". The path takes you south-west with a hedge on your right to Little Down Plantation, clinging to the chalk escarpment. Before you enter the woods, enjoy the view to your left, down the valley to the church of Milton Abbey in its perfect setting. You enter the woods at a hunting gate and bear right where the path forks immediately inside the woods. The well used path takes you up the hill to leave the woods at a second hunting gate. The map is slightly in error here, showing the woods running all the way to the road (GR 776030). You cross a field to meet the road at a stile and turn right to follow the road north for 200 yards, turning left through a hunting gate to follow the bridleway steeply down the escarpment to Aller. I noticed some severe gullying as I descended, apparently caused by ploughing up and down the slope rather than across it. Keep straight ahead when you reach the road to follow it through Aller to the T-junction below the Fox. Turn right here to reach your car.

15)   Giant Hill and the Source of the Cerne

Distance: 10 miles
Start: Kettle Bridge car park, Cerne Abbas
Map: sheet 194, GR 664014

This walk runs through some wild landscapes in the heart of Dorset's chalk country, at one point offering views as far as Glastonbury Tor, the Quantocks and the Mendips. The walk passes no pub en route, neither shop nor cafe; Cerne Abbas has pubs and tea-rooms. If the centre of the much visited village of Cerne Abbas is full of cars then you should follow the signs to the picnic site and park your car at Kettle Bridge picnic site, on the northern edge of the village. If approaching Cerne Abbas from the north, along the A352 Sherborne-Dorchester main road, turn left at the Giant viewpoint and left again after 200yards.

From the picnic site car park turn left on to the dead end road to the old stone bridge. From the centre of Cerne Abbas there is a very pleasant walk out of the village, avoiding roads. From the New Inn follow Duck Street opposite and turn immediately right into Mill Lane, following the signs to the forge. This alleyway rapidly becomes a footpath between cottages and brings you by the stream bank behind the school playing fields to reach the bridge over the chalk stream of the River Cerne.

Head east over the bridge and then left, up to a new barn. Turn right opposite the barn to follow the path between hedges to the escarpment of Giant Hill. Follow the footpath around to the right through the trees clinging to the steepest part of the chalk slope. Five hundred yards after the bridge you see the village sports field below you to your right. A sunken chalk track joins you from the right and then your path swings left, a graded bridlepath angling up the chalk slope. Three-quarters of a mile after the start you reach a gate on the left leading into a field of rough grazing; the bridleway you are on swings round to the right to meet the busy, fast Sherborne-Dorchester road just south of the Giant's Head Farm campsite. Turn left along the footpath running over the ridge to see a dutch barn by a small copse of Scots pine and beech (GR 671026). Keep heading north-west here, down the hill with a gappy hedge on your right. You enter the small coniferous wood and after 40 yards turn right to leave it at a hunting gate (GR 669027).

From here the bridleway heads along the top of the gorse-covered escarpment. After half a mile you reach the copse of mature beech by the Giant's Head road (GR 672035). Make your way through the scattered trees and follow the path northwards on the far side towards a gate in the corner of a field in front of you. Make your way along the escarpment with a fence on your left until you reach a T-junction with the unsurfaced road from Gales

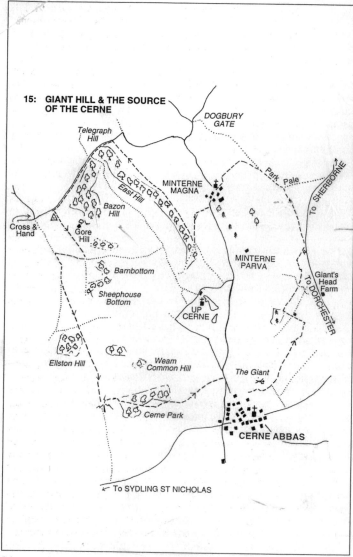

15: GIANT HILL & THE SOURCE OF THE CERNE

DOGBURY GATE

Telegraph Hill

East Hill

MINTERNE MAGNA

Park Pale

To SHERBORNE

Bazon Hill

Cross & Hand

Gore Hill

MINTERNE PARVA

Barnbottom

Giant's Head Farm

Sheephouse Bottom

To DORCHESTER

UP CERNE

Ellston Hill

Weam Common Hill

The Giant

Cerne Park

CERNE ABBAS

← To SYDLING ST NICHOLAS

Hill to Dogbury Gate (GR 669044). Turn left here, following the old embankment enclosing the medieval deer park - the "Park Pale" as named on the map. On your left, now separated from the road by a strip of felling, is a long copse of beech. This ends and the lane returns to being fenced on the left (GR 665045). Forty yards later you reach a gate on the left without any waymark on it. Turn left through this and head north-west, diagonally down the escarpment, making for a gate in a permanent electric fence. Just as the map shows, the bridleway is making for the gap between two tiny copses; in fact a thick hedge connects the two. The path now swings to the left, straight down the hill on a faint track. You reach the stream at a ford and footbridge and follow the unsurfaced lane up to the road by the church in the centre of Minterne Magna.

Turn left on the main road and follow it past the old village pump on the end of Pump Cottage. You pass the entrance to the estate farm buildings on the right and immediately afterwards turn right (GR 659040) to head west along an avenue through a patch of parkland exactly as the map shows. At the end of this field of parkland turn left through a gate by a chalk pit and head due south, diagonally up the hill, making for a small copse of Scots pine and beech not shown on the map. You pass through a gate at the top of the escarpment and walk across the end of a long field beneath some electricity poles. In the far corner of the field in front of you is a hunting gate in the tall hedge, so that you are walking through an arch. Turn right once through the hedge to find yourself walking north-west along a grassy strip between the hedge on your right and the rough woodland clinging to the escarpment of East Hill on your left.

You exit from the trees to find the bridleway continuing as a mossy track, keeping to the hedge on the right. For the next 2 miles there has been a general sorting-out and realignment of the rights of way (in autumn 1992) which actually makes navigation easier, though they have yet to be marked on the map (latest available at the time of writing). The bridleway follows a course parallel to the edge of the wood, some 40 yards to its east, separated by a strip of flinty arable. You reach the Batcombe Down road at spot height 265m and turn left. Here is the ultimate luxury - a walking route of springy moss along the side of the unfenced road. Follow this along; pause along the way to enjoy the view to the right of the road - it will not last long as this field (GR 641045) was planted with trees as part of the set-aside scheme in the winter of 1993-4. You pass the route turning right, across the narrow strip of field into the woods at the head of the Cerne Valley - a short cut return home via the beautiful manor at Up Cerne for the weary, lazy or rain-afflicted. The road enters the woods (GR 640043); your path continues on the edge of the field until the second spot height of 265m (or 868ft on the one inch map) on the road. This is by the easternmost entrance to Batcombe Down picnic site.

This road, Long Ash Lane, was the route followed by Tess, heading south-west, past Dogbury Gate (Walk 11) along the top of Batcombe Down, past Cross in Hand, which lies 500 yards further along the road. It is a relief in stone now badly worn, so much so that it is not clear what is shown. In a separate short story, *The Lost Pyx*, *Hardy* links it to the working of a miracle. It is more likely that it was a shrine connected with the monastery at Cerne.

Turn left here on a new right of way heading south-east, passing to the east of the trig point. Gore Barn (GR 641037), over to your left, stands in a tiny copse of wind-shaped beech not indicated on the map. The path brings you straight to the sharp bend in the track by a clump of beech (GR 642034). Turn right here (on a grid bearing of 280 degrees), making for the horizon just in front of you. A third of a mile of walking brings you to the unsurfaced lane across the downs at a patch of gorse. Turn left onto the lane above the hollow of Eastcombe Bottom. There follows a mile of elevated walking along an open chalk ridge.

A mile and a quarter after joining the downland track you reach the prominent radio mast on the left of the track. Immediately in front of this a path turns left through the hedge and leads to the corner of the wood of Cerne Park. Turn right along the edge of the wood, then left into the coppiced wood, keeping right immediately inside the trees. The path takes you downhill to exit from the trees over a fence into a gully. Ahead of you is a superb view of the splendid giant.

Looking around at the trees lining the chalk slopes you have an idea of the scene when this was the park belonging the abbot of Cerne. As you look at the church in the centre of the village, notice how the medieval monastic foundation was sited so as not to have a sight of the much older chalk figure. Bearing in mind the excess of prudishness abroad during the nineteenth century it is a merciful thing that the giant has survived (or at least intact) at all.

Cross over the end of the farm lane (GR 653013) and follow the path contouring along the hillside with a hedge on your right. This patch of weathered chalk escarpment can be wonderfully muddy; the path brings you to the lane leading south-west from the main road. Turn right on the road by the old workhouse, now a nursing home. Cross diagonally over the main road to walk down the lane and turn left towards the pottery to find your car in the car park on the left.

16)   Sandford Orcas to Cadbury Castle

Distance: 10 miles
Start: the Mitre, Sandford Orcas
Map: sheet 183, GR 626205

The marches of Somerset and Dorset provide some of the most enjoyable walking in the whole region. This is a walk of steep escarpments with wide

Sandford Orcas Manor

views across a good deal of the county of Somerset and south across the ridges of north Dorset. The distance above includes the walk of about a mile from South Cadbury church up to Cadbury Castle, around the innermost rampart and back to the village. The start point of this walk is the Mitre in Sandford Orcas; it then takes you past a further two pubs - the Queens Arms in Corton Denham and the Red Lion in South Cadbury.

To find the start, take the B3148 Marston Road out of Sherborne; after 2 miles you reach a crossroads; turn right and follow the lane for a mile, north-east, to a T-junction; turn right and follow the road down through the remarkable rocky cutting, a feature of the roads to the north of Sherborne, to Sandford Orcas, lying in a hollow. Turn right at the T-junction in the middle of village to find the Mitre after a few yards on your right.

The Mitre pub is named in honour of the man who wrote the first recorded science fiction novel in the English language. This was a certain Francis Godwin (1562-1633). He was rector of the living of Sandford Orcas at the time of the Armada; he went on to become Bishop, first of Llandaff, and then of Hereford - hence the name of the pub. Five years after his death The Man in the Moone, or a Discourse of a Voyage thither *by Domingo Gonsales, the* Speedy Messenger *was published. This was a major influence on Jonathan Swift's* Gulliver's Travels *and a highly innovative work in its own right, showing the author's knowledge of Copernicus's astronomical research.*

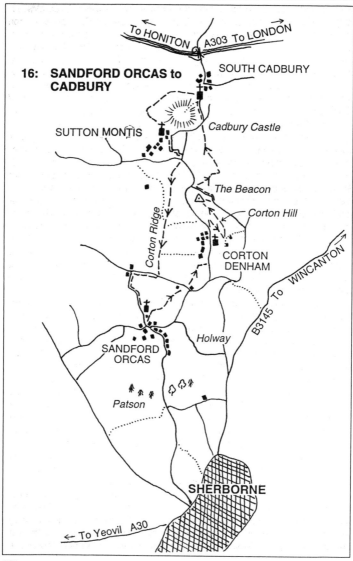

16: SANDFORD ORCAS to CADBURY

SOUTH CADBURY

To HONITON   A303 To LONDON

Cadbury Castle

SUTTON MONTIS

The Beacon

Corton Hill

Corton Ridge

CORTON DENHAM

To WINCANTON

B3145

Holway

SANDFORD ORCAS

Patson

SHERBORNE

← To Yeovil A30

You may well want to combine this walk with a visit to Sandford Orcas Manor, open on Easter Monday and from May to September on Sunday afternoon and on Monday from 10am to 6pm. The house is a delight; built adjacent to the village church of Hamstone it has been little altered since it was built in the middle of the sixteenth century. Remarkably, the present incumbents, the Medlycotts, are only the third family to have owned the house since the 1380s. A special treat is that it is usually the owner who shows visitors round. Sandford Orcas is first recorded as Sanford in Domesday; 900 years later it is still known as this by the locals. The "Orcas" suffix refers to the Norman family of Orescuils who held the manor from the twelfth century.

Turn left out of the Mitre in Sandford Orcas and make your way 400 yards to the left-hand turning to Trent. Immediately after this you will see a signpost on the right pointing the way up a bank indicating "Corton Denham 1 mile". You join a field of pasture above the road; head diagonally across this with Sandford Orcas manor ahead to your left. You pass a small reservoir in the middle of the field surmounted by a tree and a few thorns; your route continues just east of north, descending to the tiny stream flowing from Corton Denham. You climb a stile beneath a tall, ivy-mantled ash tree and then cross the stream by a plank footbridge 40 yards later (GR 626213). Follow the stream along its tree-lined gully; as you reach the farm at Stafford's Green you cross back over it - the path has been diverted in detail from that shown on the map. Bear left over the stream to walk through the farmyard and cross the lane.

In front of you lies a narrow arable field to the left of the stream; follow the thick hedge along on your left, crossing a hedge into a field of pasture with the tower of Corton Denham church directly ahead of you against the backdrop of Corton Hill. Turn right on the road at the farm and left at the T-junction to walk through Corton Denham past the Queen's Arms on your left. At the far end of the village you see the post office stores on the left; immediately afterwards a muddy track bears right off the road, up the hill under some trees. The track bears right, leaves the trees and heads diagonally up Corton Hill as an obvious grassed-over old road cut into the hillside. You reach the private road at the top of the hill; do not go through the gate but turn sharply left and head north-west along the escarpment of Corton Hill with a fence and wall on your right. Strictly, the path stops short of the Beacon at the trig point, but there is a customary right of way to this locally well-known viewpoint with its stone bench. Directly to the west glow the runway lights of the Royal Naval air station at Yeovilton.

From this vantage point you have a fine view of the topography of much of the county of Somerset. The grassy knoll just in front of you to the north-west (summit GR 628238) is Parrock Hill. In the middle of the low-lying Somerset levels beyond rises the steep cone of Glastonbury Tor; to the left of the levels, beyond Yeovilton, lie the Quantock Hills, to the left of them the

Brendons. The hills to the right of the Levels as you look are the Mendips, famous as the site of Cheddar Gorge.

When you can tear yourself away from the view head south-east for 300 yards to reach the road at a gate. Turn left on the road and walk down the steep hill beneath the trees. Turn right at the T-junction at the bottom of the hill and then immediately right again along the lane to Whitcombe. The farm lane becomes a muddy, hedged-in track which ends at the base of a bracken-covered hillside. Turn left at the end of the track to follow the fence along the hillside; the perspective of the main runway at Yeovilton changes as you align yourself exactly with it. A couple of rudimentary stiles mark the passage of the path towards South Cadbury and you join another muddy farm lane (GR 634246) to turn almost immediately right off it as it turns left by a barn. The path leads you down to cross the small stream by a footbridge and you turn right on the road, bearing left at the fork into South Cadbury.

The way up to Cadbury Castle turns left after the first house on the left; there is an information board on the wall on the right. The climb to Cadbury Castle - an out and back detour from the walk - is more than worthwhile. The map shows a footpath running round the hill below the summit.

In practice you are allowed to walk over the top of the fort to savour its spirit of place. It is the second largest Iron Age fortress settlement in the country, after Maiden Castle, outside Dorchester. (A walk around the ramparts of that is well worthwhile, but needs no explanation in this book.) For several summers as a child I was taken by my father to visit the diggings at Cadbury under Leslie Alcock whose painstaking research was detailed in his "By South Cadbury - is that Camelot?" The extensive archeological excavations on the site showed that indeed Cadbury had been reoccupied during the period when there was effective Celtic resistance to the Anglo-Saxon advance westward - a period of history also covered in the Bokerley Ditch walk. The mysterious figure of Arthur is generally accepted as the leader of this resistance and so Cadbury may be considered a possible prototype for the mythical Camelot. It was one of the largest and most developed of the Iron Age hill forts; a walk around its highest and innermost rampart is a lesson in the clever siting and massive engineering work deployed so long ago.

Return to the road and turn left to head into the village past the church. Turn left at the Red Lion along Folly Lane which becomes a green track and leads into a large arable field beneath the northern side of Cadbury Castle. This stretch of the walk gives the best perspective of the almost impregnable nature of the fort; do not be misled by the stone wall which is a later addition. To your left the barn marked on the map (GR 626255) is now an obvious ruin next to an old ivy-clad ash tree. Follow the hedge along on your right, heading south-west across the flat field - the path has migrated slightly from that shown on the map - to reach the southern end of an apple orchard. Follow the hedge round to meet the road at a sign telling you that you are on the Leland Trail; turn left on the road into Sutton Montis. At the entrance to the church on the right you see a footpath sign; almost opposite this sign you turn left to walk across a small orchard not marked on the map. On the far side you meet the public road and the path continues straight ahead - or rather it did. It would seem that, naturally enough, the path heading south-east towards Girt (GR 626246 to GR 629243) is being ignored in favour of the farm track zig-zagging along just to the west. Unless the path has been waymarked and re-equipped with stiles I recommend that on reaching the road on the far side of the orchard you turn right and then immediately left along the farm track between high hedges, past the grey breeze-block farm buildings. Turn right when you reach the road, bringing you immediately to a T-junction (GR 629241).

At the T-junction you cross over the road and head south-west along the bridleway, initially a sunken green lane. It soon turns to a faint grassed-over track making its way round the hillside. The knoll above you to your left merges as you walk into the northern end of Corton Ridge and you head south along the ridge with Corton Denham below you to your left. Ahead you can see two sets of masts on the horizon; on the left Bulbarrow, on the right the more numerous cluster of Rampisham. You have your final glimpse of the wide views behind you and enter a hedged-in lane (GR 625221), bringing you to a T-junction of tracks on Windmill Hill. Turn right here, down the hill and turn left at Weathergrove Farm to follow the road back into Sandford Orcas and your car.

17)   Between the Cale and the Stour

Distance: 9 miles
Start: the Ship Inn, West Stour
Map: sheet 183, GR 785226

South from the notable viewpoint of Alfred's Tower above Stourhead in Wiltshire runs a limestone escarpment facing west across Blackmoor Vale, its gentler dip slope facing east. Astride this escarpment to the west of Gillingham is a tight, confusing network of narrow lanes and an even denser network of paths. It is an area of almost perfectly preserved post-enclosure landscape with none of the hedge removal found elsewhere. This area of north Dorset is often overlooked by walkers in the belief that its landscapes are dull and frequently all but waterlogged. In fact the north-south ridge which this walk traverses is enough of an obstacle to cause the only tunnel on the Waterloo to Exeter railway between Salisbury and the Devon border. Nevertheless it is dwarfed by the chalk heights of Wiltshire to the north-east and around Blandford to the south. There are views of both on this walk. The unexpected literary aspect to this walk is East Stour church (visible from the start point - look east). In the former rectory here Henry Fielding wrote *Tom Jones* - the work that perhaps did most to establish his later reputation as the father of the English novel. The Rectory has now gone; in its place is Church Farm.

The walk starts at the landmark Ship Inn, 6 miles west of Shaftesbury on the A30 main road towards Sherborne and Yeovil. Starting at a pub, the walk passes the Stapleton Arms in Buckhorn Weston about a third of its way round; a mile before the end you pass the Royal Oak in Stour Provost. There is a post office stores in Buckhorn Weston opposite the pub. This walk (an alternative title could well be "hedges and stiles of north Dorset") takes you through an intricate *bocage* of enclosed pasture fields grazed by dairy herds. I recommend the use of a 1:25,000 map for this walk, although a 1:50,000 is perfectly adequate if you are a seasoned navigator.

Cross the main road from the car park of the Ship Inn and head up the road signed "no footway for 500 yards". After 400 yards the road turns sharp left around the churchyard on the left. Turn right here, a sign pointing the way to Harpitts Bridge. You walk down a narrow path beneath trees and turn left at the bottom at a private drive passing a dutch barn. Turn immediately left off the drive, over a stile and head north with a row of conifers behind a post and rail fence to your left.

Ahead you can see the houses of Bugley; your route lies directly north, marked by gates and stiles. You cross a fast-flowing stream-ditch over a plank bridge just to the right of a row of trees in a hedge. In the final field before the prominent footbridge of girders, corrugated iron and concrete you walk across a boggy patch by a lone tree before crossing a tiny clear tributary of the Stour by the bridge. Turn right along the road (Nations Road) and left after 500 yards at Wool House. Follow the road west-south-west past the fine Georgian House at Bugley and notice the letter box attached to the telegraph pole on the right. A hundred yards later the path turns left off the road to head almost parallel to it past the front of a fine south-facing house. You climb a stile and maintain your heading with a thick hedge on the left, climbing another stile before reaching the public road (GR 777245).

Cross the road and follow a thick tree-lined hedge along on your left. The next stretch is marked as parkland on the map, although it is scarcely any different from the surrounding fields. It is not waymarked on the ground; your course is marked by crude stiles in the post and rail fences - for the remaining walk to Hartmoor you have a thick hedge on your left. Four hundred yards west of the road you meet what the map marks as a drive south from Sandley Stud House - in fact if it were not for the fencing it would scarcely be visible on the ground. At the far end of the next field take care. You reach an unusual two-bar gate in the left-hand corner of the field leading into a hedged path

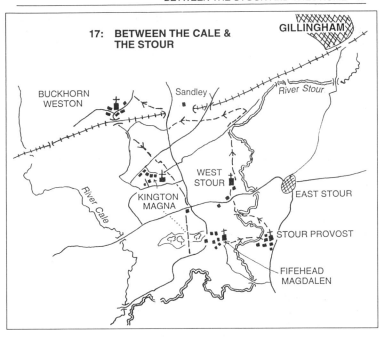

17: **BETWEEN THE CALE &
THE STOUR**

GILLINGHAM

BUCKHORN
WESTON

Sandley

River Stour

River Cale

WEST
STOUR

EAST STOUR

KINGTON
MAGNA

STOUR PROVOST

FIFEHEAD
MAGDALEN

beneath a feature which cannot decide whether it is a narrow copse of pines or a thick hedge with pines. Do not be tempted along this shortest of paths but turn immediately right off it, over a stile and make for the corner of the hedge in front of you. Follow this hedge along on your left, heading west-south-west and just before the corner of this last field before the road turn left over a stile into a small pine copse bringing you on to the road by the turning to Buckhorn Weston (GR 770243).

Turn right onto the road and follow it due north for 400 yards to the mast by the tunnel exit - or "tunnel head" as it is named on the footpath signs. Turn left off the road by some tatty sheds on the far side of the tunnel and head down through a long field of rough grazing. At the bottom, in the next field, you cross a tiny brook at a fine old culvert and head up the hill through a gate. Notice the red brick and red tiles of Hardings Farm away to your left. As you look up the hill in front of you, notice a cattle drinking trough in a long gap between hedges linked by a fence. Make for the gateway just to the left of this trough and follow the hedge up the hill on your left. At the top you climb a stile to join the road to see a footpath sign pointing the way back to tunnel head.

The path down the hill parallel to the road through Buckhorn Weston, past spot height 126m, appears to be disused so follow the road down through the village to the pub on your left.

Buckhorn Weston is first recorded in Domesday as Westone. The "western farmstead" may refer to an outlying settlement from Gillingham which would then to a great extent have been surrounded by untamed woods. The present day prefix to the name is first recorded in 1275 and would appear to refer to a family called Bouker.

Turning left out of the pub follow the road beneath the railway bridge, past the left-hand turning back up to Hartmoor.

Two hundred yards further the road swings to the right between thick hedges of blackthorn. Just after this bend is a double stile (rather dilapidated) through the hedge on the left (GR 761240). Make your way diagonally across the field towards the left-hand end of a post and rail fence. Climb the stile and turn left through the farm gate; bear across to the right-hand side of this field - there is a stile 50 yards up the hedge from the gate. The exit from the third field after the road is through a narrow gate laid with sleepers beneath trees in the hedge; above you is a stile through a thick hedge with large bramble patches. This field marks the top of the hill. Make your way right along the top of the hill and cross over the lane (Barton Hill) coming up from Kington Magna (GR 766235).

Over the road is a wide entrance to the field; climb the stile on the left-hand side to find yourself in a narrow field with a row of young trees surrounded by squares of protective fences. Follow the left-hand side of this field, exactly as the map shows; in the corner of the field you find a hunting gate through the fence. Go through this and bear right to head south-east with the fence on your right past the modern farm buildings. Turn right on the road for a few yards to the entrance to Kington Manor Farm and climb a stile to the left of the entrance. Follow the path around some pig houses, keeping the hedge on your right to bring you to the road with a row of cottages facing you (GR 771229).

The path leaves the road from the southern end of the cottages (very slightly at variance with the map); follow the cottage garden on your left and turn left at the end through a hunting gate and make your way diagonally across a small paddock to a second hunting gate. To the left of the dilapidated barn in the middle of the field (GR 773228) you see a stile near some modern farm buildings not marked on the map. Turn right on the road here for 200 yards, past a large ash tree in the hedge on your right. Fifty yards after the ash tree you turn right through a farm gate to head south across the field with a fine view across Blackmore Vale with the villages of Stalbridge and Henstridge on the low ridge on the far side.

Make just to the right of the red brick house to join the main road at the farm gate. Now take care on this narrow stretch of main road. The traffic tends to arrive in bursts due to traffic lights on the A30, so that you can time your hundred yard dash to the right along the road to avoid them. Keep to the verge on the south side of the road and follow it past the barn on the left to the end of a low ivy-clad wall, where with some sense of relief you turn left through a gate. Follow the post and rail fence on your right around the back of the house to make your way down the hill exactly due south along an all-weather horse track to a stile at the bottom and across the flat field to the gate leading into Fifehead Wood.

So rare has woodland become in this salient of Dorset north of a line from Shaftesbury to Sturminster Newton that such woods as there are (there are only two of any size - Duncliffe and Fifehead) have been declared to be nature reserves.

The path through the wood runs south on a narrow forest ride beneath the oak trees. Leave the wood over a stile and head south towards the perfect frontage of Manor Farm, reaching the road opposite the thatch of My Lady's Cottage. Turn left along the road and head up the hill into Fifehead Magdalen and turn right off the road at the top of the hill following the sign for the public telephone. Continue past the church, ignoring the sign immediately afterwards pointing along the footpath to West Stour and turn left into the next gate, heading west, down the hill with Stour Provost visible on the far side of the valley. You reach the alluvial valley floor, using the church tower as a land mark to reach a footbridge by Stour Provost Mill. Cross over this and bear right to the sluices damming the millpond. Cross this bridge and keep the mill house with its explanatory stone plaque in the wall to your left and make your way through the hunting gate at the end of the lane to the mill. Make your way up the lane past the Royal Oak, bear left along the main village street and follow this past the dead-end sign as it becomes a grassy track.

The path to West Stour leaves the track to the left rather to the north of the last house in the village, Riversdale Farm. Follow the lane past the farm; 100 yards north it forks. Take the left-hand fork taking you immediately into a field to make your way diagonally across it to a gate and footbridge over the tiny stream flowing along a ditch at the bottom. Look to the right, up the tiny tributary valley of the Stour to see East Stour church, in the shadow of which Henry Fielding worked on *Tom Jones - A Foundling*. Ahead the narrow footbridge across the Stour comes into view. From the footbridge follow a fence up the hill on your right and just before the cottage at the top turn right through a gate and climb a stile into the Ship Inn car park.

18)   Tolpuddle, Dewlish and the Downs

Distance: 10 or 12 miles
Start: near the Martyrs' Tree in Tolpuddle
Map: sheet 194, GR 792945

Tolpuddle is a village as attractive as it is famous. This walk is a circuit across the open empty downland, now largely arable, around Milborne St Andrew. It takes you past the Royal Oak pub in Dewlish and starts and finishes near the Martyrs Inn in Tolpuddle, but passes no shop. It is popularly held that the Trade Union movement started in Tolpuddle; this is a bold claim - what is certain is that events in the village in 1833 certainly had an influence on the later development of Trades Unions. Tolpuddle can be found on the A35 main Poole-Dorchester road, 7 miles east of Dorchester. Turn south off the main road in the village, signed to Affpuddle; if you cannot park by the tree continue across the river and park on the side of the road.

The background to the incident of the Tolpuddle martyrs was the great agricultural depression following the Napoleonic Wars. The result of this was a reduction in wages for farm workers very nearly to starvation level. The six "martyrs" were led by a certain George Loveless who worshipped at the Wesleyan Chapel rather than at the Anglican parish church. This was significant, for all nonconformists were viewed in those days by the landowning classes (of which the Church of England was a part) rather as wandering hippies are today by the same classes - potential upsetters of the rural status quo. However it was the incumbent of Tolpuddle church who had chaired a meeting between the farmers of the parish and their labourers, arranged because of general concern that labourers' wages would slip below subsistence level. At this meeting the farmers agreed to 10 shillings a week, but the following week's pay for each was just 9 shillings and this was soon cut to 8. When the vicar was approached he, Judas-like, denied all knowledge of any agreement. A natural reaction to this state of affairs would have been unrest; in George Loveless's words the reason for his creation of a Friendly Society was due to the fact that it was "impossible to live honestly on such scanty means...". The Friendly Society immediately gained about forty members, but only six were arrested, all Tolpuddle men, and five of them, like Loveless, Wesleyan Methodists. They were roughly handled and sentenced to be transported for seven years. It is perhaps significant that the outcry that grew up in London at these events was not from the labouring classes at all, but from a sense of fair play among those who created and administered the law at what was certainly a vicious injustice. All were pardoned and eventually returned from their forced labour in Australia. The most obvious memorial to these men is the thatched shelter erected beneath the martyrs' tree by the philanthropist Sir Ernest Debenham in 1934. He was responsible for much work for the welfare of farm labourers in the early part of the twentieth century. Many of the good cottages he had built can still be seen around Tolpuddle.

From the Martyrs Tree in the centre of Tolpuddle make your way west along the main road for 300 yards to a green lane signed as a bridleway

The Martyrs tree and memorial

97

immediately before the TUC memorial cottages. At the back of the cottages the lane forks; bear right to head up the hill along an old hedged-in track which brings you to a field of arable; keep straight ahead with a hedge on the right, taking you over the hill with fine views up the Piddle Valley. As you descend across Lord's Down on the far side, the bridleway returns to being a hedged-in ancient track, well supplied with bluebells in spring; it brings you to the main A354 Blandford-Dorchester road (GR 784966). Cross with care as this is a fast stretch. You bear slightly left as you cross the road to resume walking just west of due north, now on a sunken lane well supplied with bluebells and ramsons. On the north side of the main road you find yourself with a field of seeded grazing on your right, rather than Milborne Wood, as the map shows. After 100 yards or so you enter the wood. A footpath joins from the left and then departs again, to the right as you reach Dennet's Bottom, running along the side of the wood as your path maintains its course on a sunken lane, taking you up the side of Park Hill to meet the road just above Dewlish (GR 779980). Follow the road down the hill in the trees for 200 yards to a footpath sign on the left immediately before the end of the wood. It takes you very steeply down the hill, across the Devil's Brook on a wooden footbridge. You join the road in Dewlish just by the church; walk along the road to the crossroads by the war memorial; the Royal Oak lies just along the road to Puddletown, to your left.

Turn right at the crossroads in Dewlish and follow the road along for 400 yards, to the last house on your right - a new one, completed in 1994. Turn right immediately after this house and follow the path around the field, keeping the high hedge to your right. You pass a house on your right; go past this, along the river and then cross it at a footbridge to go steeply up the hill, joining a chalky track heading up the valley; keep right at the fork and follow the track to the top of the hill where it passes through a high hedge and bears right. There is no waymark here; you may find a number of electric fences hereabouts. Turn left off the track to keep heading north, up the side of the valley; your course is marked by a number of hunting gates in the hedge. There appears to be a path continuing due north to meet the track that runs across the downs, north-east to Gallows Corner (GR 786005). What the map shows is the bridleway turning left, down the hill to meet this track. The lane to Gallows Corner is a hedged-in byway for its entire length, rather than part of it, as the map shows.

Gallows Corner is a lonely meeting place of muddy lanes, far from any house and hidden among trees growing in the hedges; turn right here and follow this lane, heading just east of south for 100 yards, whereupon you come to a gate on the left marked as a bridleway. This is the point where you have to decide whether you wish to head straight back, through Milborne St Andrew, or to continue over the downs. If you opt for the former, keep straight ahead at the gateway and follow the hedged-in byway just east of due south

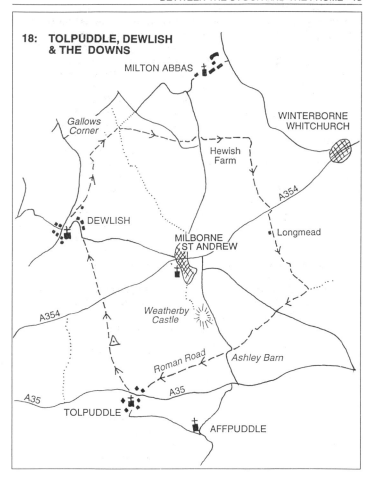

18: TOLPUDDLE, DEWLISH & THE DOWNS

MILTON ABBAS

WINTERBORNE WHITCHURCH

Gallows Corner

Hewish Farm

A354

DEWLISH

MILBORNE ST ANDREW

Longmead

A354

Weatherby Castle

Roman Road

Ashley Barn

A35

A35

TOLPUDDLE

AFFPUDDLE

for half a mile to the wood (GR 789996). Turn left and then right at the fork to head south-east to Frogmore Farm (GR 794991) and on, south-east to the road junction just north of Milborne St Andrew. Follow the road south, through the village and then past Manor Farm (GR 804971) on your left to reach the junction of tracks (GR 802966). From here Snag Lane leads up to the left, to the road. Keep straight ahead here, south along the stream-ditch and left at the end of the field, up to Weatherby Castle. Follow the path through the trees of Weatherby Castle with its dramatic rookery and descend to the road to turn right on the road down to Ashley Barn. Now pick up the directions below to follow the Roman road over the hill back to Tolpuddle.

The real route, continuing across the downs from Gallows Corner, turns left through the waymarked gate just south of the track junction and runs straight across the downs, just south of due east. You keep a hedge on your left and descend into and climb out of a chalk dry valley near its source, where you cross the old bridleway running along its base. As you near the road (GR 801003) bear left on the descent to keep slightly north of the route shown on the map, so that you are walking round the edge of the field. You cross over the road by a gap in the copse and head west, up the hill through the gap, over a broad chalk spur and then descend to meet the road immediately north of the cottages at Hewish Farm (GR 805003); the path meets the road beneath a tall tree, one field to the left of the end cottage.

Turn right on the road at Hewish Farm and then, after 100 yards, left, over the stream and steeply up the hill along a surfaced lane, bringing you to the farm buildings on the top of the hill. Keep straight ahead past these, down the hill past the end of the lane, to a hedge on the far side of the field in the bottom of the shallow gully. Turn right here (at spot height 111m) and head south, up the hill to the copse (GR 817999) on its summit. The path takes you into the copse, rather than past it on the outside, as the map shows. From its eastern end the path takes you south, along the edge of an arable field with a hedge on your left, down to Deverel Down copse. Here the path takes you along its northern side, much as the map shows. Between the two copses the path swings to the left, not shown on the ground, and makes for a slightly strange circular platform in the middle of the field, held up by a low wall and planted with thorn trees.

Ahead of you is the path crossing the main A354 Blandford-Dorchester road by the gas board building. Cross the main road (GR 823987); fear not, you do not have to walk along the road at all, as you might have thought, looking at the map. On the far side a sunken lane beneath the trees leads beside the road, before reaching the metalled drive to Longmead. At Longmead your route becomes a slightly overgrown old trackway; you have the impression of entering a wood and making your way through it; the bridleway, little used though not impassable, is entirely hidden from the surrounding arable fields. You exit from this secretive route to turn left (GR 825976) to head south-east, with a high hedge on your left and after 200 yards, turn south, to contour along the slope, still with a hedge on the left. You go through two gates and then meet a lane going to the right (GR 832970), to a dutch barn (GR 829969). Follow this rough lane south-west to meet the road from Milborne St Andrew to Bere Regis (GR 824965) where you cross over, keeping to the left of Roke Barn, now converted to dwellings. Head straight up the low hill in front of you with a fence on the right; you come to a recently replanted copse with a gateway at its northern end. Go through this to head south-west, across the top of the hill with a fence on your left. You join a sunken lane - the Roman road - and go down the hill to join the road. Cross over the river and turn right, off the road as it makes a left-hand bend in front of Ashley Barn. Go through the farmyard and make your way up the hill to a stand of oak trees not marked on the map.

You join a farm lane above Tolpuddle (GR 796747) at a sign pointing the way back to Ashley Barn; turn left on the road to descend to the main road and your car. On the south side of the main road is an old building made of cob - now a rare sight.

CHAPTER FIVE:
Purbeck and South Dorset

As one of Britain's most spectacular coastal areas, this scarcely needs an introduction. I have included in this section that part of Dorset that lies south of the River Frome and east of the A354 Roman road from Dorchester to Weymouth, including the Isle of Portland. During the summer, especially at weekends, it is heavily visited; these walks take you away from the busier sites, so that to a great extent you can have the landscape to yourself.

The walks I have devised for this book are all of a circular nature, starting and finishing at a spot where you can park your car. However Purbeck offers one or two routes which should not be ignored because they do not easily fit into the pattern of a circuit. The two routes I have in mind are the ridge route west from Ballard Down to Corfe (7 miles), and the coast route west from Swanage as far as Kimmeridge (12 miles). In fact almost all of these are covered below as circuit walks. The first of these linear walks can be done using the reopened railway (summer only), from a base in Corfe, Swanage, or at any of the campsites along the valley between. The second is a longer walk - it can be made as long as you like - but Swanage to Corfe can be walked in a day, using the railway or the bus service. Enquire about buses before you set off; I recommend you take a bus from your start point and walk back. If you have the energy, the complete circuit - the central Purbeck ridge from Swanage to Corfe, combined with the coast route - can be walked in a day, although I recommend taking two days over it, for there is much pleasantly to delay you on the way.

None of the walks described below takes you on to the army ranges on Purbeck, so they may be enjoyed at any time. However the ranges are open every weekend of the year bar four and are open for the entire month of August. They are also open every bank holiday. I do not wish to enter into any argument about the pros and cons of the army controlling this beautiful stretch of landscape, but the fact is that it is available to be used for recreation when most people can walk there and the ranges do provide superb walking. Once you are within Ministry of Defence property, you leave behind the world of fences and stiles and ploughland and enter into a wild world of rough grass, tussocks and scrub, the range paths marked by painted posts. A spot of walking can also bring you to some good beaches, notably Arish Mell, which you will have almost always to yourself because they are relatively inaccessible. An entirely unforeseen consequence of the army's taking over of the ranges during the Second World War is that, with the widespread use of pesticides on the farmland elsewhere in Purbeck, combined with extreme visitor pressure in the summer months, its ranges have become a very valuable nature reserve. Around Bovington camp, however, there has been damage to the heath from the passage of tracked vehicles - damage that is quite reversible, unlike the areas that have been built upon. A walk across the ranges between Lulworth and Kimmeridge can be a refreshing experience if you were beginning to get the impression (easily gained) that Purbeck was starting to become a patchwork of car parks and caravan sites.

When public access to the Lulworth tank ranges was being proposed, the Ministry of Defence suggested that the paths across the ranges should be fenced off, because of the danger of unexploded munitions. Happily this was abandoned in favour of marker posts. Please do not stray from the footpath, not only for your own safety but because to do so adds weight to the argument of those who hold that walking across Lulworth tank ranges should be through a kind of barbed wire corridor. Before you embark on a walk east of Lulworth or west of Kimmeridge, telephone 01929 462 721 to check that access to the ranges is open. The range firing detail explaining the day to day access is posted at information boards at Kimmeridge, Corfe and Lulworth.

View east across Kimmeridge Bay from Gaulter's Gap to Clavell's Tower. (Walk 19)

19) Chapman's Pool, Kimmeridge and Swyre Head

Distance: 9 or 5 miles
Start: Kingston car park
Map: sheet 195, GR 953795

This walk takes in one of the most dramatic stretches of the Dorset coastline with all the ingredients for a fine coast walk; dramatic high cliffs and a secluded cove with a (albeit rather muddy) beach. The walk starts and ends at a notable pub; it passes no other pub nor any shop on its way. There is no village shop in Kingston; there is a cafe at Kimmeridge, now open all year round. There is a very steep climb of 500 feet in this walk; this can be avoided by following a diversion explained in the text. I have an especial fondness for walks in this area which dates back to school camp in 1973 at Blashenwell Farm at Kingston, for which I owe a debt of thanks to Mike Goode and Ken House. My well deserved report from that camp was "If Roberts put half the effort into doing camp tasks instead of avoiding them, he (and we all) would have a better time". However the seeds were sown and I continually impress myself with my personal admin when backpacking alone in remote mountains.

A shortened version of this walk (total 5 miles) can be enjoyed, starting at Kimmeridge car park and following the footpath down to Gaulter's Gap, then heading east along the Dorset Coast Path to Rope Lake Head, whence you take the path up the hill, inland to Swyre Head. From here there is a fine ridge walk, heading north-west to Kimmeridge over Smedmore Hill.

To reach Kingston take the A351 out of Corfe, signed to Swanage. At the end of the village turn right at a left-hand bend and follow the B3069 across Corfe Common and twisting up the steep hill to Kingston. Turn right in Kingston on a tricky bend by the Scott Arms. Park your car in the car park on the left of the road leading west out of the hamlet of Kingston and walk back down into the village.

In common with many of Dorset's villages, the name is first recorded in Domesday - it means "the king's farm". However there is a record of a grant of land in 948 by King Eadred of Wessex to the abbess of Shaftesbury. The feature which dominates the village is the high tower of St James's church, built by the Third Earl of Eldon (owner of Encombe House) during the 1870s and donated to the village. There is a second church in the village, also dating from the nineteenth century, now disused.

The Scott Arms makes a fine pub to return to after a walk, with its views from the back garden across Corfe Common to Corfe Castle, dominating the gap in the Purbeck Hills. As you walk back down from the car park, turn right in the centre of the village along the road signed to Encombe. It is becoming more popular to park cars where the road ends just after the end of the wood (GR 955786). Unfortunately this has turned a stretch of verge into a car park;

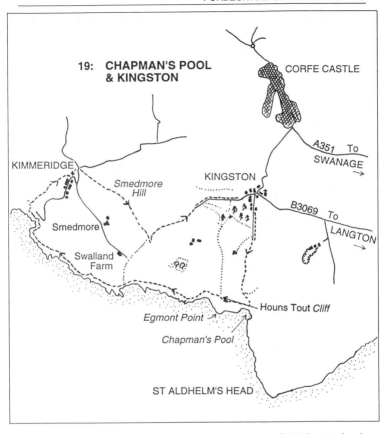

19: **CHAPMAN'S POOL & KINGSTON**

CORFE CASTLE

A351 To SWANAGE →

KIMMERIDGE

Smedmore Hill

KINGSTON

B3069 To LANGTON →

Smedmore

Swalland Farm

Houns Tout *Cliff*

Egmont Point ↗

Chapman's Pool

ST ALDHELM'S HEAD

far better to avoid retracing your steps on foot at the finish by starting in Kingston.

When you reach the gate at the end of the road (GR 955786), climb the stile and follow the private road south down the grassy valley, one of my favourite in the county, with its ever-widening view of the sea as you proceed. Kingston Down, the hillside on the left as you descend the valley, has a well preserved area of Celtic fields on its grassy summit. Two-thirds of a mile after the gate you see a track turning right to cross the stream (GR 954775). Continue following the lane here for a few yards, to turn right off it at a gate and head south-east across a sloping field. At the end of the field the path

105

Looking north up the valley towards Kingston from near Chapman's Pool

drops steeply down to cross the stream; ahead can be seen the results of repeated landslips on the southern end of West Hill. The layout of the hinterland of Chapman's Pool east of the stream has completely changed since I first became acquainted with the spot on school camps in the early seventies. By way of some tricky patches across stiff clay the path brings you to Chapman's Pool, with its few huts and launching slip.

The first record of the name comes from a later copy of a Saxon charter of 948 and refers to it as schort mannes pol; *most likely the name means just that.*

From the beach retrace your steps up the clay bank to turn left in the gully and follow the path from the stream crossing steeply up the cliff-top west of Chapman's Pool. You are starting a climb of 500 feet in less than half a mile; it is relentless and becomes even steeper nearer the top; steps have been cut in the turf. Gasping, you reach the top of the ridge running north to Quarry Wood and Kingston. You have earned a pause on the stone seat with its matchless view of a great sweep of the Channel from Portland Bill to the Isle of Wight. If you have weighed yourself down with a pair of binoculars you reap the benefit here on a clear day.

A short cut start to the walk avoids the romance of Chapman's Pool and also the ferocious climb from it to the top of Houns Tout. Walk through the trees at the back of the car park, onto the forest track which heads south-west through the Plantation. After half a mile you exit from the woods to follow a fine ridge south for a mile to the top of Houns Tout. There are very fine views across Encombe (literally hen-combe - the valley with the birds, or perhaps specifically moorhens) to the rounded outline of Swyre Head above.

Encombe clearly inspired the "Enkworth" of Hardy's Hand of Ethelberta, *but his detailed description of the house in the novel does not match Encombe at all - intentionally so!*

The route follows a dry stone wall on your left and negotiates two stiles on its way. From Houns Tout descend, almost as steeply as you climbed from Chapman's Pool to meet the stream running down from Encombe. It tumbles over the cliff to reach the sea as a waterfall landing on the tiny beach.

You now have 3 miles of relatively easy walking, above the Kimmeridge Ledges lying at the foot of the shale cliffs to your left. The first prominent landmark you meet is the now ruined Clavell's Tower.

This is a folly, built in 1831 by a certain Revd John Richards to whom was bequeathed Smedmore House and estate in 1817. He changed his name to Clavell and the tower bears his name.

From the tower you drop steeply down to cross the road by the tiny Smedmore stream. At low tide it is possible to walk down the slipway and along the beach around Kimmeridge Bay to Gaulter's Gap. This is the narrow cutting at the western end of the car park on the beach. Make your way past the public lavatories (how enlightened that they have an outside tap instead of just the handbasins that are too small to be any use to those who want to fill a water bottle). Bear right here on the far side of the tiny stream to make your way inland, with the stream on your right, making for a small dilapidated barn on the right-hand end of a small copse - Higher Stonhips. Keep along the stream bank here to a second little old barn with a rusty corrugated iron roof and bear left, up the hill to head north-east, making for a prominent copse - Kimmeridge Coppice. Bear right across the front of the coppice to head up the hill with the copse on the right and then straight ahead towards Kimmeridge Farm. Here you join the public road; there is a cafe just down the hill.

As you look at the church you will see a path leading up the right-hand side, paved with stone slabs. Follow this steeply up the hill to the notch in the ridge; it brings you to the road junction by the car park in the quarry (GR 919801). Cross over the road and walk along the Church Knowle road for 200 yards to a farm track leading up on your right; turn right here to make your way south-east up the spur of Smedmore Hill. You are walking along a track which takes you along the ridge with views inland to the Purbeck Ridge and to the fields to your right, sweeping down to the low cliffs above Kimmeridge Ledges. A mile after the road junction (and 300 feet above) you reach the viewpoint and now idle trig point of Swyre Head. *Swyra* in Old English meant a neck of land or a promontory - which it still is. If such a thing could be possible, the views from here probably surpass those from Houns Tout, with views right over the Purbeck Ridge.

Follow the path left here as it keeps along the top of the escarpment, keeping to the line of a farm track. It brings you to the edge of a narrow copse (Polar Wood) and, half a mile after Swyre Head, to the end of the public road at a small car park (GR 943793). Follow this road east across the arable fields with fine views of Corfe Castle for half a mile, bringing you back to your car.

20) Dancing Ledge and St Aldhelm's Head

Distance: 7 miles
Start: Worth Matravers car park
Map: sheet 195, GR 974776

This walk is one of the finest in the county. If you can summon up the effort to do this at first light early in the summer on a fine day when you have the world to yourself you will have memories for a lifetime. It may be combined with all or part of the Chapman's Pool walk for a fine full day's walk with a good amount of challenge. For no particular good reason I have ignored the coast walker's dictum of heading eastwards along the coast so as to have the prevailing wind behind you. If you are doing this walk on a windy day (there are few that aren't around the top of St Aldhelm's Head) then you may wish to do this walk the other way round. The walk starts and finishes at a recommended pub in Worth, which also has a good village shop and a teashop. A number of paths radiate towards the sea from Worth; if you really do not have the time or energy to do all of this walk then a shortened version (I suggest out on the Seacombe Bottom path, along the coast and back up Winspit Bottom) will probably give you almost as many smiles per mile as the full version.

To reach the start follow the B3069 from the southern end of Corfe, through Kingston and turn right a mile later, signed to Worth Matravers. Turn right into the car park after a mile. Turn right out of the car park and walk into the village. Turn left at the Square and Compass pub. In fact I recommend you go in; if you are clever enough to time this walk just right, you can fortify yourself with a pre-walk drink as you set off and celebrate its completion with an evening pick-me-up.

This is simply a very good pub and many people's favourite pub in the county - possibly mine since the sad demise of the Tiger's Head at Rampisham. A great repository of local history, it is a far cry from the all-too commonly found grimy carpets, piped music and gambling machines. Before some point during the 1830s its name was the Sloop.

Turn left out of the pub, onto the Langton road, past the Wesleyan chapel on your left and follow the road for 400 yards, past the last house on the right. You see a footpath sign on your right, indicating a path heading east-north-east across a sheep-grazed field, crossing the drive to Abbascombe Farm. Turn right to follow this path to Eastington Farm, which you pass on your right, to join the walled-in Priest's Way heading east across the plateau behind the Purbeck coast.

The Priest's Way is so called because before the Norman Conquest the incumbent at Worth had to make the journey on foot daily to Swanage to the chapel of ease there to say Holy Mass. The growth of Swanage was a recent phenomenon, based on its role as a resort.

Exactly a mile after leaving the coast you pass a small pond (GR 995780) on your right, in an area where the stone walls are carefully tended. Two hundred yards later turn right into a long narrow field of sheep-grazed turf.

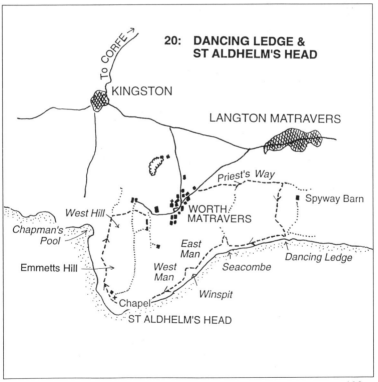

20: DANCING LEDGE & ST ALDHELM'S HEAD

The path lies along a track, heading south, towards the right-hand side of the field. The track then swings gently to the left but the path keeps to the right-hand side of the field and you pass the wonderfully isolated cottage of Sea Spray among its little stand of trees 150 yards to your right. The path becomes more obvious after the cottage and it heads steeply down, south-south-east to reach Dancing Ledge.

Formerly this was a quarry, where the stones were loaded onto boats direct, on the calmest of days. A crane used for just this is preserved on St Aldhelm's Head. Cranes for doing this can be seen on the Portland walk, and later on this walk you go through the fine quarries at Winspit. If you want to go down to the ledge and immerse yourself in Falkner's Moonfleet for a spell, there is a steep path with stone steps. There are a number of National Trust signs around here. The various stretches of Purbeck coast which are in their care came into the hands of the Trust on the bequest of the late Ralph Bankes of Kingston Lacy. There is a rash of signs which accost the walker in southern Dorset; very nearly all tell you what is "strictly prohibited" or "forbidden"; it seems to me that the only signs which are at all friendly are the Countryside Stewardship signs and those of the National Trust.

From the ledge you should follow the Dorset Coast Path west, towards the rounded chalk outlines of East Man and West Man with St Aldhelm's Head above. This is one of my favourite stretches of the coast path; take time to look behind you from time to time, along the cliffs towards Anvil Point. Where Seacombe Bottom reaches the sea the path has been diverted some way inland.

Seacombe Bottom, a narrow little valley with the tiniest of streams, is a delight; craggy at its seaward end where there was a quarry, it heads inland among gorse, bramble and thorn before reaching a confluence with Eastington Bottom. In the nineteenth century and earlier, the damp areas near the stream along Seacombe Bottom and others like it were the site of withy beds, where willows were coppiced and pollarded to grow the thin flexible stems necessary for making lobster pots. In early summer the scrub provides nesting cover to whitethroat, linnet, blackcap and others. On one occasion I was privileged to see a peregrine, carrying what appeared to be a pigeon, hotly pursued and mobbed by herring gulls, heading swiftly along the cliffs.

At Seacombe the path turns to head south-west, through the yellow blooms of sea-cabbage, along the top of the cliffs to Winspit Quarry.

Winspit is a romantic spot indeed, though on summer weekends you will find it alive with visitors, many of them groups of students from the Dorset Local Education Authority Outdoor Education Centre at Leeson House in Langton Matravers. There are the remains of two cottages right on the shore. These were built by the coastguard in the latter part of the eighteenth century when heavy liquor taxes forced the government to make a great deal of effort to prevent tax-avoidance in the time-honoured Dorset manner. Only when

Winspit Quarry

the coastguard station was built on top of St Aldhelm's Head did they become private dwellings for fishermen-quarrymen. It was here that the East Indiaman Halsewell *was driven ashore during a blizzard on the night of the 6th January 1786, with many from the village helping in the rescue, earning the reward of 100 guineas from the East India Company. The event is commemorated in the Square and Compass pub, the name of which honours the quarrying which was historically the mainstay of the village economy. At one time Winspit was the largest quarry on Purbeck. Nowadays its deserted crevices provide a site for a bat roost. If you would like to know more about the geology of the area - how the stone was quarried and worked and where it was used for building - I recommend you visit the Coach House Museum (GR 999789) in Langton Matravers. It is open daily except Sundays.*

Keep the quarry to your left as you make your way up to follow the path south-west below the now turfed-over strip lynchets of West Man; a mile of walking brings you to the top of St Aldhelm's Head. Take a farewell look behind you as you make your way up the final few steps to the coastguard lookout and the chapel, for the view henceforward is all to the west.

The square chapel on the head is mysterious indeed and there are still more questions about it than answers. Why is it square? Why is it built with each corner facing respectively north, south, east and west, rather than with the walls aligned east and west as churches usually are. There is an interesting illustration of the way that, given time, graffiti can be historically valuable, for one obvious carving of the date of 1665 on the central pillar (the style of the digits proves that it is genuine) indicates that the chapel was visited at this period. Saint Aldhelm was the first bishop of Sherborne; there is a fine view of his foundation of Sherborne Abbey in the Footsteps of Raleigh *walk.*

Rejoin the coast path from St Aldhelm's Chapel and follow it steeply down to Pier Bottom. At which point the fainthearts will take one look at the dauntingly steep pull up Emmetts Hill in front of them, and decide to take the path to the right up Pier Bottom and make straight for the Square and Compass. This would be a pity, for the next stretch is more than worth the effort.

From the top of Emmetts Hill you have the full glory of Weymouth Bay in front of you, looking clear along the cliffs, past Dungy Head and White Nothe. Immediately in front of you is the hidden cove of Chapman's Pool, happily not reached by any road, and behind it the towering mass of Houns Tout. Fatigue is a saddening thing; I would like to extol the virtues of walking north from West Hill, down into the fine valley of Hill Bottom and following the path up the side of Swanworth Quarry. However, I am quite sure that when you reach the path junction at the top of West Hill (GR 960773) you will probably consider you have had enough and take the footpath direct to Renscombe Farm and Worth Matravers.

Renscombe is mentioned as long ago as 987, when the farm was given to the Abbey of Cerne; the name means "Raven's Valley". I have seen ravens in the area; in those days I have no doubt they were breeding in the rocks.

There is an interesting approach to the car park, with good views of the church and giving your feet soft turf rather than hard tarmac. As you come into the village there is a drive on the left which has a sign saying "no footpath". Ah, but there is, 3 feet to the right of it, up the field towards the house; cross the drive at the end and turn right to follow the path along the back of the church; two stiles lead you to the car park.

Before leaving the subject of Worth Matravers, mention should be made of one Benjamin Jesty originally of Yetminster, near Sherborne, whose discovery that milkmaids who had suffered from cowpox were never infected with the fatal condition of smallpox caused him to inoculate his own family. The method of discovery seems familiar - because the school book version of history is that vaccination (the term itself of course being derived from the disease of cowpox) was discovered in the same way by Dr Jenner, but some twenty years later. Benjamin Jesty's grave can be found in the churchyard.

21)   Corfe Castle and the Purbeck Hills

Distance: 7 miles
Start: West Street car park
Map: sheet 195, GR 959818

Corfe Castle, that most distinctive of silhouettes, has become something of an emblem of Dorset. This walk takes you for an exhilarating stretch along the main spine of Purbeck and south to the hills overlooking Corfe. Beyond Corfe Castle itself is a wild area of small farms and common land. There are pubs, shops and cafes galore in Corfe, at the beginning and end of the walk; 2 miles before the end the walk brings you to the Scott Arms in Kingston, a fine pub.

Having become one of the most visited locations in the west of England, car parking is difficult in Corfe. Follow the signs in Corfe from the main square indicating the way to the car park in West Street. Unfortunately this is not free; in 1994 it cost £1 to park a car there for a day. On weekdays in the winter you may be able to park in Sandy Hill Road on the far side of the railway bridge. From West Street car park walk back into the centre of Corfe and follow the main road round the base of the castle mound to the right-hand turning leading under the old railway bridge, along Sandy Hill Road. Immediately under the bridge turn left to go over a stile and steeply up Challow Hill, with very fine views of the castle and the town, behind the now restored station. This path is a permissive path and is therefore not marked on the map. It leads due east, along the boundary between the gorse and the grazing, along the top of East Hill and Challow Hill. To your right is the view of the "Weald of Purbeck" and the high ground immediately behind the coast around Langton and Worth Matravers and Kingston.

The top of the ridge offers very fine walking across sheep-grazed turf. You cross the rough road winding over the ridge from Woolgarston to Rollington Farm and follow the ridge along its crest past the mast (GR 973822). Your passage along the top tends to be marked by numbers of rabbits darting ahead of you into the gorse. At the end of Rollington Hill you meet an ancient route going over Purbeck's dramatic central spine, from Rempstone to Woolgarston. Turn right here and take the well made track angling down the escarpment past the old stone workings to the hedge at the bottom, where you turn sharp right, back on yourself to follow the bridleway north-west along the base of the hill with a hedge on your left.

After 500 yards of contouring along the foot of the hill you turn left, a marked gate (GR 980819) indicating your way and walk down the hill for 250 yards to the public road (GR 979817). Turn left on the road and follow it for 200 yards to a gate on the right (GR 981816) bearing a footpath waymark. Go through this gate and look for the stile through the hedge on the right-hand side of the field you are in; make for this and follow this little-used path to the two old cottages hidden among the trees in their garden. The path joins the farm lane here; you turn left, down the hill past the new house on your right to walk through the modern piggery unit, keeping the buildings to your right. The gateway on the far side of these is marked with the bridleway blue arrow;

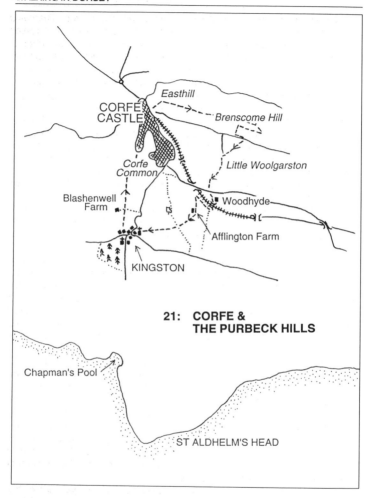

**21: CORFE &
THE PURBECK HILLS**

make for the gate in the corner of the field in front of you and follow the hedge along on your left. You are heading downhill across small fields grazed by cattle; rather sooner than you expect you meet the A351 Swanage to Corfe road opposite the entrance to Woodhyde Farm campsite (GR 974805).

Cross the main road and follow the lane downhill to the farm. There is a wonderful tangle of bramble and small trees on the right which when I walked through was obviously a nest site for whitethroat. How much more valuable as a habitat are these patches than sterile government-sponsored plastic-wrapped rows of trees in designated set-aside. You pass under the railway bridge; immediately after the bridge turn right across a patch of rough grazing and through a high hedge over a stile to follow the railway along on your right. After 500 yards you meet the drive to Afflington Farm. Turn left onto the drive and follow it up to the farm, keeping the farm to your right as you make your way up the hill, diagonally across a small paddock to the right-hand end of Afflington Wood. Among the trees the well-used farm track bends to the left; take care here and turn right off the track to head diagonally across a yet smaller paddock to pick up the vestiges of an old green lane which contours along the hillside above Scoles Farm before angling up the hill towards the village of Kingston.

There follows an enigma of navigation and cartography. Ahead of you is a Victorian Gothick church with a tower (GR 958796) - the perfect beginner's navigation feature, and yet the one marked on the map is across the other side of the village.

The fact is that the church in front of you has long since gone out of use as a place of worship and is now a highly distinctive residence. Its role as a navigation feature is unchanged; I am quite sure that nine out of ten users of Ordnance Survey maps use churches as reference points for navigation rather than to see where they may take communion on Sundays. Is there not some way that a redundant church could be shown by the same symbol, perhaps instead of solid black the pinky-brown shading used for other buildings?

The path takes you up to the former church, where you join the B3069. Turn right on the road and follow it down the hill to turn left at the Scott Arms.

Nowadays this is the only service in the village; in the early seventies I recollect receiving letters sent for collection at the then post office in the village, whilst taking part in school camps there.

The church that you have passed has been given up in favour of another nineteenth-century church which is obviously too large for the village. This is St James's which the Third Earl of Eldon had built between 1873 and 1880 for the sum of £70,000. He was then resident at Encombe House (there is a fine view of this on the Swyre Head walk).

Follow the street through the village to the small patch of grass where the road to Westhill Farm turns left. Opposite this on the right is a footpath sign, leading you down a narrow path among the houses; turn left on the drive, past three cottages, to find yourself at a track junction in the wood. Turn sharp right, back on yourself to head down the shady avenue of the drive. After about 100 yards you see a stile on your left leading to a well used path heading down the hill. Ahead is one of the classic views of Corfe, lying in its dramatic notch in the main Purbeck ridge. The path descends across some horse-grazed fields and then takes you over a tiny stream amongst the scrub before leading you onto Corfe Common.

Making your way northwards over the expanse of cropped turf, scattered brambles and gorse you arrive at the abrupt end of West Street, which you follow until the entrance to the car park on the left.

22) Ballard Down and Godlingston Heath

Distance: 10 miles
Start: Studland car park
Map: sheet 195, GR 036815

Starting along one of the finest stretches of the Dorset Coast Path, this walk leads along a relatively little-trod route with superb views south across the "Weald of Purbeck" and, more spectacular, across the heaths and woods to Poole Harbour. It finishes with a walk across a stretch of this heath, part of the National Nature Reserve of Studland. There are pubs, a cafe and a village shop in Studland; before returning to Studland the walk avoids all human habitation.

Park your car in the public car park behind the Bankes Arms Hotel (GR 037825).

The hotel commemorates the Bankes family who held the estate of Kingston and bequested it to the National Trust in 1983 - the biggest ever bequest to the National Trust.

Turn right onto the road from the car park and head past the pub down the short hill to a narrow lane leading down to the beach. Immediately after the public lavatory a lane leads up to the left; follow this south-east, turning off a drive to reach a broad path above the low cliffs with the Warren Wood to your left.

Studland is now more famous perhaps for its beach and nature reserve than for the village itself - but it is well worth visiting for its own sake. St Nicholas's church is remarkable, even in a county well supplied with fine churches. Much Anglo-Saxon work remains, the present building having been started following the destruction of an earlier, seventh-century church destroyed by the Vikings. That seventh-century church likely stood on the site of a pre-Christian temple.

During the course of this walk you pass a badger's set; I would have liked to point it out but have avoided doing so because urban badger baiters now visit rural areas of Britain in some numbers to dig out badgers in order to

The Pinnacles, near Old Harry Rocks

satisfy their grisly perversion. Incidentally, if on any of your walks you do see anyone behaving suspiciously near what appears to be a set then keep your distance. Please try and take a vehicle number, but do so surreptitiously and report it as soon as you can to the police. Talk about it to any locals you meet, for word travels on the Dorset grapevine.

The coast path leads along the top of the bright chalk cliffs for a mile, bringing you to the Foreland, where the central spine of Purbeck juts out towards the Needles on the Isle of Wight - part of the same geological feature. From the top of the turf-covered chalk stacks of Old Harry and his wife the gulls watch you with a supercilious air, knowing that no latterday mortal could make it across St Lucas Leap. The path swings to the right and heads south-west, across the springy turf of St Nick's Ground, above Parson's Barn. Here you notice how, in common with other areas of Dorset's chalk cliffs, the coast path acts as a ribbon of botanical reserve, for all the thin chalk soil with its rich habitat of wild flowers and grasses has been ploughed inland, leaving a thin strip between the cliff top and the beginning of the arable.

At the second fence after Old Harry (GR 048814) there is a gate in the corner with a blue arrow indicating the bridleway which leads diagonally up the hill, inland, heading west-south-west up to the trig point hidden among old earthworks on the top of Ballard Down. Turn right here to leave the Dorset Coast Path. As you gain the top of the gently rounded chalk ridge, one of the finest views in Purbeck - indeed in the whole county - unfolds around you.

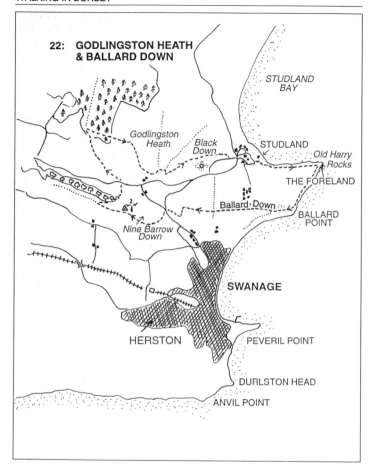

Ahead of you the path heads exactly due east along the top of the down, towards the Obelisk. Mercifully the worst and nearest modern eyesore - the Glebeland Estate down to your right - is hidden out of sight by the convex curve of the down.

It is strange, perhaps, that the dramatic landscape of Ballard Point, Ballard Down and Nine Barrows Down was mentioned by Hardy so little.

Stranger, too, that the one novel he sets in this remarkable area of Dorset's scenery should be his "somewhat frivolous tale" (Hardy's own description) of The Hand of Ethelberta, a delightful social comedy that for some inexplicable reason is much less known than his grimly fatalistic novels. Ballard Down is mentioned merely as "the lofty ridge which ran inland" ridden by Ethelberta on her donkey on her way from Swanage to Corfe (Corvsgate). In fact Ballard Down is not mentioned by name in any document from before the nineteenth century.

If you are not happy with a very steep descent on loose gravel (I have more senior walkers in mind here) then you should forsake the superb view from Ballard Down and turn left at the stone seat memorial (GR 034813) and follow the path along the bottom of the southern edge of the down due west to reach the road at the base of Godlingston Hill (GR 018813). The path brings you, after 2 miles of wonderful ridge-top, to the Obelisk, where you turn left to follow a very steep and difficult path down through the gorse. Turn right under the thorn trees at the bottom of the hill and follow the path to the road. Turn left on the road and then immediately left to join an obvious track winding up the side of Godlingston Hill. To your right is the dry chalk gully of the Giant's Trencher. The path divides at a narrow fork; keep right here as the track steepens on its way up the hill.

This track continues to the north of the trig point, past what appear to be some Second World War defence emplacements on the left. Turn left off the path here to head along the top of the ridge; keep the trig point to your right. For the time being you are walking without waymarks. The path is just visible as an old grassy track just to the south (left) of the top of the ridge. You pass through a gate and enter a long field with a prominent gorse hedge on the right, marking the exact top of the ridge. Four hundred yards into this field is a gate; go through this and head north-east, so that you are almost doubling back on yourself, making for the far corner of a deciduous wood (King's Wood). The path, now an obvious track, makes its way down through the end of the wood, in early summer the air rich with the garlicky smell of the dense beds of ramsons. Keeping to the edge of two fields with a hedge on your right you descend to the B3351 Studland to Corfe road. You reach the road at a green metal sign pointing the way along the bridleway.

Turn left along the road (there is a verge to walk on) and walk for 300 yards to the viewpoint car park on the right. At the near end of this a stile leads you down a bank and into a field of rough, damp grazing. There are no waymarks for the next stretch. You reach a rough track leading north from Kingswood Farm (GR 003821). Join this as it swings left to head north-west across some badly eroded rough grazing. The track (merely wheel ruts in the rough ground) forks, the left-hand fork heading for the corner of Foxground Plantation - young pines bordered with birch. Keep right here, descending to cross a rough patch of scrub birch and gorse to bring you to the mature firs of Kingswood Heath wood. You cross a small stream at a ford immediately inside the wood (GR 000828); ignore the right-hand turning just over the stream and follow the good track due north. Now you should turn left off this after a few yards to head along a fire break (there is a blue arrow on a tree) but nobody does so far as I can see. I suggest you follow the track north until you reach a T-junction some 300 yards after the stream.

Turn right at the T-junction and follow it past some felling to the end of the wood to a large cylindrical tank which claims to be "Frank's Tank". After a small diversion through some Scots pines to avoid a green of the Isle of Purbeck Golf Club you reach an obvious track heading south-east towards the green-roofed clubhouse on the slope in front of you. The track disappears but the path keeps on and crosses the drive immediately below the clubhouse. You keep the green to your right and head east. What looks from the map as though it might be a slightly tricky bit of path finding turns out to be very easy, thanks to the stone path indicators at every junction. The first path heading off to the left goes north-east to the Knoll House Hotel, via the Agglestone, a remnant of iron-bearing sandstone (GR 024829). Ignore this and turn right up a lane between two greens, towards the road, then immediately left off it to continue across the heath, north-east towards Studland village. The path brings you to a gravel road by a row of houses on the right; keep straight on at the end of the houses, on a path beneath a row of trees; follow this along the lane to bring you onto the public road just before the village green. A classically suburban sign proudly announces that this is "Studland Village Green" - just in case you might have thought it was something different. Keep straight ahead across the crossroads and then turn left, along a footpath towards the church. A footpath leads you due east from the far side of the church to reach the road by the Bankes Arms and your car.

23)   Durdle Door and Bat's Head

Distance: 9 miles
Start: Lulworth Cove car park
Map: sheet 195, GR 822801

This is one of the most spectacular stretches of the Dorset Coast Path. There are few finer views than the sun setting over the sphinx-like silhouette of the Isle of Portland, looking west to White Nothe and listening to the grinding roar of the pebbles below you on the shingle beaches beside Durdle Door. However, if you like your walks in relative solitude, you will not embark upon this one during a weekend in summer. There are shops, a hotel and cafes at Lulworth, as well as a youth hostel. There is a shop and cafe at Newlands Farm campsite, passed through just before the finish.

Looking down into Lulworth Cove

The start is the necessarily large car park behind Lulworth Cove. This is, or rather should be a magical spot. Dennis Kay-Robinson (*The Landscapes of Thomas Hardy*) complained in 1984 that "The Cove today is the victim of its own popularity.... a general atmosphere of lollies and Cola bottles, squawking children and fat grannies with bad feet...". Unkind, perhaps. Ten years later there is even more of the same. More pressing, perhaps, are the problems of traffic jams to and from the Cove on bank holiday weekends. This is really a walk to be enjoyed in the depths of winter (but not at the weekend). In summer, the time to do it is to arrive at the cove before first light so that you can watch the sun come up over the Isle of Wight and your companions will be larks above and the rabbits around. You may then enjoy breakfast on your return at Lulworth Cove.

From the car park follow the broad swathe of footpath heading west up the rounded chalk hill of Hambury Tout. There are good views down to the villas huddling in the trees and gorse behind on Dungy Head. Behind, there is a fine view of the Cove.

This was the last spot on English soil trodden by John Keats, in the last year of his life, en route to Italy where he died in 1821.

The path takes you due west, above St Oswald's Bay and descends towards Red Hole. At low tide state and in good weather it is possible to take

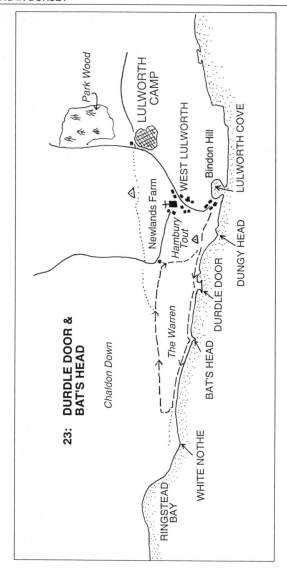

23: DURDLE DOOR & BAT'S HEAD

Park Wood

LULWORTH CAMP

WEST LULWORTH

LULWORTH COVE

Bindon Hill

Newlands Farm

Hambury Tout

DUNGY HEAD

DURDLE DOOR

Chaldon Down

The Warren

BAT'S HEAD

WHITE NOTHE

RINGSTEAD BAY

the path down to the beach and walk along the fine shingle of St Oswald's Bay, climbing up by the path by Durdle Door to rejoin the cliff-top path. A mile west of the car park the cliff-top path meets with the broad path descending from the large caravan site at Newlands Farm. The path down to the beach turns off to the left; this is the last chance you have on this walk of a dip - from here on the path runs along the top of cliffs with no access to any beach. Follow the cliff-top path west from Durdle Door as it contours along before descending to a fine chalk dry valley glorying in the name of Scratchy Bottom.

There follows a steep climb up Swyre head; as you reach the top you see the bent vertical strands of the link fence on the right bent out of true as weary walkers have hauled themselves up by it. You descend as steeply to a second chalk dry valley and climb up again to Bat's Head. Below you the stiff-winged fulmars twist and wheel in the air currents along the cliff. At Bat's Head you see two stone obelisks ahead, more or less identical. For some strange reason only one has been noticed by those responsible for the 1:50,000 map. This is the one standing back from the cliffs in the arable field. The second is at the junction of two paths along the cliffs (GR 702809). Follow the path down the side of Bat's Head to a sweeping gully on your right much grazed by rabbits. The path now angles diagonally up the hill towards the stone obelisk and contours a bowl.

Four hundred yards after the obelisk you meet a stone marker indicating a path inland (GR 779808); turn right here and follow this north-north-east. You find yourself at the head of a long chalk gully leading down to West Chaldon. Turn right, to head west along a bridleway through some fields which have been designated as having free access. This bridleway takes you for a mile and a half until you reach a walker's signpost (GR 800811) by a gate indicating a footpath bearing off to the right, towards Newlands Farm. Turn right here and follow the footpath as it becomes a chalky track, bringing you to the old farm buildings of Newlands Farm.

Nowadays any farming is rather overshadowed by the vast complex of static caravans - a visitation of the worst form of suburbia upon the chalk downs. There is perhaps a case for a kind of blue plaque on the farmhouse wall, saying something like "Bertrand Russell stayed here". In his later life he was as famous, of course, for his support of the anti-nuclear lobby as for his writings on analytical philosophy. To say that he stayed at Newlands Farm is something of a euphemism, for he used the place as a rural hideaway where he would take his mistresses - one at a time - for copiously consummated affairs. His visits were notable for scandalising the villagers of Lulworth by skinny dipping in the sea round about.

Turn right past the farmhouse to take the tarred road leading south through the caravan park, past the shop, and cafe on the right.

This central part of the site is hidden under trees, making it pleasant to walk through. However, rows of white caravans in the field besmirch the landscape in a particularly hideous way, beyond the effect of pylons or road cuttings. Whilst strolling through here early one morning I thought of a possible way of alleviating the eyesore. Surely, linked to planning permission, it would be possible to make it a requirement to paint all caravans a pleasant apple green (not military camouflage, but the effect would be the same). Secondly, if one deciduous tree - beech perhaps - were to be planted on a ration of one per caravan and the site owner made responsible for its continued presence without any pruning then the caravan site would be both pleasanter to be in and to look at after a few years of tree growth.

Keep heading due south, through the plantation; at the end you find a stile leading to a permissive path (not shown on the map) heading south-east across the gorsy top of Hambury Tout to rejoin the coast path. Ahead of you lies the car park.

24) The Land of the Trumpet Major

Distance: 9 miles
Start: Spice Ship Inn, Preston
Map: sheet 194, GR 705830

> *It was just the time of year when cherries are ripe, and hang in clusters under their dark leaves. While the troopers loitered on their horses, and chatted to the miller across the stream, he gathered bunches of the fruit and, held them up over the garden hedge for the acceptance of anybody who would have them; whereupon the soldiers rode into the water, caught the cherries in their forage-caps or received bunches of them on the ends of their switches. It was a cheerful, careless, unpremeditated half hour, which returned like the scent of a flower to the memories of some of those who enjoyed it, even at a distance of many years after, when they lay wounded and weak in foreign lands.*

Thomas Hardy, *The Trumpet Major*

The downs inland and to the east of Weymouth inspired Hardy to one of his finest novels. As a child and a young man in the middle of the nineteenth century he was able to talk to those whose memories of the Napoleonic Wars were still fresh. The action is centred on a water mill in a small village near Weymouth - the locations remain but of course the way of life has long vanished. If you have read or are reading *The Trumpet Major* I recommend that you also do the Hardy's Monument and Portesham walk. Together these walks explore much of the unchanged part of the landscape that Hardy had in his mind as the scene for his novel. There is a fish and chip shop at the start of this walk (two, in fact), as well as a pub. One third of the way along its length it passes through the garden of the Smugglers Inn at Osmington Mills.

Thereafter it passes neither pub nor shop.

Leaving Weymouth on the A353 to Wareham you pass the Spice Ship (formerly the Ship) pub on the right, heading uphill through Preston. Immediately after this turn right, south off the main road into the dead-end road to the church. Park your car in this road. Head south, down the road. When you reach the bottom of the hill the road turns sharp left and you see a prominent footpath sign pointing to the right. Ignore this and go round the bend to the left and see a second footpath sign on the right, taking you south, across the caravan site. You join a private road and head left, east, along it to a stable where you turn right to go up the hill to a second stable. Cross the stile here and make your way uphill. In the left-hand corner of the field you come to a stile and turn left onto the coast path. Half buried in the hedge is a fine boundary marker made of Purbeck stone indicating the limits of the town of Weymouth - the boundary has not changed to this day.

From the boundary marker to the "Holiday Centre" there is a walk of just over half a mile of damp fields of pasture, gorse, thick hedges and low trees.

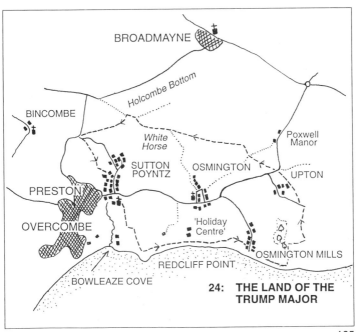

24: THE LAND OF THE TRUMP MAJOR

Ahead of you is the view along the coast, past White Nothe and the cliffs towards Houns Tout and St Aldhelm's Head. Below you to the right is a tangle of gorse and scrub with tussock grass running down to the sea.

It is a fine bird habitat, enhanced by its location, a few minutes' flight from Portland Bill. I have walked this on a misty, mild day in May, with parties of newly arrived swifts wheeling over the cattle in the lush grass and the strident, staccato song of the whitethroat calling over the gorse. True to its grimly Orwellian naming on the map, the "Holiday Centre" presents a rather prison-like aspect as you approach, with its chain-link fencing and grey portakabins. A tiny path leads down to the water. If you do fancy a dip on a hot day I recommend you wait until after Osmington Mills, where you can find a relatively secluded (if steeply shelving) stretch of beach.

A mile beyond the "Holiday Centre" the path turns inland after some landslips and reaches Osmington Mills a few hundred yards inland from the car park. Just before you reach the road you cross a stile. This point marks the reunion of the coast route and the inland route of the Dorset Coast Path. Turn right on the now unified path as you reach the road and walk down to the Smugglers Inn.

It was to Osmington Mills that Britain's favourite painter, John Constable, came for his honeymoon in 1816. One result is one of the most admired paintings in the National Gallery, his View of Weymouth Bay. *Nowadays, on summer bank holidays, Osmington Mills vies with Lulworth in being almost more car park than village.*

Turn left, down the steps to the pub, across the tiny stream running through the garden and make your way round the left-hand side of the pub. The path takes you uphill and over a stile into a field. Over a number of stiles and past an old Second World War pillbox the path brings you past Bran Point - not that you would notice it. Half a mile after Osmington Mills you pass a stone marker indicating a route to the left, inland. Keep straight on here and continue for a further 400 yards, into a wood and down to a tiny stream not marked on the map. You come to a clear T-junction of paths at the stream crossing. To the right is a short path (not marked on the map), leading down to the pebbly beach and a fisherman's hut piled with lobster pots.

Turn left at the path junction in the trees and follow the tiny brook upstream, into the wood, crossing it. You reach a tarred drive; turn right and walk east along it with a field on your left. A grassy lane joins from the left and then you meet the public road (GR 746814) immediately after a modern bungalow hidden in the trees on the right. Turn left on the road to follow it uphill, past some modern barns and a new slurry pit on the left. It takes you up a dry gully to a barrier as you cross the top of the ridge and then down to the road at a T-junction (GR 747826). Turn left here and follow the road downhill for a hundred yards. You meet a farm lane turning right through a steel five-bar gate. Turn right here and follow it down to Upton dairy, with the wood on your right. It becomes a tarred lane and takes you up the hill, past some cottages at Plantations to reach the main A353 Weymouth to Wareham road (GR 742834).

Directly over the main road is a bridleway sign beneath a tree. Take this, heading west, up the hill across the pasture fields; the path becomes quite faint across the grass. After a quarter of a mile the path drops to meet the track heading up the gully from Poxwell Manor by Pixon Barn (GR 735839). Suddenly you are very close to the scene of Hardy's action in his superb novel of Dorset folk facing the threat of Napoleon, *The Trumpet Major*.

One of the lighter episodes in this novel is the besieging of the heroine, Anne Garland, by her laughable buffoon of a suitor-tormentor Festus Derriman at a deserted (because of the imminent threat of invasion) shepherd's cottage on the downs between "Oxwell Hall" and "Overcombe". Pixon Barn brings this episode very much to mind. Poxwell Manor has changed little since Hardy used it as his model for "Oxwell Hall", the home of the Scrooge-like Benjy Derriman. It lies less than half a mile's walk down the dry valley to the east; it is not open to the public, although a good view of the exterior can be had from the road.

Keep straight ahead past Pixon Barn, leaving it on the left. You may be able to find the "Poke's Well" which gave rise to the name of the manor. The path takes you up, along a bridleway, onto the arable downs, through a hedged drove way for a stretch.

Nothing can be seen of the Osmington White Horse as you make your way along the top of the hill above it; what you do have, however, is a superb view out across Weymouth Bay and across to the Isle of Portland. This is easy, delightful walking along a broad chalk ridge, with a view far inland across the Frome Valley, as well as out to sea. The bridleway becomes a chalky farm track and then descends slightly to meet another farm track coming up the side of Holcombe Bottom (GR 710848). Keep left here; you are now on the top of Broadmayne Beacon. There is a new plantation behind a fence on the left of the road. You meet the ruins of a farm 50 yards to the left of the track; turn left here to keep the ruins to your right and follow the obvious grassy track south-west.

The track becomes deeply rutted, descending steeply with a fence on the right, bringing you to the public road by the Combe Valley road junction. Turn left on the road here and then immediately right off it, over a stile in the fence. The path takes you down a sheep grazed slope, into some thorn trees and across an arable field; a headland is left for you to walk on. You see a small scruffy copse in the bottom of the gully; make for this and find yourself on an obvious track heading south-east through the trees - the copse is not marked on the map (GR 703836). You meet a rough, untarred public road (nevertheless marked yellow on the map). Turn left on this and follow it to a T-junction. If you turn left here you will reach the dead-end upper part of

Sutton Poyntz village, which is generally held to be the inspiration for Hardy's "Overcombe". To complete the walk, turn right at the T-junction and follow the road for a quarter of a mile to the main road opposite the Spice Ship pub. Cross to reach your car.

25)   The Isle of Portland

Distance: 8 miles
Start: the Verne car park
Map: sheet 194, GR 692732

> *And this I thought: that never again will I look on London with quite the same eyes. Always at the back of my mind will be, as I walk the streets of London, knowledge of a white island lying out to sea like a great whale. When I see Portland stone in London I shall think of the sea breaking against high hills; I shall hear the scream of the gulls; the suck back of pebbles on the little stony beaches; the white dust lying over the road in the little mysterious Isle of London.*
> H.V.Morton, *In Search of England*

On a clear day this walk gives excellent views of very nearly all of Dorset's coastline and beyond - into Devon and eastwards to the Isle of Wight. Very little of the Isle of Portland is attractive in its own right; however its coast path is a superb walk with much wildlife and history. Hardy's *Isle of Slingers* has an especial atmosphere all its own; I am sure it is no coincidence that he chose it for his most bizarre novel. It has frequently been compared to Gibraltar - knowing both, I consider the comparison very valid. There is a feeling here distinct from Dorset - distinct, too, from England - almost in the way that there is in Cornwall. This is due to something more in its history than quarrying, the Royal Navy and the prisons - the three keys to Portland which remain its mainstay. This walk is very nearly a complete perambulation of the island. No shops are passed, although, nearing the halfway stage, it passes the Pulpit Inn and a number of small cafes at The Bill.

To reach the start take the A354 signed to Portland out of Weymouth; the road climbs steeply out of Fortuneswell and round a left-hand hairpin bend; immediately after this turn left by the Portland Heights Hotel (GR 690731) to park your car at the Verne car park. Turn right on the Verne road and follow it south-west, back to the main road, where you cross over. After 50 yards turn left onto the cliff-top coast path, taking you south along the top of West Cliff above West Weare.

Instantly you leave the traffic behind and find yourself among the delights

Looking west to Golden Cap from Seatown

View east from above Winspit *(Walk 21)*
Looking down into Lulworth Cove from the slopes of Hambury Tout *(Walk 23)*

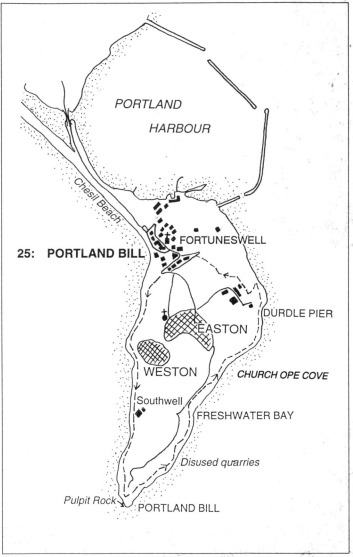

PORTLAND HARBOUR

Chesil Beach

FORTUNESWELL

25: PORTLAND BILL

DURDLE PIER

EASTON

WESTON

CHURCH OPE COVE

Southwell

FRESHWATER BAY

Disused quarries

Pulpit Rock

PORTLAND BILL

of walking here; there are magnificent views across Lyme Bay, along the great sweep of Chesil Beach and over the Fleet, inland to Hardy's Monument and the hills beyond. Below, the fulmars, stiff-winged, circle and wheel against the cliffs, whilst acrobatic rabbits dart into fissures in the old quarry-workings. There are various rock arches over the path and views below to a great tangle of thorn and scrub at the base of the cliffs - much used as a pausing spot by migrating birds on their landfall after the 70-mile crossing of the channel. For some parts of the path you are walking along ancient stone-paved trackway that served the quarrying; deep grooves are worn in the stone, testament to the passage of horse-drawn iron-tyred vehicles in the past.

After a mile you emerge from the endless quarrying to find yourself walking across open grassy sward with a large modern housing estate to your left - it seems as if a little piece of Greenock or Hamilton has been deposited in Dorset. Beyond you is a large, apparently concrete-built complex behind a fence. This is the Royal Navy's underwater weapons establishment; in fact it is not concrete at all but built of Portland stone quarried not a mile from the site; it is the architecture that makes it look as though it is made of concrete. Do not despair of Portland; there is inspiring walking to come. The path starts to head downhill towards The Bill and its lighthouses, ancient and modern.

The Upper Lighthouse (no longer in use) was once the home of Dr Marie Stopes, the pioneer of contraception, who would flaunt her youthful lovers before her husband, to the outrage of the locals, and indeed her husband. She is encountered later in the walk as well. One surprise is an art gallery; during the early summer of 1994 there was here the first posthumous exhibition of Derek Jarman's work, some of it being hung in the lighthouse itself. The working lighthouse is frequently open to the public.

You keep the radio mast to your left and follow the path across the grassy area just to the west of the car park, bringing you at last to Portland Bill itself, where on spring mornings the birdwatchers huddle with their binoculars and tripod telescopes, peering across the waters of The Race for incoming migrants.

Now begins the best of the walking as you turn to head up the lee side of the island. You pass a scattering of beach huts and make your way across several small fields bound by drystone walls which slope down to the low cliffs. You pass a crane formerly used to load the lighters with the stone blocks direct from the quarry. It still has a chain around a fine block of the limestone, as though waiting for a ghostly hand to winch it aboard a spectral vessel. Ahead of you lies the glory of Dorset's coastline facing Weymouth Bay. You can make out the wide curving chalky track bringing the masses down to Durdle Door beach from Newlands Farm campsite and car park. To the left are the chalky faces of Bat's Head and White Nothe. Given a clear day and a pair of binoculars you can study the inlet of Lulworth Cove, just east of Durdle Door.

The enormous seascape around you has witnessed the passage of some important events in our country's history. The rounding of Portland Bill marked an important stage in the running battle between England's defenders and the Duke of Medina Sidonia's Armada in 1558. In his brilliant The Trumpet Major *Thomas Hardy works a fine pen-portrait of Anne Garland gazing at the departing HMS* Victory *passing on its way from Portsmouth to again defeat the Spanish, allied with Napoleon's France off Cape Trafalgar in 1805. In between these two battles, much of London as we know it had been constructed from the quarries you are walking over. Now the air is alive with the chatter of the Lynx and Sea King helicopters from the naval base as the modern Royal Navy goes through its training.*

All this contemplation of your surroundings is brought to a temporary halt as the path brings you to the road above Freshwater Bay. Turn right and walk northwards along the road, past a working quarry; there is a pavement and a good wide verge on the left of the road. *H.V.Morton, a very popular travel writer of his day, recounts a visit to Portland in 1927, quoted above. He narrates being shown the beginnings of a pillars intended for St Paul's Cathedral, and the source of the stone that became The Cenotaph, then a fresh cut in the quarry.*

After a quarter of a mile of walking northwards up the road you pass a

Quarrymen's crane near Portland Bill

footpath sign on the right. Three hundred yards further on you turn right to descend, zigzagging down the cliff towards Church Ope Cove. Early in the morning you can gaze right onto the crab boats as they haul the pots in, tossing the unwanted crustacea overboard and the crabs and lobsters into their boxes for sale in Weymouth later.

From here Hardy's Anne Garland, heroine of The Trumpet Major, *took a small ferryboat back to Weymouth on her way home from sighting HMS* Victory *setting forth to Trafalgar. If you were to stay on the road instead of descending to the path above Church Ope Cove you would come to the museum of Portland, located in the house that Hardy used as Avice Caro's house in his strange tale* The Well Beloved. *This was once the property of the contraceptive pioneer Dr Marie Stopes and was donated to the Isle of Portland by her.*

The path takes you north-east, between cliff-top and shore; after a third of a mile you reach Rufus Castle (not built by William Rufus but by the Duke of York in the middle of the fifteenth century) where some concrete and tarmac steps lead upwards. Now take care, because the next section is a little tricky to follow; it is almost entirely without waymarks. Turn right at the bottom of the concrete steps to follow a narrow path through low bushes across the tangle of old quarry-workings which brings you around to Durdle Pier. In fact there are a number of paths snaking through the knee-high bushes - on a wet day your legs are in for a soaking. A recent embankment appears above you and eventually the principal path zigzags up to join it above some small boat huts.

There is now a stretch of easier walking. A large-section sewage pipe joins you so that you are walking with it on your left. You pass a sign saying "Military Firing Range Keep Out". Rest assured the right of way continues and there is no danger at all on the path. The sewage pipe disappears under an earth bank about 4ft high. Make your way onto the top of this bank and soon afterwards you come to a concrete block with an angle-pipe leading out of the right-hand side. There is a coast guard lookout resembling a small outhouse toilet nearby - the first of two such. Turn left at this pipe junction to follow the obvious path along the top of a similar small embankment, leading towards the trees and the base of the cliffs below the gaol. If you reach the 30ft high back-stop wall of the old small-arms range you have gone about 300 yards too far.

This path dives into a tangle of low trees and bushes and passes a small apple tree. It then leads you steeply up towards the cliff to the "hole in the wall" along an ancient well-graded path twisting up beneath the low cliff. You pass through an old gateway (GR 703725) and suddenly find yourself on a public road beneath one of the "stone walls" which "do not a prison make". Well, this one certainly does. You turn right on the road and follow it north-west, with fine views over the wall to your right. You pass the HM Young Offenders

Prison Farm and its paddock of sheep and Friesian cows. The road, now private, swings to the left at the end of the paddock and leads through an old gateway with an open area in front of you, looking towards the two naval transmitting masts. You are now standing at the road junction (GR 700727). Follow the good track indicated by a green sign as a footpath, leading north-west towards a quarry. You pass some enormous boulders placed across it. Behind a 5ft high wall on your left is Portland's remarkable sunken sports field, surrounded by trees growing on the old quarry walls; it is well worth a peep over.

The track forks (GR 697728); bear right here and follow the track due north-west towards the left-hand of the two masts (GR 695734). You reach a small car park and may well feel tempted by a short-cut across the grassy mounds to your left to reach the Verne car park. It leads to the lavishly constructed high-angle batteries where deep trenches, revetted with fine stone walls, lead to the gun platforms - still looking as though they are capable of being used. You join the Verne road where it turns steeply to head down the hill and follow it for 400 yards south-west to your car.

CHAPTER SIX

West Dorset

This section covers that part of Dorset which lies to the west of the River Frome and the A354 Roman road from Dorchester to Weymouth.

26) Golden Cap, St Gabriel's and Chardown Hill

Distance: 7 miles
Start: Langdon Hill car park
Map: sheet 193, GR 413932

Golden Cap is remarkable - the highest cliff on the south coast of England and visible on a clear day from almost any point along the coast from Portland Bill to Start Point. This is one of the best walks in the county, but if you like to have the landscape to yourself in summer I recommend you do it as early in the morning as possible, for the stretch of coast between Charmouth and Seatown attracts large numbers of car-borne visitors. This walk takes you past the tiny National Trust shop on Stonebarrow, where you can buy sweets and drinks. It passes no pub, although it could easily be extended to pass through the village of Morcombelake, which has a pub. Alternatively you could start at The Anchor Inn in Seatown (meaning that you start off with a steep climb of 600 feet to the summit of Golden Cap).

To reach the start in Langdon Hill Wood, turn south off the A35 main road less than a mile west of Chideock (GR 412935) towards Norchard Farm and St Gabriel's. A National Trust sign beseeches "No cars beyond this point please" and subtly points the way to the left, immediately off Muddyford Lane. You follow Langdon Lane, rutted and potholed (surely a much more effective speed limiter than well-spaced sleeping policemen), around the edge of the wood, then turn right off it to head up the hill into the wood on a gravel road to the car park at the top.

Go through the gate at the far left corner of the car park and follow the track southwards along the eastern side of Langdon Hill Wood. After a third of a mile it swings to the right, keeping inside the wood; at the south-west corner of the wood an obvious track turns off to the left, downhill to the edge of the wood where you turn right and go uphill across the field to the obvious stile ahead. Directly in front of you the path takes you straight up the furze-covered summit of Golden Cap; an easier path goes round to the right.

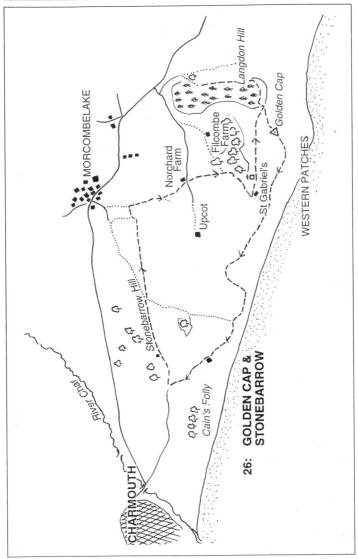

CHARMOUTH

River Char

MORCOMBELAKE

Stonebarrow Hill

Cain's Folly

Norchard Farm

Upcot

Filcombe Farm

St Gabriel's

Langdon Hill

Golden Cap

WESTERN PATCHES

26: GOLDEN CAP & STONEBARROW

Suddenly you have made it to the top - it almost seems too easy. The fact is that Langdon Hill National Trust car park is the highest point to park your car near to Golden Cap and offers the easiest approach.

Golden Cap is considered by many to be the crowning glory of the National Trust's Enterprise Neptune. There is no finer point from which to contemplate the work being done by the Trust than from its summit. There is a strong impression along this section of coastline that the entire landscape may be divided into two categories; it is either a caravan site or it is owned by the National Trust. The work being done by the Trust poses some fascinating environmental questions. There is a campaign to remove a deal of the bracken from the summit and grass it over. The presence of bracken on the summit plateau concentrates people's passage into well-defined paths which rapidly lose their grass cover and gullying results, which in a short time could irreparably scar and eventually erode away the entire hilltop. However, some people complain that removal of the bracken spoils their view of the hilltop itself.

Immediately below you to the west you see a time-honoured agricultural landscape of dumpy fields, hedges and gorsy hill-tops; these are the valleys of the St Gabriel's stream just below you and Ridge Water and Westhay Water just beyond. Behind them, inland, lies the long ridge of Stonebarrow Hill. Notice how the car park marked on the map on the summit in fact extends all the way along the summit. Here the Trust is planting gorse in an attempt to hide the cars parked there. And yet people like to park their cars with a view, which therefore means that they can be seen from far and wide.

The land between Stonebarrow Hill and the sea is farmed in a "traditional" way, which in fact means using methods that were in universal practice until around the time of the Second World War. Meadows are not ploughed and seeded for improved grass production; hay is cut instead of silaged, damp meadows are left undrained, bramble, bracken and gorse patches are left uncut. Which all sounds very well except that the Trust depends to a great extent on the income generated by the land for its revenue, and land thus treated generates considerably less income than land farmed in a more modern way, so the Trust has less money to buy and protect sites or set up expensive traditional wooden gates and stiles. Undrained pasture contains liver fluke which badly affects sheep and can kill them (and with the bilharzia virus in the Third World can kill people); bramble, bracken and gorse are host to a plague of ticks which afflict sheep in hot weather and visitors and their dogs as well. A book could be written about the acquisition and management by the National Trust of Golden Cap, and possibly will be.

From the summit of Golden Cap, go down the very steep zigzag steps taking you to the west; you reach a signpost at the beginning of the grass field; keep left here to follow the coast path west, down the hill to cross the St Gabriel's stream at a footbridge. Follow the path westwards, keeping the

Looking inland from the north slope of Golden Cap to Hardown Hill

landslips of Broom Cliff (not named on the map) to your left. The path is moving by stages northwards at around a yard a year as the land slips away towards the beach. You can see the cracks starting in the sheep-grazed turf, indicating the alignment of the next slip. At the lower stages the ground is covered in scrub, replacing the turf and providing a particularly good nest site for linnet and whitethroat.

You reach the top of a gentle spur with a banked hedge on your right; behind this on the far side is Ridge Barn. Follow the path down to cross the Ridge Water and then over a steeper spur. At the top of this a path heads inland, across two fields, following a hedge on the right. As you look inland you can see it zigzagging up through the rough grazing near the top of Stonebarrow Hill, above the pasture fields. (This offers a short-cut of almost a mile, missing out the information centre and shop on Stonebarrow.) Continue on the coast path down to cross Westhay Water; immediately after crossing it you see a signpost, pointing the way uphill to a wet patch in a field and joining a prominent track at Westhay Farm.

Follow the farm lane directly up the hill, heading north-west; after 200 yards the lane turns sharply to the right in the gorse and you turn left to head up the hill on a grassy track. A number of tracks turn right near the top of the hill, so that you make your way through the gorse to reach the National Trust information centre and shop in the building of the old radar station

(GR 383933). From the shop head west along the track across the car park. This offers much better walking than it might sound; the car park is entirely turfed and is so large that it very rarely fills right up. At the end of the car park you come to a signpost just before a clump of pine trees (GR 390935). A sign points east to Chardown Hill; go through a gate in a hedge to find yourself in a sheep-grazed field by a second signpost and keep left, heading due east. You keep a hedge on your left for a third of a mile before you come to the steep, east-facing escarpment of Chardown Hill. Follow the footpath down the hill, with a thick hedge on the left, to reach a track at the bottom at a stile. If it is a hot day you may wish to throw some water over yourself from St Wite's well (GR 399927); to reach this turn left through the gate and walk a few yards to the north. St Wite (or Candida) is also encountered in Walk 31 - Marshwood Vale and Hardown Hill, as her shrine is in the church at Whitchurch Canonicorum.

Follow the track south from St Wite's Well past the second cottage on your left. A few yards after this you see a hunting gate on the left in a natural arch in the high hedge. The path down the hill to Norchard Farm is clearly marked with gates and stiles. You reach the track with the converted barn on your left. Cross over the track and go through a gate to find yourself in a damp field; on the far side you see a stile by a large oak tree. You continue with a hedge on your left, over a stile in the corner of the field and a footbridge. You find yourself in a wet field with St Gabriel's Wood facing you. The high hedges behind you give you the impression of being in a clearing - this is Copse Mead. In the middle of this is a pond, enlarged by the Trust in 1985. In the far left corner you see the path coming down from Filcombe Farm; keep right, to a footbridge, and follow the path south along the edge of the wood on your left. This is a particularly attractive stage of the walk, with field irises, kingcups, red campion and various rushes flourishing in the damp ground.

At the bottom of the hill you reach the ancient track at St Gabriel's; formerly this was a fishing village, Stanton St Gabriel's. The immediate cause of its decline was the rerouting inland of the main road from London to Exeter in 1825, so that it dwindled to a few cottages (now rented out as holiday cottages) and a ruined church. Turn left up the track and go through the gate to the ruined church on the left. Directly in front of you is the path up to Golden Cap; I assume you will not have the energy for this and suggest you take the path heading east, diagonally up the slope, to the saddle between Langdon Hill and Golden Cap, following the footpath round into the wood and back to the car park.

27)   Four Short Walks on the Golden Cap Estate

The National Trust has created and signed a number of walks around its land on and near Golden Cap. The term "estate" is perhaps somewhat misleading, since there never was an estate here in the usual sense of the word. The

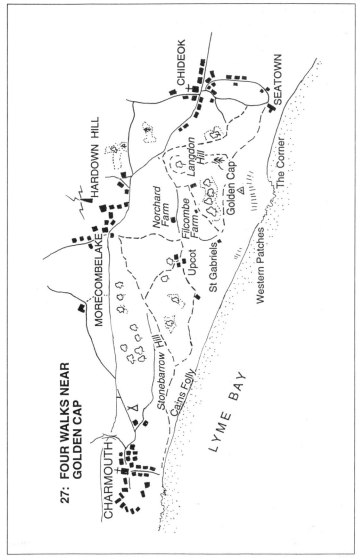

27: FOUR WALKS NEAR GOLDEN CAP

CHARMOUTH

Stonebarrow Hill

Cains Folly

LYME BAY

MORECOMBELAKE

HARDOWN HILL

Norchard Farm

Filcombe Farm

Upcot

St Gabriels

Langdon Hill

Golden Cap

Western Patches

The Corner

CHIDEOK

SEATOWN

Trust has had to buy up piecemeal, sometimes field by field, all the land which is now available for the public to enjoy. These walks, each of them much shorter than the average in this book, are arranged to show the walker a particular part of the landscape of the environs of Golden Cap. With signposts marked with their particular "animal" symbol they are obviously very attractive to families with children. However, do not think that you are guaranteed to see the animal (or bird) whose symbol you are following. (In fact at the time of writing it is difficult to avoid the plague of rabbits here and elsewhere in Dorset.) Since the routes are graphically marked on signposts the directions below are an outline only. The walks are shown on the laminated display maps in the car parks around the Golden Cap Estate. There should be further information available from the information centre in the old radar station on Stonebarrow Hill although none was at the time of researching.

The "Rabbit" Route

This route starts in the sea-front car park at Charmouth (GR 365931) and takes you across the bridge east from there, following the signs steeply up Stonebarrow Hill and along its gorsy ridge to the end of the car park by the pine trees (GR 390935). From here it takes you along the path down the hill, south-west, to the east end of the wood behind Upcot (GR 394933) and from here across the valley of the Ridge Water to Ridge Barn and then down to the Coast Path and westwards, back to Charmouth.

The "Butterfly" Route

This starts in the village of Morcombelake, clustering around the south side of Hardown Hill. From the A35 it takes you west along the dead-end lane which makes its way up onto Stonebarrow Hill to the track junction and gate under the pine trees (GR 390935). From this point it is the same as the path above and the signs carry both symbols as far as the east end of the wood (GR 394933). From this point you head east, to Upcot and the crosstracks (GR 400930), and due north, past St Wite's Well (GR 399937, but not marked on the map) and back to the start.

The "Roe Deer" Route

This is a circuit route from Langdon Wood car park (GR 413932). It takes you south along the track along the east side of the wood and then, from the south-west corner of the wood, down the hill to St Gabriel's, then north-east up the valley through St Gabriel's Wood and across the fields to the north of Filcombe Wood, to Filcombe Farm, back to Muddyford lane and so to the car park.

The "Kestrel" Route

This is a climb of Langdon Hill from the start point at the car park in Seatown (GR 421917). It takes you west along the coast path and then inland to Langdon Hill Wood, around the wood on the track (a permissive path and therefore not shown on the map as a right of way). From the north end of the wood you head down the track (Langdon Lane), past Knell Coppice on your left (GR 415926) and continuing on the old coach road (Cambrey Lane) down to Seatown.

28) Thorncombe Beacon, Quarry Hill and Eype Down

Distance: 7 or 3 miles
Start: Eype's Mouth car park
Map: sheet 193, GR 447911

This is a "something for everyone" walk, with matchless views, both out to sea and inland, some good stiff hills to climb and a perfect village whose perfection is enhanced by a delightful pub. The walking is very varied, including lofty cliff-top, hill-tops covered in furze and tussocks, grass fields, hidden valleys and sunken ancient lanes. It can be extended by walking a mile to the start along the Coast Path from West Bay to Eype's Mouth. It can also be started from Bridport; I recommend you take the footpath that heads north-east along the River Simene to Symondsbury and pick up the directions below from there.

To reach the start take the well-signed turning to Eype from the A35 Bridport bypass (GR 451924) and from there follow the signs to Eype; you can also reach Eype by heading south from the centre of the town, down South Street, which becomes West Bay Road (the B3157). Half a mile down this road you cross the Mangerton River on South Bridge by the Old Brewery into Skilling Hill Road. A mile from the bridge you cross over the bypass on a new bridge; turn immediately left and follow the twisting narrow road down to Eype's Mouth.

The car park at Eype's Mouth is a paying one; the good news is that however long you stay you pay the same amount (£1.50 in 1994) so by going for a good walk you certainly have more value for money than those who pause for a picnic and a paddle. Newcomers to the area should note that Eype is pronounced "Eep". On the west side of the car park at Eype's Mouth you see a cream-painted wooden chalet house. The coast path sets off uphill behind this and takes you steeply up the sheep-cropped turf. You descend equally steeply into a short gully and then make the climb to the beacon. At the summit is a replica of the firebaskets erected in 1588 and used as a message-carrying system to send news of the sighting of the expected Spanish Armada. The replicas (many other hill-tops were and are again so

141

Golden Cap, with Lyme Regis and the coast of Devon beyond

adorned) date from the celebrations of the 400th anniversary of the event, in 1988.

The views from Thorncombe Beacon are as good as from Golden Cap - better perhaps, because you can see Golden Cap itself, a great hill which is being eaten away by the sea. One wonders why Thorncombe was chosen for a beacon and not its higher neighbour; I think the answer may lie in the fact that it is much closer to habitation and therefore much more accessible. Its command of the view out to sea is almost as good as Golden Cap; you can see Portland Bill and Start Point, given good visibility. When you have had your fill of the view, turn inland and walk north, around the head of the gully that leads down towards Great Ebb. It takes you straight to a very prominent tumulus; go over a stile to the right of it and keep heading inland on the well-worn path. This becomes a track along the side of the wood and brings you out onto the gorse-covered top of Eype Down.

On the top of Eype Down you reach a crosstracks on the summit - this not being quite as the map marks. There is a magnificent view from here across the valleys that drain towards the River Brit, reaching the sea at West Bay. On your left, and higher than you, is the grassy summit of Quarry Hill, which you are about to climb. Immediately to the right of it is Colmer's Hill, a stand of spindly pine trees surrounding the trig point on the summit. Directly behind it you see the wooded summit of Lewesdon Hill, while just to its left

142

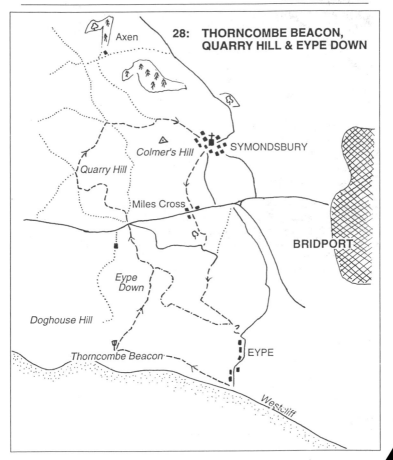

28: THORNCOMBE BEACON, QUARRY HILL & EYPE DOWN

Axen

Colmer's Hill

SYMONDSBURY

Quarry Hill

Miles Cross

BRIDPORT

Eype Down

Doghouse Hill

Thorncombe Beacon

EYPE

Westcliff

along the horizon is the smaller rounded outline of Pilsdon Pen, the highest summit in the county. This cross-tracks is the point where those who opt for the shorter version of this walk depart (for the longer route miss out all the rest of this paragraph and start reading at the beginning of the next) turning right and following the track through the woods, bringing you d to Down House Farm. Turn left on the farm lane for a few yards until you to a gate on the right, opposite the entrance to the house named "Dow Turn right here and follow the bridleway steeply down the slope, thr gates. At the bottom of the hill you meet the end of a track by a black wooden holiday cottage. Follow the drive down to the public road and turn right along it to return to your car.

To continue to Quarry Hill turn left at the crosstracks on Eype Down, descending as you head north-west across the gorse, bracken and tussocks. The path brings you to the lane from Eype where it meets the A35 main road at Turnpike Cottage (GR 437928). Take very great care in crossing the road; the A35 is busy and fast. Take especial care with traffic coming from the right.

At the time of writing (summer 1994) discussions are in progress about improvements to the A35 on the stretch from Bridport to Charmouth, bypassing Chideock and Morcombelake. Newcomers to the area should note that Chideock is pronounced "Chiddock". It remains to be seen if these will be implemented and in what form. The stated plan is for a two-lane dual carriageway, which seems a little excessive, bearing in mind that the bypasses for Bridport and Lyme Regis, on either side of this stretch, are single carriageway, as are the recent Dorchester and Axminster bypasses on the same road. Whatever form the road improvements and bypasses take, they will probably affect the alignment of the paths along this route so be aware of this when reading the directions. Meanwhile the houses, lamp-posts and cars in Chideock and Morcombelake are alternately emblazoned in stickers saying "No Bypass!" and "Bypass Now!" and everyone watches the progress of matters at Solsbury Hill outside Bath.

Now safely over the road, follow Quarr Lane north, past a footpath turning left; the lane forks. Turn left at the fork along a track with a strip of grass up the middle and turn left at the end after just a few yards to follow the ancient grassed-over track up the side of the hill and over the summit. The path descends very steeply on the western side of the hill with a small wood on your right and then turns right and follows the hillside round so that you are heading north across the head of a gully that leads down to Chideock. Make for the downhill side of the second wood and follow the path down the hill, heading north-east to Quarr Cross (GR 434939), the junction of Hell Lane (west), Axen Lane (north), Quarr Lane (south) and Shute's Lane (east), ancient, sunken, rutted cart tracks all. However it is not quite a simple crossroads, as the map marks. Turn right; you are now in Quarr Lane, which ⌐u walked the southern end of by the main road.

⌐⌐diately after the crossroads turn left at a fork and head down the hill
⌐⌐⌐d track running around the north side of Colmer's Hill - not that
⌐⌐⌐⌐ng of it as for some of its length you are in a cutting and
⌐⌐⌐⌐⌐ from the surrounding landscape by high hedges
⌐⌐⌐⌐⌐s you past a fine thatched cottage on the left,
⌐⌐⌐⌐dsbury. Less than a mile from Bridport, this is,
⌐⌐⌐⌐vorld". You reach the church on the left and the
⌐⌐⌐⌐after; your path turns right through a wicket gate

View of the centre of Symondsbury

to the left of a drive gate immediately opposite the turning to Broadoak in the centre of the village. It would, however, be a shame to miss out on the Ilchester Arms pub, just beyond.

Leaving the pub, turn right on the road and then left through the above-mentioned gate. You find yourself in a lane beneath trees, which twists around and reaches a field by a muddy patch. Head south-west, along the left-hand side of a narrow gully. You climb the hill, keeping the copse to your left above you; go through a stile and descend on the far side to a high hedge with a tiny brook running through it; a footbridge and a stile marks your way, whereupon you head straight up the hill with a large turn-of-the-century red brick house at the top of the field. There are two gates to the left of this house; go through the left-hand one and cross diagonally over the road, bearing right. The path continues south, along a short drive and then past a large thatched house on the right, down into an orchard through a gate. At the bottom of the orchard turn left through a gate in a high overgrown hedge and walk downstream along the valley for a few yards with a wood and a steep bank down on your right (GR 443927). Turn right at the corner of the wood and descend to cross the small stream. Ahead the path takes you very steeply uphill towards some trees and reaches the road in a small copse - it's a secretive little path leading onto the road, where high hedges hem it in on either side.

Of the footpath heading south-west to Down Farm, I could find no sign, although this may hopefully have been reopened and waymarked when you come to walk it; the track leading up to the small barn marked on the map has "private" written plainly, so I suggest you turn left and follow the road along for 300 yards and turn right, down to Higher Eype. After a third of a mile you come to an obvious wide steel gate (GR 444920) just before a scruffy shed on the left. This gate was painted black the last time I saw it and no doubt will remain so for years to come. Turn left through this and make your way down the hill, over the stile, to find yourself in a muddy, hedged-in track which brings you to the narrow lane running through Lower Eype. Turn right on the road and walk back to your car.

29)   The Lyme Regis Undercliff Forest

Distance: 5 miles there and back to Pinhay
Start: Coram's Tower car park
Map: sheet 193, GR 337920

> *with its green chasms between romantic rocks, where the scattered forest trees and orchards of luxuriant growth declare that many a generation must have passed away since the first partial falling of the cliff prepared the ground for such a state*
>
> Jane Austen, *Persuasion*

This walk is unique in this book insofar as it is purely an out-and-back walk, returning by the same route as you departed. In principle this is something I try to avoid; it makes for a less enjoyable walk. However in this case there is no choice at all for once beyond Underhill Farm you have to continue the full 7 miles to Seaton, well into Devon. This walk is so delightful it is very worthwhile returning the same way you set out. Even if you were lucky enough to have an accomplice with a boat this would not help, for there is no right of way access to the shore either.

To find the start follow Broad Street uphill from the centre and bear left into Pound Street, up the hill towards Seaton. The car park is on the left, well signed, opposite Coram's Tower with its stone-mullioned windows. If you want to try and find a free parking space for your car, turn right, off Pound Street, into Pound Road at Coram's Tower; at the bottom of Pound Road turn left, up the hill past the Kent House Hotel on your right; there are a number of free parking spaces on the left of the road facing uphill. After Underhill Cottage the walk passes not one habitation.

The Undercliff Forest is a fantastic landscape; enormous landslips in the forests, tall trees, occasional glimpses of the sea below or crags above, beds

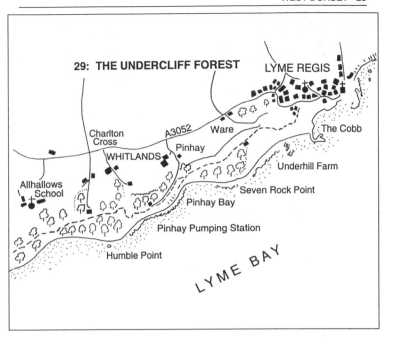

29: THE UNDERCLIFF FOREST

LYME REGIS

Charlton Cross

A3052

Ware

The Cobb

Pinhay

WHITLANDS

Allhallows School

Underhill Farm

Seven Rock Point

Pinhay Bay

Pinhay Pumping Station

Humble Point

LYME BAY

of ferns and hidden springs - all this produces an atmosphere that makes you think yourself something of an intrepid explorer. There is no way to discover the Undercliff woods other than an out-and-back walk, unless you can arrange transport to or from Seaton; the woods are more than worth exploring on an out-and-back walk, and you can make the walk any length you like. The woods are now managed by English Nature (formerly the Nature Conservancy Council) as a national nature reserve. The sense of this being a wild landscape is enhanced for me by the fact that the 1960 edition of the OS one-inch map shows none of this as woodland! And yet the woods have been here for centuries and more.

The Undercliff Forest is unique in many respects. Firstly the forest has never been managed - extraction of more than firewood on donkey panniers was just too difficult. It therefore represents climatic climax vegetation - except that here there is a micro-climate quite different from that which prevails on the cliff-tops above. J.Mead Falkner mentions blackberries bigger and earlier-ripening than elsewhere, growing on the sheltered south-facing cliffs of the Dorset coast; the same is true of the Undercliff woods, so that almost every plant breaks into leaf and blooms earlier and grows taller. It is a magical habitat; on humid spring evenings the lithe coppery slow-worms glide across the path and the nightingale pours out its song from the luxuriant undergrowth. To whet your appetite for this walk you should really read John Fowles's vivid description in *The French Lieutenant's Woman*, for he perfectly captures the spirit and nature of the place.

Let us set forth and discover this landscape, unique in all the British Isles. At the far side of the car park from the road you see a black walkers' signpost pointing the way along Pinewalks to Ware. Walk along this lane to the end and through a gate into a small paddock running up the hill to the right. A sign points the way to the Cobb; this path turns off immediately down to the left through the trees. Continue south-west, along a grassy slope and then up the side of a long copse to your right to meet a private road at the top. Turn left on the road, past two cottages on the right and follow it to Underhill Farm. The drive turns left to the house - until the 1960s this was the home of John Fowles, who then moved into the town. For more about him, see the following walk - The Lim Valley.

Turn right off the drive by the information board and follow the path into the forest. These are about all the directions that need to be given. From here to Axmouth or Seaton there is no right of way to the shore or inland. Moreover the path itself is an entirely mobile thing, rarely following exactly the same line from one year to the next. The reason for this is that the landscape itself is continually moving. There are stretches where you have the impression of being in an old building site in the woods, with piles of bright gravel exposed by the landslips.

The first stage of the walk takes you across Ware Common - a natural enough location for a lovers' retreat; the French Lieutenant's Woman scandalised the prurient Mrs Poulteney by walking there alone. A mile from Underhill Farm, having passed below Ware Cliffs, you reach a tarred drive beneath the trees (GR 317909); bear left on this and follow it down the hill. This is the access route for the pumping station at Pinhay, where some 2,500 cubic metres of drinking water are pumped back up the cliff from the springs. To the left you can see the path worn through the trees as people have made their way down to the rocky shore. There is no right of way here and the path, if such it can be called, is very tricky; when I was last there a length of rope had been attached to some tree roots by which you could lower yourself down a bank. On a hot day you may be glad to learn that the water outflow which goes down a canvas pipe to the beach is purified drinking water.

On the far side of the pumping station you head up the hill away from the sea and turn immediately left to follow the Undercliff path through the woods, past a gully descending from Whitlands; the path continues past Whitland Cliffs, behind Humble Point. A mile further west you meet a private lane descending from Allhallows School, but there is no right of way inland here.

Around Culverhole Point the seaward slope becomes less abrupt and the path exits from the trees and the coast path heads inland round a golf course to cross the River Axe into Seaton. If you can arrange to be dropped here to walk back to Lyme, well and good; if not, you will have to walk back the way you came.

30) The Lim Valley

Distance: 7 miles
Start: Charmouth Road car park, Lyme Regis
Map: sheet 193, GR 345926

This walk is an exploration of the intricate, hidden landscape immediately inland of Lyme Regis. When you are tired of the summer crowds in the town, this is the perfect respite. I have walked this on a sunny Sunday afternoon of the May Bank Holiday weekend and, apart from the small stretch that is in the town itself, saw not a single soul. The route sneaks into Devon for less than a mile, but the landscape of steep narrow twisting valleys, woods, hidden cottages and small fields is wholly Devonian - and quite delightful. Apart from the start, it passes no pub or shop on the way, although it is hard to avoid these in the centre of Lyme.

To reach the start follow the signs for the A3052 to Charmouth. From the traffic lights at the narrow corner where Bridge Street turns into Church Street, head steeply up Church Street, out of the town. Four hundred yards after the church you reach a car park on the right (GR 344926); park here. The price of parking here for all or part of a day in 1994 was £1.50. If you really want to park in Lyme for free, I suggest you try in Silver Street, just above and on the other side of the street from the Kent House Hotel (GR 334926). The price of this is half a mile of walking through the town to the start.

Lyme Regis is a town that seems to have invited literary figures to it down the ages. Jane Austen was here from the autumn of 1803 to 1804 and elements of Persuasion *are modelled on what she witnessed here. A plaque fixed to the wall of a house on the promenade between the Marine Parade and the town announces the Jane Austen Garden, opened to commemorate the bicentenary of her birth in 1975. At present, however, Lyme is more famous for its contemporary literary connection, as the home of John Fowles. The fact that he set* The French Lieutenant's Woman *in Lyme has given the town greater standing.*

Unusually, when the media moguls came to film the book, Lyme was used as the location. The film is still available on video (starring Jeremy Irons and Merryl Streep) and is well worth watching; the book is more highly recommended. I remember leaning on field gate above Lyme whilst they were filming and hearing from a local about such matters as the spreading

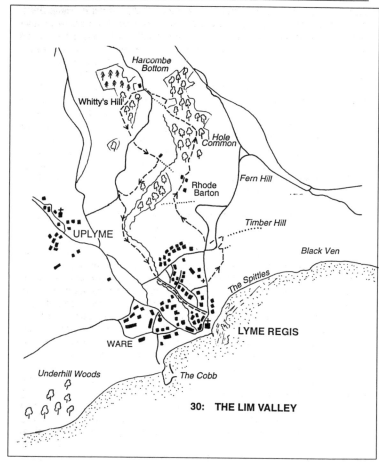

30: THE LIM VALLEY

of straw in the streets, the hiring of extras, the thatching of bus shelters, the erection of a false array of masts in the harbour behind the cobb to give an authentic background and so on. He went on to explain ".. there's zome American woman in it, neame of Ztreet urr zummat". Fowles had lived in Lyme long before the publication of the popular French Lieutenant's Woman. He was something of a cult author in the United States and France, for his darkly fascinating The Collector and The Magus. Fowles combines bestselling status with intellectual respectability in a way that perhaps no other living author does. The French Lieutenant's Woman *is a highly entertaining read and has a valuable insight into a Dorset (indeed an English) social scene long vanished. The filmmakers brought this up to date with the portrayal of an easily arranged affair between Irons and Streep, contrasted with the long-running tragedy between Sarah Woodruff and Charles Smithson.*

Walk uphill from the car park with the football pitch on your right. At the top of this a stile in the corner of a high hedge leads into a field which you head steeply up, to a gate through a hedge, then due north, straight up the hill to the conifer wood on Timber Hill immediately above you. You reach a track running along the bottom edge of the wood (GR 345932) and turn left along this. As you reach the road turn right, into the wood, and follow the well-used path twisting up through the wood, well supplied with bluebells in the spring. At the top of the wood, turn left by a coast path signpost and follow the path down to the road. Cross over and head down a narrow path between gardens, taking you down to the main road.

Cross over the main road and follow the tarred drive north-west along the bottom of the residential caravan site. You reach the crosstracks at the end, after the tennis court on the right (GR 339937); you are now walking along the Wessex Ridgeway. Keep straight ahead at the crosstracks and walk along the tree-lined drive to Rhode Barton. You find yourself with some old farm buildings by the track on your right and a large house in a spacious garden on the left. Take care here. You bear slightly left by the house and follow the ancient sunken track heading through the conifer wood of Hole Common. You drop steeply down the hill and exit from the wood by a ruined corrugated iron shed. Do not cross the river here but turn right, off the track, along a little used path with the river on your left. As you reach the gate leading back into the wood turn left, across a footbridge, and up the hill with a hedge on your left, to join Harcombe Road (GR 336950).

Turn right when you meet Harcombe Road and walk up the hill for a hundred yards to a drive on the left between two cottages beneath overhanging trees. Turn up this and follow it into the wood; it is an ancient trackway bringing you up to something of a perfect dream cottage hidden in the wood. Happily this path is still used as all paths were originally intended - for access rather than recreation - so keep left as it forks before the cottage to keep the hedged garden on your right and continue up the hill. You exit from the wood to find yourself in a square arable field sloping up to your right towards the top of Whitty's Hill and bounded on two sides of the wood; follow the path along the headland with the wood on your left for a hundred yards to bring you to a gate on your left (Hodder's Corner, GR 332947).

Turn left through the gate to find yourself in a perfect lane heading down the hill with the wood on your left, back to Harcombe Road. Cross over the public road, diagonally to the left and head south-east, down the hill on the drive past the red brick and sandstone pile of Rhode Hill on your right. You reach a farm at the bottom (GR 337942) and turn right off the drive to head south-west, contouring along the hillside towards a trio of oak trees. A second such brings you to within sight of a hunting gate leading into a small wood; go through this to follow the track through the wood to bring you to a drive with a cottage wall on the left. Follow the drive round to the public road (Rhode Lane) by the Edward VII letter box in the hedge on your right and turn left on the road and then immediately left again off it down another drive twisting southwards along the valley between hedges.

At the end of the lane by the cottage you pick the waymarkings for the combined Wessex Ridgeway and Liberty Trail which have joined you from the left. The path takes you across the field to a kissing gate and stile on the far side, leading to a footbridge over the River Lim. Immediately after the footbridge the path joins a track and takes you south-east a third of a mile to reach the public road by a narrow stone arch bridge. You find yourself at the end of two roads; continue down the left-hand one, past the well tended gardens of the council-built houses. Follow this street all the way to its end where it meets Church Street and turn left up the hill to return to your car.

31)   Marshwood Vale and Hardown Hill

Distance: 9 miles
Start: the Five Bells, Whitchurch Canonicorum
Map: sheet 193, GR 399953

This walk is an exploration of the hidden world of Marshwood Vale followed by a superb view of what you have just walked over from a series of excellent viewpoints - the tops of Denhay Hill, Coppet Hill and lastly Hardown Hill. Whitchurch Canonicorum lies a mile north of the main A35 Lyme-Bridport road. Travelling from Lyme, turn left off the A35 just over a mile east of the junction with the A3052 and follow the lane past the crossroads in the centre of the village, up the hill past the church and keep left at the fork; the Five Bells is at the end of the village on the road to Ryall. Travelling from Bridport turn right as you enter Morcombelake just over a mile west of Chideock church. Follow the lane twisting through Ryall along the east side of Hardown Hill and then steeply down the hill into Whitchurch to see the pub on your left. By the time you come to read this these directions may be out of date due to the proposed improvements to the A35 along this stretch. If you do not intend to visit the pub you can find space to park your car just down the hill on a wide patch of gravel at the side of the road. This walk starts and finishes at a pub and passes close to the well known Shave Cross Inn nearly half way round.

Turn left out of the pub and walk down the hill to the sharp left-hand bend. On the right-hand side a wooden signpost next to the farm gate points the
152

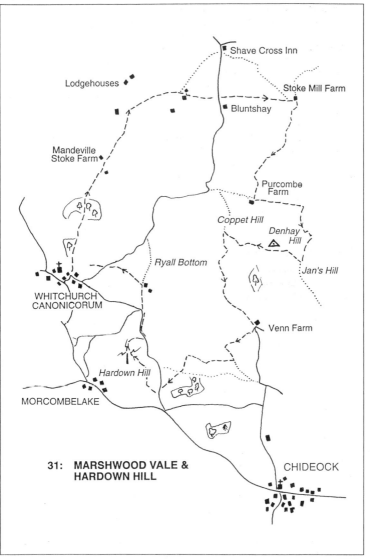

Shave Cross Inn

Lodgehouses

Stoke Mill Farm

Bluntshay

Mandeville
Stoke Farm

Purcombe
Farm

Coppet Hill

Denhay
Hill

Jan's Hill

Ryall Bottom

WHITCHURCH
CANONICORUM

Venn Farm

Hardown Hill

MORCOMBELAKE

CHIDEOCK

**31: MARSHWOOD VALE &
HARDOWN HILL**

way north, "Bridleway to Mandeville Stoke Lane".

The farm of that name is recorded in the Middle Ages as having its names reversed, so that it had the same name as the village and hospital near Aylesbury associated with Sir Jimmy Savile.

Head north down the hill on a lane hidden beneath the trees and wet underfoot. It brings you to a gate and a stile at the bottom leading into the field by the church over to the left.

On the far side of this field you see the deciduous copse ahead; make for the right-hand side of it and follow the edge along, down into a tiny valley; you cross a stream-ditch in a hedge by a footbridge. Keep straight ahead in the next field, heading north towards the distinctive silhouette of Pilsdon Pen on the horizon. The stile leading into the wood (GR 399961) is hidden by a minor kink in its edge. Over the stile you find yourself on a footpath heading north down a ride; on your left is Lower Coppice and on your right Higher Coppice, though they are really one wood. This is largely of oak with coppice hazel; should you walk this in the spring I recommend you pause and listen to the birdsong.

On the far side of the wood you descend to cross a tributary of the River Char and then head north-north-east towards the cottage in the trees at Mandeville Stoke. In the field before the cottage descend to your left to a footbridge over the river; turn right on the far side of the footbridge and cross the small paddock to the farm lane. On the far side go through a gate to find yourself in a large arable field to the north of the farm. In the high hedge in front of you now is a gateway; this does not mark your path. Keep well to the right of this and make for a stile in the hedge a few yards to the left of the river. The path follows the east bank of the river upstream to Middlebrook Farm (GR 404973), south of Lodgehouses Farm. Cross the stream on a footbridge (GR 404973) and turn right; the path keeps close to the river bank, crosses a second tributary and heads east to a former farm now a builder's yard (GR 411975). The path is indistinct here; do not head for the left-hand side of the house as you approach, as the map would indicate, but walk into the complex of old barns below the new house to the right.

Make your way through some piles of junk; turn left and immediately before the new house turn right so that you are walking east, with some old cowstalls on the right and a new barn on the left. A gap in the hedge conceals a stile; walk east from the farm with a hedge on your left. If you would like to divert to the Shave Cross Inn, a well known local landmark and an excellent pub, then you should bear left as you approach the new house to head north and then north-west across three fields to reach the pub. The path heading directly to Buckett's Farm (adjacent to Stoke Mill Farm) is difficult to find so I recommend you head south along the road for half a mile and turn left at the new stile described below (GR 415974). Heading east to Bucket's Farm from the builder's yard you see the somewhat ruinous barn directly ahead (GR

413974). Formerly the footpath continued straight ahead (there is in fact an old footbridge entirely buried in the thick thorn hedge on the line of the path). Bear slightly to the right and go through the gate into the yard by the barn and follow the farm track east from it to the public road.

On the other side of the public road (Bluntshay Lane) is a stile used more, I suspect, by those staying in the caravan just behind the hedge to the left than those walking through. You see a gap in the thick thorn hedge on the far side of the field; make for this and climb the stile and continue due east past the barn on your right (GR 418973). As you head east across the flat fields you keep a hedge to your left until, with Bucket's Farm (immediately north of Stoke Mill Farm) visible in front of you, you are confronted by two gates. There is no indication of which is the right of way; I suggest you pick the left-hand one so that you approach the farm with the thick hedge on your right. The occupants of Bucket's Farm have no idea of the exact alignment of the path either. Cross the yard and turn right on the tarred lane heading south to Stoke Mill Farm.

The path marked on the map heading in a dog-leg route across the fields towards Denhay looks tempting. If you are addicted to such route-finding, the beginning of the path is over a white stile up to the left immediately before the cottage at Stoke Mill; good luck. When I last walked this way there was no waymarking or sign of the route being much used. I hope it does not disappear off the map. However the lane that takes you south-west from Stoke Mill is fascinating. It soon deteriorates into a green lane between hedges and as it goes under the overhead pylon lines (GR 422968) it dives into something of an arboreal tunnel. For the next stretch it doubles as a watercourse beneath the overhanging trees - the woods of Marshwood Vale may nearly all have been felled but the marshy stretches remain and no doubt always will. You exit from the trees, the lane bends to the left and becomes a farm track leading up to Purcombe Farm.

Turn left on the now tarred farm road and follow it just south of due east along the base of Coppet Hill and Denhay Hill, passing the water tank on your left. Half a mile from Purcombe Farm you come to two massive new barns (built summer 1994) on the right. Turn right immediately after them to head up the hill towards the established wood on the hill (Denhay Rookery) with the new plantation on the right. The path takes you into the old wood and up the hill on a track. On the uphill side of the wood you continue up the hill with the dramatic gully with the wood in its base (GR 427977) down to your left. Bear right once out of the wood to go through two gates into a long field, a fence on the left and a thick hedge with ash trees on the right. You are now on an old byway running from Lower Denhay, over Henwood Hill all the way to Quarry Cross. Make your way to the top of the long field, through a gate at the top (Denhay Cross, GR 424955) and turn right to head north-west with a hedge on your right to the far right-hand corner of the next field.

The bridleway across the top of the hill runs just to the south of the summit, so that the grassy hill-top slopes up to your right with the trig point (spot height 157m) out of sight. Heading west you descend steeply across the western face of Coppet Hill, going through a very thick hedge by a double stile and down a steep bank. At the bottom of the next field turn left so that you are heading south across the hillside with a thick hedge on your right. For this stretch your passage is marked with the plastic discs with blue bridleway arrows fixed to the gates. This is an area of rough grazing with tussocks, gorse and bracken - if you are walking this with a dog in hot weather in summer, you might want to check for ticks when you finish.

The final descent, heading south-east to Venn Farm, is along a wet overgrown track beneath trees. You exit from this to continue downhill with a hedge on your right; it is preferable to walk in the field up to your left. As you splash through the bittercress approaching Venn Farm you go through a gate to find yourself back on a reasonable roadway. The bridleway heading south-west from Venn Farm is not waymarked but is easy to follow. Turn right through a farm gate on the far side of the farm building and head up the hill with the River Winniford on your left. The route does not cross the river as it might appear from the map, but joins an unfenced track descending across an arable field from Ryall (GR 416945). This is Butt Lane - but it is not named on the map. Turn left along this track, heading south-east between hedges; a footpath joins you from the left after 200 yards. A few yards after this you see a gap in the hedge on the right and a stile waymarked with the number "33".

From the track turn right over the stile and head just south of due west, across the arable, keeping parallel to the river across to your right. Make for a prominent gate in the fence with thick fenceposts; follow the hedge on your left up the hill; the route taken by the path is more of a dog-leg than the map shows. It runs due west along the side of the Winniford Valley with a hedge on the left with an arable field on the far side, and at the end of this turns left and heads almost due south across a small spur again with a thick hedge on the left. It drops into a small gully with a tiny stream running along the bottom, following a row of trees and a fence; cross at a stile and head south-west, diagonally up the rather steep hillside, through a gate before reaching the public road (GR 408940) where you turn left.

A very few yards along the road you see the drive turning right up to High Bullen. Follow this steeply up the hill, the track becoming rather overgrown (but quite passable) as you pass the entrance to the house. The old track finishes and your route continues as a path, steeply up the hill to the summit. Make your way due north across the top, keeping the transmission mast to your left. You reach a sunken track with a scar running east-west across the summit; this is perhaps the best viewpoint from Hardown Hill, right across Marshwood Vale to the escarpment that bounds it to the north. The obvious summits along this escarpment that create the "bowl" effect of Marshwood Vale are, from left to right, Coney's Castle, Lambert's Castle, Pilsdon Pen and Lewesdon Hill. Due south you have an unusual view of the landward side of Golden Cap.

Bidding farewell to the view from Hardown Hill you turn right on the track and head down the hill to join a steep track that returns you to the road - Ryall Road. Turn left on the road, a cottage hidden behind a hedge on the right. Follow the road steeply down the hill; it turns left where two drives turn off to the right, signed as dead-end roads. Immediately after this turn right, heading exactly due north down the tarred drive to Beerlands Farm. At the bottom some temporary sheep fences lead you into a field and you turn left, opposite the farm, heading north-west down the side of a gully. A stile beneath and overhanging tree in the bottom right corner of the field leads you to a small field; a gate leads you into a field by the road. Do not be tempted to go through the gate leading onto the road, but head diagonally across the field to go through a gap in the high hedge over a stile (GR 402955).

You find yourself opposite the entrance to the drive to "Griddlehays". Turn right off the road, over a stile on the corner of the drive which leads you onto a path heading west, down the hill through a number of gates in high hedges; there is a tiny stream hidden down to your left. You find yourself in the field in front of the church. Turn left at the beginning of this field in the corner to see a rickety gate and a stile on its right. Go over the stile, cross the stream and head up the hidden track (retracing your steps at the start) to the road; the Five Bells pub is just up the hill to your left.

Note on the Shrine of St Wite at Whitchurch Canonicorum Church

Even if poking round rural churches is not your passion you may care to look inside the church here to see the shrine of St Wite. There are plenty of settlements with the name "Whitchurch" in the region - generally this means just that. However here the name refers to its dedication - to St Wite and St Cross. There is no clear indication as to exactly who St Wite was. St Blanche of Brittany has been suggested. It seems more likely that she was an Englishwoman who was killed by the Danes. An Archbishop of Canterbury of the time was murdered by drunken Vikings sportingly hurling ox skulls at his head by way of after-dinner entertainment.

St Wite's shrine is remarkable not only for its antiquity, but for the fact that the saint is English (as a nation I tend to think we excel at things other than saintliness) and the shrine survived not only the Reformation but also the depredations of Cromwell's soldiers and the zeal of nineteenth-century church restorers. The shrine itself is thirteenth century and takes the form of a stone chest with a top made of Purbeck marble. Beneath this are three tunnel-shaped holes, oval in section, into which the arms of the afflicted would be placed. In 1900 the wall behind and the shrine itself developed a large crack (readers of *Moonfleet* will be interested to learn) and the stone coffin had to be moved to repair it. Inside was found a lead casket containing St Wite's bones; they showed that she was a rather small woman who died around the age of forty.

The village itself was mentioned in the will of King Alfred the Great, as *Witan-cercian*; he left the property to his son Ethelward. Had royal ownership continued down the centuries we would no doubt talk of Whitchurch Regis, but in the year 1240 the living was divided between the canons of Salisbury and Wells, in the dioceses of which Dorset lies.

32)   Beaminster, Netherbury and Gerrard's Hill

Distance: 7 miles
Start: from centre of Beaminster
Map: sheet 193, GR 4701

Using as its start point the "sweet Be'mi'ster" of William Barnes, this walk explores the intricate *bocage* landscape around the head of the valley of the River Brit. It is a walk rich in ancient picturesque villages of Hamstone, hidden in folds in the land; it takes you through small copses and hedged-in fields grazed by prize Holsteins and Friesians and finishes with a fine ridge walk over Waddon Hill and Gerrard's Hill, with views into Somerset and Devon and southwards down the Brit Valley towards Bridport. The walk takes you within an easy mile of the Hare and Hounds at Waytown, south of Netherbury; better perhaps to contain your thirst until the New Inn at Stoke Abbott, by which stage the walk is more than half done. Beaminster has shops and pubs galore and a cafe; there are no other shops passed on the way. Beaminster lies 6 miles north of Bridport, along the A3066. This walk may be combined with the walk over Pilsdon Pen and Lewesdon Hill, for a full day of good hill walking.

The picturesque market square of Beaminster now has a disc parking scheme which rightly enough discourages long-term parking and encourages visits to the shops. I suggest you leave the market square along Church Street and park there, or turn left into Mary Well Street and park there. Do not miss the town's main square and shops or indeed pubs. It is a superb small town whose role is still to serve those who visit it from round about in quest of their daily needs rather than those who descend on summer weekends in quest of cream teas, ice lollies and antiques.

Beaminster (newcomers to the area should note that it is pronounced "Bemminster") is first recorded in a charter dating from 862 as Bebingmynster. By the time of Domesday (1086) its name had more or less reached its present form, being spelt Beiminstre. The first element is taken from a woman's name - Bebba - who may well have been the founder of the minster. For much of its life as a settlement, Beaminster acted as the market town for

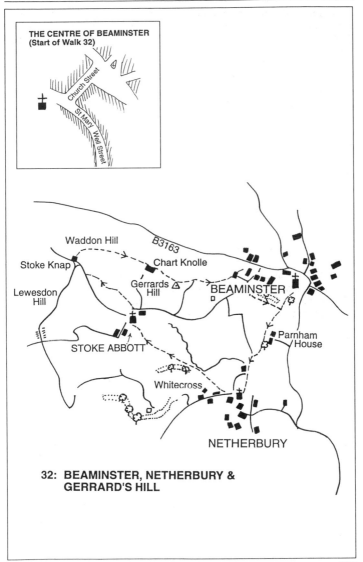

32: BEAMINSTER, NETHERBURY & GERRARD'S HILL

this area of west Dorset, a role now largely taken over by Yeovil, across the county boundary to the north. The medieval wool trade brought early prosperity to the town, reflected in its church. This is very much worth a visit; it was one of the last churches built in the area before the Reformation and, more remarkably, its statuary escaped the iconoclasm of the mid seventeenth century. Local lore has it that supporters of the ill-fated Monmouth's rebellion of 1685 were hanged from the tower. In the latter part of the eighteenth and early nineteenth century the flax industry brought prosperity to the town; the factories remain, as do a number of fine houses from this period. It is certainly one of Dorset's most attractive towns, beautifully situated and with fine buildings clustered around its church - the chief glory of the town. Ringed by hills, the town gives the impression of being in a bowl.

Walk southwards down St Mary Well Street; at its end you see a sign pointing the way to Netherbury. Follow this lane until you come to a gate which leads into a field. Beyond this the lane becomes a drive; follow it as it swings down to the left with a narrow copse on your right. It brings you to a cottage with a stile on its right. Climb this and resist the temptation to follow the bank of the River Brit along the left-hand side of the field. Follow the path diagonally across the field to join a green lane at the end; the path is well trodden. The lane forks at the beginning of a small wood. Bear left at the fork; if you want to visit Parnham House (better to do so at the beginning of a walk when relatively unmuddied) then follow this path down to the footbridge.

Parnham House is open on Fridays, Sundays and bank holidays from April until October. It is a little different from most country houses that can be visited owing to its sad neglect following its use during the Second World War as the headquarters of the American 16th Infantry Division prior to D-Day. It was rescued by John Makepeace following his purchase of it in 1976. Accordingly, instead of glowering family portraits, ancient oaken furniture and old masters, what you find inside is the quite superb modern craftsmanship of the John Makepeace School for Craftsmen in Wood.

From the footpath at the end of the wood, just across the river from the house, follow the footpath through the wood (the right of way is marked on the map as running southwards along the track on the western side of the wood, but the path through the wood is pleasanter and is apparently used as a right of way). The woodland path, beneath yews planted under the ancient beeches, home to a small rookery, gives good views across the gardens and lake at the bottom and runs through some pleasant bluebell beds. At the end of the wood the track improves, being joined by one coming down the hill. As you reach a flat paddock by a small weir on the River Brit you find the track on the ground very slightly at variance with the map. Turn right off the track just before the bridge over the river below the weir and keep left past a large dutch barn by a fine old ruined farm. Just after the dutch barn the track forks;

View of Lewesdon Hill from Pilsdon Pen *(Walk 33)*
Looking across Abbotsbury from Abbotsbury Plains, with the tithe barn behind
the church and Chapel Hill on the right *(Walk 35)*

Cottage in Melbury Osmond *(Walk 36)*
Hooke Court *(Walk 38)*

Steps leading up to Netherbury church

bear left to follow the well used path contouring the side of the valley to Netherbury.

This is one of the most picturesque villages in Dorset. Sadly, however, the "PH" confidently marked on the map closed for good in the autumn of 1984. Within living memory the parish had four pubs, the Hare and Hounds a mile to the south, the Happy Return at Whitecross and the Shepherd's Crook on the way to Beaminster. Now only the Hare and Hounds at Waytown remains. Also gone are the village school, post office and shop - is Netherbury too pretty for its own good?

Turn right at Netherbury church to follow the path beneath the churchyard wall. Turn right at the end to go steeply up the hill and round the sharp left-hand bend. A hundred yards after the bend turn right by the entrance to Tower Hill Cottage (GR 469995) and follow the footpath along the back of the cottage with an arable field on the right. You reach a stile at the end of the field; turn right immediately after this and follow the path past a stable block and along the side of some horse-grazed paddocks. The path now takes you steeply down to the confluence of two tributaries of the River Brit in a wooded dell beneath a line of poplar trees.

The steep descent is across an example of very bad management of horse grazing; when I last walked this way the field had a number of bare patches alternating with weeds and recent heavy rain had caused a good amount of gullying on the steep slope; a few more years of this maltreatment will see all the topsoil here washed away into Lyme Bay.

At the bottom of the hill the path takes you into Lower Woods Coppice and over a railway sleeper for a footbridge. Immediately after this footbridge the path forks; turn right to follow the path through the copse. You leave it at a stile in the corner of a field. Make your way straight ahead, up the hill with a patch of scrub hiding a rabbit warren to your right. A gate leads into a green lane running north-west across the top of the hill.

Immediately after the top of the hill the lane turns sharp left (GR 456003) to become Beech Lane (not marked on the map); there is a turning to the right leading to a hidden sunken lane; turn into it. Unless it is very dry underfoot I recommend you bear right almost immediately, up a bank to a hunting gate to walk down the hill in the field. Cross the field by the sewage farm and climb a stile behind it. Make your way up the steep little hill, keeping the church to your left and turn left past the ivy-covered ruin of a cottage into the farmyard to walk past the village hall to the road.

Turn right on the road to go down the road through Stoke Abbot, past the spring flowing into a fine old stone trough on the left-hand side. Follow the road round the bend to the excellent New Inn with its attractive sign. From the New Inn the path heads north from the opposite side of the road, along an old lane with some well laid hedging on the left. You exit from the lane at a gate beneath a tree. The path runs straight ahead, up a grassy spur between two "bowl" features on the hillside. You reach a stile at the top ~ hill which leads to a short steep path beneath nut-bushes taking you do~ to the sunken public road (GR 446014). Turn right on the road and follow it uphill, past Stoke Knapp Cottage on the right, to Stoke Knapp Farm; turn right through the farmyard, a sign informing you that you are now on the Wessex Ridgeway (see Chapter Two).

At the back of Stoke Knapp Farm is a pair of gates; go through the right-hand one and follow the obvious track angling up the hill. It takes you up to an old quarry-working across to the left and then through a gate so that you are heading east, across the top of Waddon Hill with a fence on your left. As you approach Chart Knolle you are on a clearly defined track with a bank of bluebells and bracken above you to the right. A hundred yards before Chart Knolle, turn left through a steel hunting gate in the fence to make for the drive; walk along this for a few yards and then turn right through a gate way to find yourself in a small paddock with a line of cypress trees on the right. Make your way up to the top corner of this and go through the waymarked gate so that you are heading south-east over the top of Gerrard's Hill with a thick hedge on your left. At the top of the hill is a small stand of wind-blown beech trees with the trig point hidden on their far side. From the top of Gerrard's Hill is the most superb view, not least of Beaminster lying in its bowl in the green landscape. I wonder if it was the view from here that inspired William Barnes to write,

> *Sweet Be'mi'ster that bist abound*
> *By green and woody hills all round,*
> *Wi' hedges reachen up between*
> *A thousan' vields o' zummer green,*
> *Where elems lofty heads do show*
> *Their sheades vor hay-makers below,*
> *An wild hedge-flow'rs do charm the souls*
> *O' maidens in their evenin' strolls.*

You can trace much of the walk you have done from the top of Gerrard's Hill, along the hidden valley of the River Brit and through the villages of Netherbury and Stoke Abbott. Keep the beech hanger on your right and follow the path steeply down the hill, across the end of the hedged-in lane (GR 463012) and on down the grassy hill. The path goes up the gentle hillside in front of you, towards Higher Barrowfield Farm (GR 470013). It is well marked through the grass to the farm; bringing you to a steel stile. This is the point where you leave the Wessex Ridgeway.

Head down the drive from Higher Barrowfield Farm and turn right on the road at the end to turn immediately left, up a well trodden path along a slightly sunken lane. At the end of the hedged-in track bear left to find yourself in a

...mall wood crowning a steep little hill on the left. The path
...f this with a hedge on the right; go through the gate at the
...k tree and you find yourself looking at the cottage in the
...at you passed as you started the walk. Do not walk down
..., making for a gateway commemorating two flying officers
...killed in the First and Second World Wars. The path from
this gate is well trodden across the field to the gate leading into St Mary Well
Street in Beaminster and so back to your car.

33)   Pilsdon Pen and Lewesdon Hill

Distance: 7 miles
Start: Broadwindsor
Map: sheet 193, GR 437026

In a county crammed with wonderful walks, this is without question one of the
finest. It takes you over perhaps the best viewpoint in the county - its highest
summit - and through fine woods, hidden lanes and streams and past some
very fine vernacular architecture. There is a pub and very good post office
stores in Broadwindsor; thereafter the walk passes neither pub nor shop.
Broadwindsor is 7 miles north of Bridport along the B3162 which eventually
winds its way all the way to Chard in Somerset.

From the centre of Broadwindsor head down the hill, following the signpost
in the centre of the village, indicating the B3164 to Lyme Regis. At the bottom
of the hill you see a modern pine workshop in the old chapel. Immediately
after this turn left by the old Toll House, following a wooden footpath sign to
Lewesdon Hill (properly pronounced "Lew'sdon Hill"). A gate leads you into
the end of a field of pasture; make your way due south, straight up the middle
of it, to find yourself walking up a broad spur, through a gateway in a hedge
and then a second field, past a lone ash and holly tree in the middle of the
field. In the second field the transmitting masts at Rampisham come into
view. As you near the beech woods on the northern side of Lewesdon Hill you
find yourself walking beside the remnant of a very ancient hedgerow - now
mature beech trees showing signs of early hedgelaying and holly trees at
their base.

At the beginning of the woods you meet an ancient track running along
their edge; turn right along this by the National Trust sign (GR 436015). On
your left is an ancient embanked hedge, now a row of beech trees; in the
spring the woods here are full of bluebells. Follow this track for 500 yards
beneath the ancient beeches until, by a metal farm gate on your right, you
see a footpath turning left, through a gap in the earth bank beneath the trees.
You turn almost back on yourself so that you are heading up the eastern spur
of Lewesdon. There are a number of paths here; the one you want is well

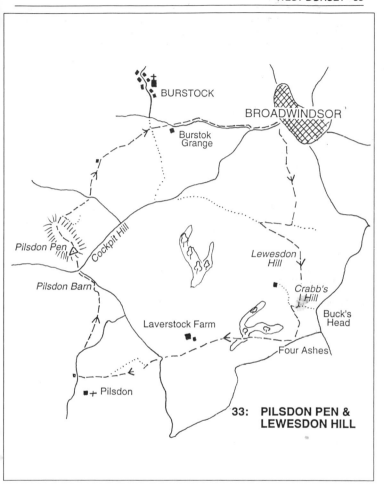

BURSTOCK

BROADWINDSOR

Burstok
Grange

Pilsdon Pen

Cockpit Hill

Pilsdon Barn

Lewesdon
Hill

Crabb's
Hill

Buck's
Head

Laverstock Farm

Four Ashes

Pilsdon

**33: PILSDON PEN &
LEWESDON HILL**

worn and takes you up the spur. You climb steeply across a patch of bracken
to meet a second National Trust sign. Just to the right of this is a small spur
giving a superb view. Follow the path south-east across the wooded summit
of Lewesdon; the drop through the trees to the right is dramatic.

At the end of the summit of Lewesdon the path swings to the right and descends very steeply through the trees and follows a line of old beech trees southwards; this is Crabb's Hill. At the bottom of the hill you meet a concrete farm road where you turn right for 100 yards before turning left through a gateway. The bridleway is not well shown on the ground here; make your way south-east, following a line of electricity poles to the gateway at the far end of the field. At this gate bear right to head diagonally across the next field to the gate you see in front of you leading onto the public road. Turn right here and walk a few steps along the road before turning right off it into a large arable field.

For the next 2 miles there are very few waymarks and little indication of the way on the ground. However the rights of way do exist. Head west from the road, over the brow of the hill to a gate as you descend. Notice the yellow arrow waymarks on a fence by the corner of the wood in front of you (GR 433003). Follow the side of the wood for a further hundred yards after the corner and look for a stile on your right, hidden in a small dip below the level of the field. Cross this to make your way down a bank beneath a felled patch of wood, the ground now supporting a luxuriant growth of dog's mercury, nettles and bracken. At the bottom of the bank, find more waymarks nailed to the trunks of trees among the wet woodland floor and cross the stream at the plank footbridge.

Leave the strip of wood along the stream bank at a stile and head west, up a slope to meet a thick hedge on your right. Follow this along on your right for 400 yards before turning left, to head south to meet the drive to Laverstock Farm at the stone gateway. Turn right along the drive for a few paces and turn left as it swings to the right. Make your way across the paddock, heading for a lone birch tree just before the stream. Cross the stream and find yourself heading up a green lane to the road. Cross over the public road (GR 423000) and go through a gate on the far side, following a hedge on your left across an arable field. The map marks the path going through the triangular copse on the far side (GR 421999), but there is no sign of this on the ground. Bear right as you near the copse and descend to a gate at a culvert over the stream between the two copses. Go through this gate and make your way up the hill with the hedge on your right. At the top of the hill go through the gate so that you are continuing to head west now with the hedge on your left.

Pilsdon Manor comes into view, with its small chapel. The path keeps slightly further to the right of it than the map shows; leave the wooden sheds well to your left and make for a gateway leading into a small paddock before the road. You meet the road at an old red brick milking parlour with a wooden building to its left (GR 414998). Turn right onto the narrow hedged-in road and walk up to where it bends to the right with a small copse on the left (not shown on the map). On the far side of this copse is a modern barn on the left (GR 415001). Turn left off the road here and make your way up the hill to the gate in the hedge in front of you. On the far side of the first gate after the road you find yourself in an arable field; make straight across it to the prominent gate in the hedge on the far side and bear left to head up the hill towards the almost entirely glass fronted house attached to Pilsdon Barn; the view of Marshwood Vale and beyond begins to unfold. As you approach Pilsdon Barn turn left through the hedge and follow the old banked hedge round on your right through the new trees. On the far side turn right and cross the grass to join the road. Ignore the waymarked post on the opposite side of the road and turn left to head north-west up the road to the road junction at Lob Gate; it looks as though someone has stolen the ring from the top of the signpost with the name and grid reference (GR 414009).

Turn left on the road here with the car park on the left and then cross the stile by the National Trust information board and climb the gorse-covered escarpment of Pilsdon Pen by the made path. This brings you to the flat, grassy platform of the iron age hill fort on the summit.

The turf within the ramparts of Pilsdon Pen hill fort is of a particularly fine quality, testament to good soil and repeated sheep grazing. This fine turf came to the notice of one William Lord who laid out the first cricket ground bearing his name in London. The ground later moved to its present location in St John's Wood, by Regents Park. The turf was moved each time; there is something poetic in that the most famous and hallowed turf in the land should have come from such a beautiful spot.

It need not necessarily follow that the highest point in the county is also the best viewpoint - but Pilsdon Pen is. It presents a dramatic escarpment towards the south and so from the trig point the most striking view lies across Marshwood Vale and - further left - the lower part of the valley of the River Brit and Bridport. Almost directly due south rises Golden Cap with Chardown Hill, Hardown Hill and Stonebarrow Hill to the right of it. The prominent conical hill with Scots pine around its summit and on the far side, rising to the east of Marshwood Vale, is Coney's Castle (bearing 228 degrees, GR 372975).

A mile and a half to the west is Birdsmoor gate, where one Martha Brown murdered her husband in 1856. She was hanged in August of that year at Dorchester - the last public execution there. The event was witnessed by the sixteen year old Thomas Hardy - he had made a point of going there. As an old man he wrote that he was "ashamed" of what he had done by watching the hanging. If one central event can be said to have inspired Tess it was this.

The dip slope of Pilsdon Pen runs north, presenting a much gentler gradient down towards the valley of the River Axe and beyond, with views deep into Somerset. To the east is the summit of Lewesdon Hill, mantled in beech trees. Very nearly all of your route from Lewesdon to Pilsdon Pen can be followed - more easily if you have binoculars. The season and the weather will probably be what dictate the amount of time you spend here enjoying the view of most of west Dorset laid out before you.

The name "Cow and Calf" was given to these two hills by sailors who used them as a landmark when afloat on Lyme Bay. The old Dorset expression "as much alike as Pilsdon Pen and Lew'sdon Hill" is an expression of dissimilarity, rather like using the saying referring to "chalk and cheese". The expression is, of course, lost on those who do not know the hills, so close in distance and height but so utterly contrasting in shape and character. There is an unexpected literary connection here, with a poet more usually associated with the Lake District. William Wordsworth stayed for two years at Racedown Lodge on the north-west slope; he wrote The Borderers *there. Coleridge visited him there in 1797 and their friendship grew from that point on. Dorothy was particularly enchanted with the scenery here.*

Make your way north over the springy turf of the top of the hill fort to the prominent bank of gorse on the rampart at the northern end. Go through the gap in the rampart just beside it and walk down by the line of the old hedge with the fence on your left enclosing an arable field. At the end of the fence you find yourself at the top of a very steep grassy slope; there is a minor footpath diversion here; turn right to contour along the top of the slope for a few yards and at the end of the electric fence on your left turn left, down the slope (these last few steps may have been a temporary diversion when I last walked the route). You are now following the green Wessex Ridgeway signs; make for the stile at the bottom of the hill and follow the recently made farm track down to the public road, which you cross to follow the drive down the hill to Lower Newnham Farm. Bear right at the farm to follow the track around the right-hand side of the field behind the farm, rather than make your way straight across it. At the bottom of the hill you cross a tiny brook and make your way uphill, diagonally across the field in front of you, to the gate at the top, continuing north-west across the top of the hill to meet Sheepwash Lane, a green hedged-in farm lane (GR 422025).

At Sheepwash Lane the Wessex Ridgeway signs point the way south, over Lewesdon Hill (if you have the time and energy you could return to Broadwindsor this way). Cross over the lane here and make your way across the field to Burstock Grange Farm, where you join the public road (Grange Lane) and follow it west, on to the B3164 and so back to Broadwindsor.

34)   The Bride Valley and the Downs

Distance: 8 miles
Start: Little Bredy
Map: sheet 194, GR 590890

This walk is an exploration of the villages in and the downlands around the Bride Valley. It goes through two delightful villages and the third of the Bride Valley trio (Long Bredy, Little Bredy and Litton Cheney) can be enjoyed by starting at the Youth Hostel or the White Horse pub at Litton Cheney, for which directions are given below. Apart from this the walk passes no pub or shop, although there is perfect small village stores in Litton Cheney.

To find the start turn south off the A35 a mile west of Winterbourne Abbas, west of Dorchester. Follow this road south-west down the hill, steeply into Little Bredy and park just uphill from the telephone box on the opposite side of the road.

 With your back to the church you see the road fork by the telephone box; take the right-hand fork and follow the road out of the village, heading south-east. Trees on the right overhang the road; a drive turns off at the end of these. This is the entrance to Bridehead House (not open to the public) and

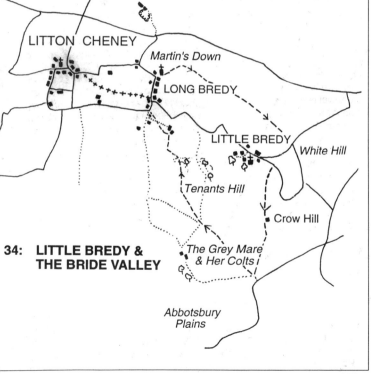

34: LITTLE BREDY & THE BRIDE VALLEY

the lake which is accepted as the source of the River Bride, although it is fed by a number of chalk streams. Immediately after the drive you see a gate on the right leading to a track running along the side of the cricket ground with the pavilion by the road on your right.

Now when I last walked this way this was as far as I got for an hour as I sat on the grass and enjoyed a keenly contested village cricket match, played in the most sublime of surroundings. The ground gives the effect of being in a bowl, which extends to the ground itself; in whatever direction the ball is hit, it has to negotiate a considerable slope to roll up to the boundary, enhancing the braking effect of the lush grass of the outfield. It all helps walkers-turned spectators who have a good view of the ground wherever they sit, which is more than can be said for Lord's, with its seats on the south side facing up the famous slope. Wait for the change of overs before walking down the track behind the bowler's arm.

Follow the track south from the ground, through a gate and up the hill beneath a stand of trees, where you keep left at a fork. It heads due south as a pronounced old grassy track running up the chalk spur (a good view behind you to Bridehead House and the lake) to reach the trees at the back of the farm on Crow Hill (GR 590879). Bear right as you approach the copse and follow the grassy track around its edge past the farm (becoming derelict when last I saw it). You now join a well used farm track heading just west of due south over the top of the downs with a hedge on your left. It takes you past the steel barn on your right (GR 589871). Five hundred yards further on the track turns sharply to the left and a metal walkers' signpost points the way to "Kingston Russell Stone Circle" (GR 588867). Follow the bridleway north-west with a hedge on your left for a third of a mile to bring you to a stile marking the junction with the path heading west, down the gully to Gorwell Farm (bed and breakfast - see accommodation guide). This leads you on an out-and-back route to the long barrow known as the Grey Mare and her Colts.

Return to the path and continue heading north-west, your route signed to the stone circle, identified by the English Heritage sign.

Sadly none of the stones is now standing, although it is recorded that one remained upright in 1815, the year of Waterloo. It is generally held that it was built around 1500BC. The fact of it now being an English Heritage reserve has helped preserve the flowers growing in the grass here.

There is a superb view from here, westwards to the coast and along it to Golden Cap. From here your path lies north-west; a chalk dry gully opens up below you to your right (GR 575882). You find yourself walking on the boundary of grassland below you to your right, and arable uphill to the left. Continue north-east, down the hill until you meet the end of an old hedge with a gate just beyond (GR 575886). The path lies due north, straight down the hill through three gates to the east-west strip of wood lying east of Lower Kingston Russell. Go into the wood (GR 575889) by a hunting gate; it is a fine little wood, principally of oak and ash, and your path northwards through it lies between old banks set far apart on either side.

You leave the wood by a hunting gate in a wet patch and see a small recently-created lake in front of you. A tiny stream runs down to it which you can either cross by the farm gate or by a gravel patch as it enters the lake. Continue north-west to meet the lane at a farm gate and turn right. You head north down the lane, with a narrow copse on the left and continue straight on into the drive to Watergate where the road turns sharp left by some cottages (GR 572894). Down the drive you come to a neat ford over the infant clear-running River Bride and turn left through a gate before the house, past the swimming pool on your left. Ahead is a stile beneath a high hedge as you continue north-west across the flat fields of the valley floor. You climb a gate to find yourself in what the map shows as parkland and continue through the grass to cross the drive diagonally.

Pause on the drive to look at Kingston Russell House. It was here that Admiral Thomas Masterton Hardy was born in 1769, he who is now remembered in history only as Lord Nelson's companion at his death. His monument stands on Black Down Hill (see Walk 39). Viewed from the road on the north side the house looks as though it is more frontage than house itself - it was lengthened in 1913. Certainly it is at its most impressive when viewed looking down the drive. It is not open to the public.

On the far side of the drive you see an old grey lodge to the right of some new brick houses. Go over a stile beside the lodge to find yourself in a small paddock used as a children's playground. On the far side a stile leads you onto a tarred path between some new houses, built in 1992 by the Raglan Housing Association. Turn right on the road with its stream running by the side and walk north through the village. A hundred yards after the turning on the right (signed to Long Bredy and Dorchester) you see a track turning off on the right as the road goes round a left-hand bend. Turn right here to go past a tiny old barn on the left and the track ends by something of a perfect thatched cottage with unusual hand-made wooden gutters. The path continues across two tiny paddocks to some black-painted corrugated iron sheds and you turn left down the stony lane to reach the road leading up to the church.

Your path turns off after 70 yards to the right, along what the map marks as a black pecked line. This is in fact a county road and is a right of way. However it would be a shame to miss St Peter's church in a perfect situation by two old cottages and the old school (notice the stone plaque high on the wall) at the foot of the chalk slope. A wooden footpath sign points the way due north to Long Bredy Hut; it looks enticing and offers an extension to this walk, through the wealth of tumuli north of Martin's Down. Long Bredy Hut was many years ago a pub, just north of the Dorchester-Bridport road (now the A35), mentioned by Hardy. Go up the sunken rutted lane heading north-east up the hill from the lane leading to the church. It brings you to the end of a well used farm lane (GR 574907); turn right along it with a row of wind-sculptured trees on your right. After 200 yards it turns left by a walkers' signpost to go down to Kingston Russell. Turn right at the bend and follow the fence into a gully, past a large silage pit on the right. The bridleway leads you up the slope to a prominent tumulus by a thorn tree on the right where you go through two gates (notice the signs on the reverse of the rails by the gates). To your right a track descends the gully to the west of Whatcombe Down. Through the gates bear slightly left, so that you are heading south-east along the fine ridge between Whatcombe Down and Black Down.

The fact of this ridge having been used as a defensive feature is shown by the number of Cross Dykes. You go through two fences following an old hedge and then a stone wall on the right. This ends at a gate at the top of the steep bowl above Pitcombe Farm.

You are looking across a very broad saddle with views ahead to two tumuli made more obvious in summer because the silage cutters leave them uncut - if only all farmers were as caring of their archaeological heritage. East of Bronkham Hill I have seen a number of tumuli rapidly disappearing under the repeated passage of the plough.

Go diagonally across this field to the left to a prominent gate (GR 589899) which marks the beginning of the track leading you south-east to the road junction on White Hill (GR 595892). Turn right on the road and walk back down to your car.

Directions from Litton Cheney Youth Hostel and the White Horse pub

Starting from the youth hostel or the White Horse pub in Litton Cheney extends this walk by around a mile and a half. Turn right out of the hostel, past the White Horse pub, and walk up the lane into the village with the clear chalk stream on your right. Bear right at the end and follow the Long Bredy road out of the village, past the village shop on your right. You reach a long barn on the left, almost the last building in the village - if you get as far as the fine Georgian farm with the wisteria you have gone too far. Turn right through a waymarked gate; a well used footpath runs away, due south towards the river. A less well used one bears off to the left, almost parallel to the road you have just left. Look for a prominent gap in the hedge marking a stile beneath; make for this and look ahead as you climb over, across the flat fields to see your path marked by several more of these, taking you across the hedged fields all the way to meet the road at Long Bredy (GR 568901). Turn right on the road and then immediately left up the stony track between hedges. Now follow the directions above from Long Bredy, over the downs to Little Bredy and then start reading the directions at the start when you reach there and once you are back at Long Bredy retrace your steps to the hostel. An alternative return route might be to take the bridleway north-west along the ridge from Kingston Russell stone circle on Tenant's Hill and follow the footpaths to bring you to the road junction east of the hostel (GR 555899).

35)   Abbotsbury and Puncknowle

Distance: 10 miles
Start: Abbotsbury Castle car park
Map: sheet 194, GR 556865

This walk explores some of the best areas of the hinterland of Chesil Beach; it takes you along the top of a dramatic escarpment with views right down Chesil Beach and to Portland Bill and right out across Lyme Bay. This walk takes you through one of the most attractive villages in the county (no less attractive for having a picturesque old pub) and includes the best of both inland and seashore sections of the Dorset Coast Path. The village, tithe barn and swannery of Abbotsbury need no introduction. To find the start, drive out of Abbotsbury on the B3157 steeply up the hill in the direction of Bridport. A mile out of Abbotsbury, shortly after the viewpoint laybys on the left of the road, you see a signpost pointing to the right, to "Ashley Chase only". Turn right here and park your car in the small car park on the left at the top of the hill. This walk can also be enjoyed using the youth hostel at Litton Cheney as your base, adding a total of 2 miles to the distance. Since this is located next to a pub (the White Horse) you may care to use this as your start point, be you a dedicated hosteller or dedicated quaffer. Turn to the directions at the end of the walk for this. In fact the walk itself is well supplied with pubs, passing the Crown in Puncknowle and a number of pubs in Abbotsbury.

A footpath from the south side of the car park takes you up onto the heather-covered ramparts of Abbotsbury Castle and past the trig point. Suddenly, with almost no effort involved in getting there, you have a superb view, inland across the Bride Valley and out to sea. Looking north, notice how the villages of the Bride Valley are carefully sited, south facing, off the valley floor but at the bottom of the chalk escarpment.

The furthest west of the three villages, Litton Cheney has a remarkable set of medieval strip lynchets which are well worth studying, particularly if you have a pair of binoculars. The level terraces remain grass covered but there are strips of scrub between - it is a medieval landscape almost unchanged.

Immediately to the north are ramparts around the summit of a hill (GR 556871) almost as impressive as those of Abbotsbury Castle itself. Happily this is not one of those viewpoints where you leave to descend and lose the view. Make your way west along the escarpment with the road below you to your left. You cross the protective earthworks at the western edge of the Iron Age hill fort and continue along the hill-top across a field of grazing.

Half a mile west of the trig point the path meets the road at a National Trust sign and crosses with the help of two stiles; you are now on Tulk's Hill. After 500 yards of walking on the south side of the road you see a footpath signpost on the road pointing north-west and stiles either side of the road; cross back over the road here and head north-west, keeping the wood well to your right; you cross two stiles before you find yourself in a large arable field between the two woods - Green Leaze. Continue north-west, descending diagonally across the slope to the middle of the wood facing you and then turn right, to head north along its eastern edge. You come to a farm track with a footpath sign (GR 544876) pointing the way north to "YHA Litton Cheney" and west to "The Knoll". Continue northwards down the side of the wood on a headland left on the edge of the plough. A thick hedge of thorn runs diagonally away from the corner of the wood; keep this on your left to bring you to a stile and a gate to find yourself looking into a wooded gully. Bear left, down the valley side to a grey concrete pumphouse in the field and make your way to the farm gate at the bottom corner of the field where you cross the stream beneath the trees (GR 545882).

On the far side of the stream turn left to head due west, up the hill, over a gate and then contouring across the hillside with Puncknowle in front of you and Shipton Hill (GR 5092) directly behind it. You turn right, down the hill on a bridleway for a few yards and then left, off it at a stile to make your way across an arable field and over another stile into a small paddock behind some new houses. It looks as though the back boundary of the gardens has been dictated by the right of way, so that the house nearest the village has a back garden a fraction the area of the one furthest away. I wonder why the right of way was not diverted round the back. The path takes you, hidden, through some trees and then into a road through a small housing development. Keep straight ahead through the centre of the village to the Crown, a fine old thatched pub.

Turning right out of the pub, continue past the turning on the right to Litton Cheney with an attractive old farmhouse facing you on the right-hand side of the road. Immediately after this turn left up a muddy lane beneath trees in which there is a rookery; the sound of rooks in the trees is one I shall always associate with childhood visits to Puncknowle. A sign points up the lane with a long list of exotic delights that can be found by following its directions. Bear left in the trees at the top of the lane to follow a very wet grassy track out into a narrow paddock leading uphill. You are looking more or less due south at Puncknowle Knoll. At the top of the paddock turn left at the signpost on the farm lane taking you south-east to Clay Lane; turn right on the public road. Four hundred yards later, over the brow of the hill a footpath crosses the road; a short diversion to the right brings you to the top of Puncknowle Knoll.

The village takes its name from the knoll, or stubby hill; it is first recorded in Domesday. The first element of the name may refer to a plum tree.

The right of way that follows the track to the top of the knoll (you have to return the same way) brings you to the revenue hut, built as a deterrent to smuggling liquor landed on Chesil Beach. Later its fine view across the

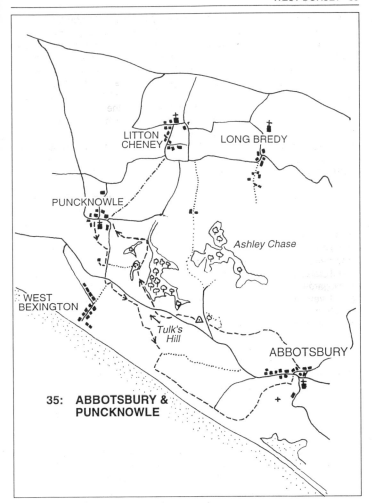

LITTON
CHENEY

LONG BREDY

PUNCKNOWLE

Ashley Chase

WEST
BEXINGTON

Tulk's
Hill

ABBOTSBURY

**35: ABBOTSBURY &
PUNCKNOWLE**

eastern part of Lyme Bay was used in order to spot the shoals of mackerel.
It is well worth the detour just to enjoy the view.

Continue south to cross the B3157 and head down the well surfaced old
track through the gorse down towards West Bexington. A few yards down the

track turn left at a Coast Path signpost to head back up the hill to the main road (yes, it really is preferable to taking the short cut straight along the road). The footpath now crosses into the National Trust property of Limekiln Hill. The path is not well defined across this as, in common with other such National Trust properties, there is free access across it and so walkers are not confined to walking a single route. The limekiln itself can be found at the head of the escarpment. Follow the edge of the grazing area along with the gorse on your right; you see a recently built stone wall ahead of you; keep right here and look for a marker post leading you to a stile. Keep following the edge of the gorse and thorn scrub on your right along the edge of the hill; this starts to lead you down the hill to the right and you come to a three-way signpost (GR 545867).

Above you and slightly east is another signpost on top of the hill; however the one you want points south-east, down the hill to "East Bexington and Beach 1". Follow the track down the hill among the gorse and thorn scrub to the old barn (GR 546865). Take the path with the thorn and gorse scrub on the left and a field to the right. Below you is a white painted house surrounded by conifers; from here the path sets off diagonally across two fields to East Bexington Farm. Keep the farm buildings to your right and follow the path straight down the hill to the gravel track following the inland side of the gravel embankment of Chesil Beach.

A mile of walking along the coast path, latterly on a road, brings you to the car park at Abbotsbury Beach. Continue on the coast path south-east from the car park; it begins to bend to the left, inland, and you notice to the right the beginnings of West Fleet, starting as a small reedbed. The track is barred with wooden posts and a stile and you follow it as it heads towards Chapel Hill. This offers easy, level walking, taking you around the side of Chapel Hill. You reach a track junction (GR 570851) shortly before some new farm buildings; avoid these by turning right, through the gate and up the hill along a stony track towards the village of Abbotsbury. The turning to the left to the main road through the village (GR 574852) is not quite what you might expect from the map; you actually have to turn right to continue east along Chapel Lane, bringing you to the high street by Chapel Lane Stores.

Look across Abbotsbury High Street and you will see the old school buildings which now house a gift shop and cafe, predictably enough. Setting off up the hill from here is Back Lane, the road that takes you up past the Limekiln picnic site (GR 589859) to White Hill; you pass the chapel marked on the map, now a studio. Fifty yards after the chapel you turn left, just before Spring Cottage, opposite the entrance to a residents' only car park. This track takes you past a house called Copplestone on the left and immediately afterwards turns left, an old track heading up the hill. It finishes at a gate and takes you past a spring feeding into a cattle trough; the bridleway is clearly marked heading up the hill to a gate, then towards a crude wooden dutch

View west across the north of Lyme Bay from Puncknowle Knoll

barn with an asbestos roof (GR 574860). You go through a gate into the hill-top field which is a nature reserve and follow the grassy lane to the top of Wears Hill where you continue west, along the ridge with much the same view as you had when you started the walk, continuing all the way back to the car park.

Starting from Litton Cheney Youth Hostel

Litton Cheney Youth Hostel lies half a mile south of the church on the road to Puncknowle, at the turning left to Kingston Russell house by the White Horse pub. From the footbridge across the stream by the verandah in front of the hostel look across the road to see the path following the bright chalk stream to the left of the cottage. Go down this and climb a stile to find yourself in a flat field of pasture in the bottom of the Bride Valley. Follow the stream on your right for 50 yards and then turn right to cross over it at a footbridge and stile. Look ahead, south-west, towards the village of Puncknowle on the slope of the far side of the valley; the path takes you through a gate and crosses the River Bride at a waymarked footbridge and stile among the trees and continues up the hill to Puncknowle, joining the road from Looke Farm; continue up the road for a few yards to the junction in the village and turn right. From here follow the directions through Puncknowle above. When you reach the end of the directions above, turn back to the beginning and follow them to the signpost at the edge of the wood on Green Leaze. Follow the path indicated down the hill from here and along the valley to Looke Farm, then due north across the flat fields of the valley bottom to the youth hostel.

36) Evershot and the Melburys

Distance: 7 or 10 miles
Start: Evershot
Map: sheet 194, GR 575046

This walk takes you past one of the finest houses in the county, Melbury House. There is the tiniest of detours to see Lewcombe Manor, enchantingly hidden away, tucked in the valley in the trees. This walk is tailor-made, too, for those who like to discover ancient rustic churches, hidden away from any through road. It takes you past four: Melbury Sampford, Melbury Bubb, the exquisite St Edwold's at Stockwood and Lewcombe Manor, as well as the parish church of Melbury Osmond, where Thomas Hardy's mother was baptised and married. Nowadays the church houses a fine collection of kneelers stitched in the 1970s. If I were forced on pain of something terrible to name my favourite village in the county, I think it would be difficult not to name Evershot. It has a good pub, the Acorn, and the one remaining shop, the post office stores, is big, well stocked and friendly. The superb architecture to be found in the village is more reminiscent of some perfect small town than a rustic village. Strangely, it is not named in Domesday; the name is thought to have originated from the Anglo-Saxon *eafor*, meaning wild boar.

"Great Hintock" in Hardy's *The Woodlanders* had its initial prototype as Melbury Osmond; later he introduced other aspects to the fictitious village to link it to Minterne Magna. The village has certainly had a profound influence on Hardy for his mother (born as Jemima Hand) was a pauper child brought up in a family of seven, children of a widow. What made the situation bizarre was that Jemima's own father was a wealthy farmer who disowned his descendants; Jemima and her family all lived on the parish dole, ignored by their wealthy grandfather, a fellow dweller in Melbury Osmond. A number of Hardy's short stories use incidents in and around Melbury Park (*The First Countes of Wessex, The Life, The Duke's Reappearance*). Evershot is, famously, the "Evershead" of *Tess*; the Acorn Inn appears as "the Sow and Acorn". In terms of its buildings, little has changed in Evershot since Hardy's day.

This walk may be taken from Chetnole halt as a day walk, arriving and departing by train. Reaching the road at the top of the stairs turn left to walk into Chetnole. Turn right at the T-junction as you arrive at the village, to walk south-west, initially along a grassy track, then along a footpath across the fields to a bridge over the railway line to bring you to Melbury Bubb. Now pick up the directions from Melbury Bubb below.

The true start point for this ramble is the village of Evershot; walk down to the bottom of the village and turn left into Melbury Park. The road forks; keep left, up the hill on the tarred lane to enter the park by a lodge on the left. A few

Looking up Evershot High Street to the Acorn Inn

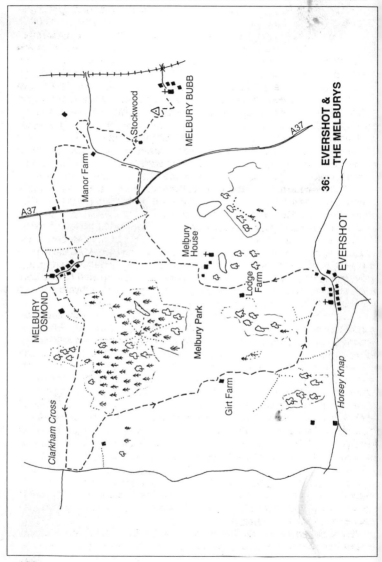

Stockwood

MELBURY BUBB

A37

36: EVERSHOT &
THE MELBURYS

A37

Manor Farm

EVERSHOT

Melbury
House

EVERSHOT

Lodge
Farm

MELBURY
OSMOND

Melbury Park

Horsey Knap

Clarkham Cross

Girt Farm

hundred yards later you enter the deer park proper and keep right at the turning to Lodge Farm on the left.

The park has a herd of red, fallow and some sika deer, but they are most frequently to be found in "wilder" stretches of the park, over to the left on the hillside as you approach the house. Dorset has been spared the grandiose piles of ostentatious stately homes; no Chatsworth, Holkham, Blenheim, Castle Howard et al to be found here. What the county specialises in are more modest manors and country houses, the perfect embellishment to the landscape - this is a good example. The proximity of the great house to the village was, of course, a key to the action of Hardy's The Woodlanders. *Despite the proximity of Melbury Park to Melbury Osmond, Hardy makes it plain by his description of Mrs Charmond's residence that Melbury House was not hers. It is generally held that Turnworth House (many miles away, near Okeford Fitzpaine) is the model for the "Great House" at "Hintock".*

Follow the tarred drive round the back of Melbury House and follow it due north; 400 yards later you come to a fork, helpfully signed to the A37 to the right, to Melbury Osmond straight on. Here you have to decide whether or not you want to extend your walk by 3 miles, as far as Melbury Bubb and the Welcome Inn pub on the main road (GR 582078). If not, continue north, down the hill with a fine view of the thatched cottages of Melbury Osmond in front of you. You pass through Clammers Gate to exit from the park; the first group of cottages around the sharp left-hand bend in the road is called Town's End. At the top of the lane through the village go through the churchyard and turn left on the lane on the far side. (Now continue at * below.)

To walk to Melbury Bubb bear right at the fork and follow the drive downhill towards the stream marking the edge of the deer park. Follow the drive up the hill to the lodge and the junction with the busy main A37 Yeovil-Dorchester road. Cross the road and follow the road to Stockwood and Chetnole for half a mile until you reach the sign for Church Farm. Turn right down the drive to the farm and Stockwood church and turn left at the bottom, through a gate across the field, leading to a rather ornamental bridge to the church. (The path to Melbury Bubb is an out-and-back excursion to visit Melbury Bubb church, with superb views en route across to the downs - if you don't think this is for you, bear left and follow the path downhill by the stream on your right.) Keep the brick bridge to the church to your right and cross the stream on the next bridge and make your way across the field to the wood. (Formerly the path went up the hill to the right, past the water board pumphouse.) Follow the path up through the wood and up the hill to the trig point on the spur. From the old trig point the path heads south and twists down the grassy slope to the church. The interior of the church is well worth visiting, not least for its font.

The decoration around the outside of the font is of typically Anglo-Saxon entwined beasts - but in this case upside down. It is generally held that what is now the font was originally a pillar capital or the base of a sculptured cross which was reworked as a font by Norman craftsmen. The fact that the stone was inverted for its reuse may indicate that the Norman stonemasons felt that its previous use was heathen.

From the church retrace your steps to Stockwood Church and turn right over the stream down the western side of the wood and down through the farm at Stockwood Mill. At the bottom of the short farm lane you reach the public road (GR 592075); turn right along it for rather less than 100 yards to a second farm lane where you turn left to Bragg's Farm. Head north down the farm drive with a new plantation on the left for 200 yards before turning left, across a stile. Bear left, up the hill towards the fine thatch of Manor Farm on the ridge immediately in front of you. As you reach the farm you find yourself on a track leading down the hill to the north with a hedge on its left.

Turn right, down the track (the footpath that is marked on the map as going from Manor Farm to the Welcome Inn round the left-hand end of the copse seems to be no longer used and, besides, is less attractive). Five hundred yards down the track (GR 589079) it turns sharp right; turn left here, crossing two poles laid athwart the entrance to a shady drove-road. Suddenly you are walking beneath trees on an old hedged-in trackway with grass now overlying the damp ground. The copse to the left is full of bluebells in spring and I have heard the nightingale singing from the scrub here in May. At the end of the copse the track, now faint, takes you straight up the hill with a hedge on your left to bring you to the main Dorchester-Yeovil A37 at the Welcome Inn (GR 582079).

Cross over the road here, bearing left, up towards the second-hand car dealer's. The path takes you west, down the hill with a hedge on your right to cross the stream at a wooden footbridge to bring you to the concrete drive to Melbury House. Cross this and bear slightly left, towards the back of the nearest cottage. You find yourself in a short lane with a cottage garden on your right bringing you to a T-junction with the main street through Melbury Osmond. Turn right, crossing the tiny stream to follow the road up to the church.

This is the church where Jemima Hand, already three months pregnant, was married to Thomas Hardy in December 1839; the baby she was carrying who was to do so much to spread the fame of his native county was born in the upstairs room of the now famous cottage by Higher Bockhampton, near Dorchester.

Walk across the churchyard and turn left on the lane on the far side, a telephone box on your right.

*The lane leading west from the north side of Melbury Osmond churchyard, a small conifer plantation on its south side, brings you to the crossroads at the top of the village (GR 573079); head straight across along the gravel lane marked "no through road". Immediately before Melbury Dairy, the house at the end of the lane, turn left over a stile and make your way through a new small plantation. Turn right on the track and follow this uphill with distant views of the outskirts of Yeovil away to the right. The track takes you across the south side of a delightful wood of mature oak and coppiced hazel known as Annesley's Plantation; you descend to cross a stream at a bridge in the trees. The lane ends at the end of the next field as you go through a gate and head down the hill towards Lewcombe with the wood on your right. Avoid the stile in the corner of the field and go through a metal hunting gate 50 yards to the right and descend through the brambles and trees.

Please note that from this point there is no access to the church at Lewcombe Manor nor down the drive; the alignment of the paths is accurately shown on the map. Cross the Lewcombe stream at a tiny footbridge and follow the muddy path up the slope to join the track running along the north side of the wood before Clarkham Cross. This stretch is, regrettably, along the worst sort of horse-chewed bridleway; there is some relief at this stage with a parallel path through the massed bluebells under the old coppice on the left.

Turn left on the road and walk to the end of the wood. There are fine views across to the right, over the catchment above Sutton Bingham reservoir; the prominent hill, largely covered in mixed woods, is Birts Hill (GR 516087). Turn left down the tarred drive to Lewcombe Manor. (A right of way leads to the church and back, should you wish to visit it and the manor house.) You reach a cottage with a stepped roof on the right; turn right here, over a stile, looking towards the modern attempt at a stately home one field away. A gate at the corner of this field brings you to a steep slope overlooking the woods on the other side (North Holt Copse).

Make your way to the right-hand corner of the wood and go through a stile to cross the stream at some rudimentary stepping stones before a pull up a high bank. Ahead of you is an area of grazing fields with scattered trees. Make your way across the long field to the south of the wood with the stream down to your right. There are no waymarks now until you reach Girt Farm. At the end of the field is a tributary brook in a gully full of trees and undergrowth. Cross this; after 200 yards you come to the second such. From the top of this one you can see the path heading diagonally up the slope across the field to a gate, from where a track leads you down to the corner of the deer park and another tiny stream. Follow the path which has been diverted to the left of Girt Farm and join the tarred farm drive, apparently with some ramparts above you in the deer park.

The drive leaves the trees and heads up the hill with fine views of the Norman Motte and Bailey and West Chelborough.

The slight escarpment you are making your way up faces west and, modest as it is, still provides enough updraught for the area's birds of prey to enjoy. One blustery day I saw a flock enjoying the breeze - in the distance, so numerous were they I took them to be rooks. On closer examination, standing almost beneath them, I realised I was looking at half a dozen buzzards. I have also seen a pair of sparrowhawks here in the spring.

Follow the tarred Girt Lane south to a stile almost opposite a telegraph pole. Turn left here and make your way downhill with a fine view of Evershot with Wardon Hill behind with its landmark squat tower on the summit. Just before the houses you cross a green farm lane. Keep the farm buildings to your right and join the back lane in Evershot just by the old chapel. Turn left along the road and then right, crossing the tiny stream along a right of way to bring you into the car park of the Acorn Inn, in Fore Street, where you find your car.

37) Askerswell, Powerstock Common and Eggardon Hill

Distance: 8 or 5 miles
Start: the Spyway Inn
Map: sheet 194, GR 529934

This is a delightful walk of varied scenery and interest, taking you over the contrasting chalk downland and west Dorset-Devon scenery and through the quietest and most picturesque of villages and a nature reserve wood. From the top of the Iron Age hill fort of Eggardon Hill there are views out to sea and across much of western Dorset. The walk starts at the Spyway Inn and goes near two other pubs after 2 miles; it passes the post office stores in Nettlecombe.

The start, at Askerswell, is 9 miles west of Dorchester and 4 miles east of Bridport, just north of the main A35. If you do not intend to visit the Spyway Inn at the start, then I suggest you park your car by the parish noticeboard in the centre of Askerswell (GR 529928), where the bus and travelling library draw up, or at the village hall car park, easily found by following the signs (GR 531929). Make your way up the lane past the row of houses on the left with a datestone of 1943 to the Spyway Inn.

The Spyway used to be its nickname, generally held to commemorate its use by smugglers - the "real" name was the Three Horseshoes.

Leaving the pub turn left and walk down the lane for 100 yards. Turn right along a gravel lane (a feature of this part of Dorset is that the right of way signposts have their grid reference marked down the stem of the post); strictly the footpath you follow crosses the field but most people now seem to follow the lane to the kennels. At the far end of the field it turns sharply to the left and goes through a hedge before turning right over the stream. You are looking at a new asbestos-roofed barn beside the hound kennels; keep

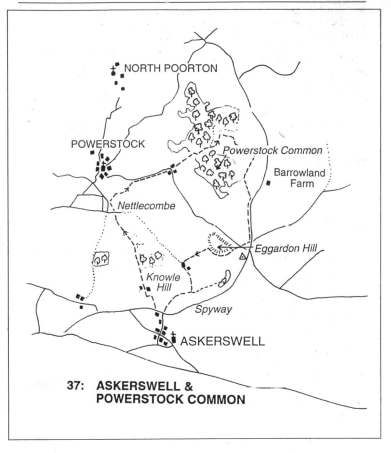

**37: ASKERSWELL &
POWERSTOCK COMMON**

to the left of this and make your way up the hill to the obvious gateway at the top, heading just west of due north.

From this point there is a good illustration of the dramatic change in the landscape; to your right are the sweeping turf slopes of Eggardon Hill, surmounted by the ramparts of the Iron Age fort. This is the westernmost point of England's chalk country; behind Eggardon Hill stretches the great sweep of downland right across southern England. From the summit of Eggardon you could walk east and north, staying on chalk across the Dorset

Downs, Salisbury Plain, the sweep of downs above Andover in Hampshire, over the Hog's Back and Box Hill and along the North Downs all the way to Kent. There could scarcely be a more contrasting scene as you look west; the view is of dumpy hills and intricate valleys where the ploughlands show the red soil - a landscape that stretches unchanged right across Devon.

As you approach the patchy woodland around Knowle Hill you find yourself walking along a well used farm track; at the end of the wood it dips to cross the track that now follows the line of the old Maiden Newton-Bridport railway. At this junction you will find a stile on the right of the track. Beyond it the path heads diagonally up a slope with a recent plantation, of beech, larch and oak. At the top of the slope a second stile leads you into an arable field which you cross to reach a gap in the hedge about 300 yards to the right of the gate in the far left corner. You find yourself on the public road (GR 519953) opposite the gate leading onto the cricket ground - the home of Powerstock and Hooke cricket club.

Assuming there is no match in progress head straight across the ground, keeping the square to your left. If there is then keep to the boundary and keep still during the bowler's run-up. At the corner of the ground you go over an old stone slab stile and find yourself in Nettlecombe. From an electricity pole hangs a time-honoured sign indicating the way to the post office. If you would like a drink, then ignore this sign to turn left and walk 200 yards along the road to the Marquis of Lorne. If you really feel like spoiling yourself you could walk on to the Three Horseshoes in Powerstock and follow the road round to rejoin the walk on the Eggardon Hill road.

Head north along the dead-end road through Nettlecombe, past the post office stores on the right to find a three-way signpost at the end. Take care here; cross the stream - step over it or use the footbridge - and walk along the path sandwiched between the hedge on the right and the stream on the left, past a very rustic farmyard on the right. At the end of the farm buildings, by a tiny ancient quarry-working, turn right to follow the path along the valley with the farm buildings on your right. Strictly, this path keeps up the side of the valley, but despite some effort at clearing I have found it overgrown and impassable. Should you find it thus, then follow the alternative path at the end of the old farm buildings down between the old barn and a very new one to walk up the little valley. You come to a fence with a hunting gate by the stream, just before a small waterfall hidden beneath the overhanging trees. Turn left after this fence to make your way up the very steep bank and turn right along the top to follow a grassy track which swings to the left to reach the slightly sunken Eggardon Hill road running east from Powerstock (GR 524959).

Turn right along the road and follow it for half a mile, over the steel-sided bridge over the old railway (this offers a pleasant and interesting point to point walk, from Maiden Newton to the outskirts of Bridport). You reach the drive to Whetley Orchard; turn left off the road here and walk down the drive, through some impressively easy-to-open gates. The bridleway runs straight ahead, north-east, past some good old-fashioned wet patches, and enters the woods of Powerstock Common. On your right is a plantation of young Scots pine, on the left a tangle of thorn. You pass the sign announcing the beginning of the Dorset Naturalist's Trust reserve and the path, quite muddy, heads up the slope beneath coppiced hazel.

The fact that this wood is a nature reserve is largely due to the efforts of the writer and broadcaster Kenneth Allsop who lived at West Milton, a mile west of Powerstock.

The right of way through the woods of Powerstock Common is well worn, taking you up out of the valley of the River Mangerton. The path starts to level out beneath low overhanging oak trees - this stretch would make a fantastic walk at dawn in May - and the wood starts to thin as you reach the end of the track from the left. Continuing north-east along the edge of the wood (just outside it, rather than as the map shows) the path brings you to the cast iron Dorset Naturalist's Trust sign (GR 541969) where you turn right, through a hunting gate to find yourself entering a field of seeded grazing.

Barrowland Farm is very obvious, ahead of you, with the tree-lined track running up to it. Just to the left of the farm as you look at it you see a clump of deciduous trees in the bottom of the valley. Make for these as you descend the slightly convex slope and you find yourself at a gate in the fence. Turn right on the far side of this gate and follow the fence down the hill on your left to cross the tiny stream and head up the hill on the farm track to Barrowland Farm. As you climb the hill the field on your right, well supplied with scattered oaks, looks as though it should be marked as parkland on the map. The 1960 edition of the OS one inch map marks all this land to the east and south of Barrowland Farm as being wood, so this may be a remnant.

At the far side of the farmyard turn right and follow the farm lane contouring along the side of the hill; after 300 yards the track turns sharp left to go up the hill. Keep straight on here, across a field of seeded grazing towards the top of the hill, the edge of the wood facing you. At the top of the hill you come to a hunting gate; go through this and turn right to follow the headland along the edge of the field. There has been a realignment of the bridleway here; follow the headland along the edge of the field for about a quarter of a mile until you see a fence crossing the top of the plateau to your left. Turn right to follow the fence; go through a waymarked gate and follow the fence along on your left to bring you to the road up from Toller Porcorum onto Eggardon Hill. Turn right on the road at spot height 216m (GR 547955) and follow it south across the chalky plateau with ever-improving views of Eggardon Hill until you reach the Eggardon Hill signpost indicating the way to Wynford Eagle. A thick hedge runs away to the right here; climb a stile on the far side of it and follow the well used footpath across the field to the stile at the end; there has been a very slight realignment here, for strictly the footpath should take you to the far corner of the field. However you find yourself crossing the road back down to Powerstock opposite a stile; climb the stile and follow the footpath across the field to reach the ramparts of Eggardon Hill. This is National Trust property and so having crossed the boundary fence you are free to wander the ramparts at will; I recommend a walk all round the ramparts, to enjoy the view in all directions and contemplate the labour of those who created these and Dorset's other mighty Iron Age fortifications.

The bridleway right of way along the southern edge of Eggardon Hill is not well trodden, but is nevertheless easy to follow. You descend gradually, on springy turf with a dramatic view down to your left, to the head of the valley leading down to Eggardon Farms. Following the edge of the hill fort you pass one thick hedge running down the hill to the right and then at the next you see a hunting gate with a yellow disc waymark (I have a feeling it should be blue); go through this and follow the path down the hill, improving to a track as it descends to bring you to Eggardon Farms. Turn left on the lane at the bottom of the hill and follow it along with the great old barn on your right; turn right at the end and pause to admire the stonework of the barn on the right, around its great door. Now bear left and follow the drive down the hill and keep the farmhouse with its delightful windows (and even more delightful view from them) to your left to see a five-bar gate in front of you. Go through this and descend across a rather damp field of old pasture to find a hunting gate at the bottom; a hedged-in byway and a second damp field brings you to a slight realignment; the path turns right before the pond in the bottom of the valley to cross the valley just downstream of it, rather than as the map shows. You reach the farm lane below an old sycamore tree and turn right on it to walk half a mile down it to Spyway.

38) Far from the Madding Crowd: Kingcombe and the Hooke Valley

Distance: 11 or 6 miles
Start: the Old Swan, Toller Porcorum
Map: sheet 194, GR 563980

The phrase "the hidden heart of Dorset" sounds like the sort of thing one might read in the worst kind of holiday brochure. If there is such a thing then I think there is a strong case for advocating the Hooke Valley. In a county where the village names are poetry in themselves Toller Porcorum must surely rate as the most euphonious - though the village itself is perhaps not as picturesque as its name may lead you to believe. The valley is well wooded and copiously supplied with hidden ancient tracks still used (though

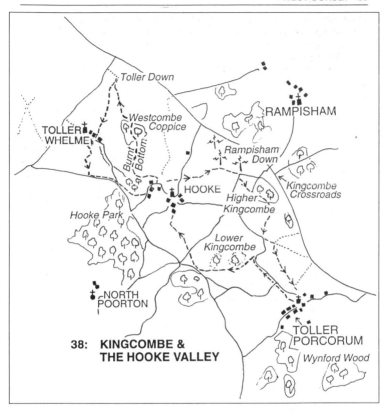

Toller Down

Westcombe Coppice

RAMPISHAM

TOLLER WHELME

Burnt Bottom

Rampisham Down

HOOKE

Higher Kingcombe

Kingcombe Crossroads

Hooke Park

Lower Kingcombe

NORTH POORTON

38: KINGCOMBE & THE HOOKE VALLEY

TOLLER PORCORUM

Wynford Wood

not much) as rights of way. This is a figure-of-eight walk so you have the opportunity to decide en route whether or not to walk the whole thing, or merely the first section. There is a post office stores in Toller Porcorum but no other pub or shop is passed on this walk.

Turn right out of the Old Swan and then right at the church, to follow the road around past the village hall on the right. There is a small development of new houses on the left and the road bends sharply left and right at the end of the village. At the end of the road you turn right over a stile to head north-west with a high hedge on your right to go down to the road; the path turns sharply right at the end of the hedge and turns left on the road to leave Toller

189

Porcorum.

Toller Porcorum was known in the Middle Ages as Swine Toller. It would appear the presence nearby of the Knights Hospitallers (hence the hamlet of Toller Fratrum) meant the name had to be elevated and Latinised to disguise its earthy origins - a touch of humour in Dorset place-names.

There now follows two-thirds of a mile of road walking towards Kingcombe, but this is a quiet hedged lane.

The name of Kingcombe does not, as one might expect, refer to any royal connection. It is first recorded as Chimedecome *in Domesday and refers to the plant wall germander - this being a valley where it grew. See below for information on the Kingcombe Centre.*

As you approach Lower Kingcombe the road bends to the right, down the hill and an unsigned track turns left off the road to go up the hill, marked "Nature Trail" on the map. The track leading south-west up the hill is beneath trees growing out of old overgrown hedges. You pass a traditional wooden farm gate on the right, complete with field names. Continue up the track to the new hunting gate at the top and bear right to head west, contouring along the hillside towards a small group of pines on the horizon at Mount Pleasant. The path lies through some farm gates waymarked as though they were permissive paths, whereas in fact you are on a statutory right of way. You continue with a hedge on your left all the way to Mount Pleasant; instead of going on to the road here turn right to continue to follow a hedge on your left, heading just west of due north. Go through the first gate on the left and continue to follow the same hedge on the right hand side to reach Common Lane (GR 539990).

Cross over Common Lane, leading down to your left to Higher Kingcombe, and follow the track heading just west of due north; cross the field over the top of the hill, going more steeply down the hill to cross the stream flowing down to join the River Hooke in the village of the same name. The track swings to the right and then up the hill to meet the road at Green Lane, opposite a row of cottages. Turn right on the road and walk down the hill to the church, where you turn left at the junction in the centre of the village.

I think I have rarely seen an uglier intrusion to the front of a churchyard than the BT telephone on a post, more at home on the hard shoulder of a motorway than outside the church in an ancient Dorset village.

This is the point where you have to decide if you are to walk the full figure-of-eight walk to the source of the River Hooke; if you have the time and energy, I recommend it. If not, then cross over the road in the centre of the village and make your way steeply up the hill for 500 yards to turn right along a hedged-in green lane at Chalk Corner (GR 537005). (Continue at * below.)

To continue up to Toller Whelme, turn left in front of the church and walk along the lane upstream along the bottom of the valley. It bends to the right with a cottage on the corner on the left and a pond on the right behind a high embankment. Look back to your right to see the white-painted Hooke Mill - used by Hardy as Trewnell Mill in *Far from the Madding Crowd*. At the northern end of the pond you see a house facing you with a row of old close-set iron railings (GR 533004). Cross the tiny stream on your right here and head straight up the hill on a track beneath trees whose bed has become extremely wet; it supports a lush growth of bittercress. You reach the end of the track beneath a tree; look diagonally up the hill to your left and you will see the downhill end of a small copse. Go through a gate below this and follow a hedge along on your right to see two gates ahead of you, remnant of when a hedge continued on the far side. Go through the right-hand of these and you find yourself with an expanse of arable in front of you. The route of the old track is visible as a crop mark - darker soil in this chalky field. You keep straight ahead, due west and then follow the shoulder of the hill round to the right to find yourself looking up a gully towards Westcombe Coppice.

The bridleway drops down the hill to meet the farm lane descending from the spur to cross the stream. Keep the stream on your right and head straight up the valley to enter the wood at a hunting gate. Westcombe Coppice is a highlight of this stretch of the walk - richly supplied with bluebells in the spring, it is a fine old coppice now largely of mature oak. You exit from the top and turn left to find yourself on top of the high downs. At the end of the wood a hedge bears to the right; keep this on your left and follow it as it heads just to the west of due north, somewhat less straight than the map shows.

Of the lonely barn on the downs marked on the map (GR 523024) there is now no sign. There has been a diversion of the bridleway, sensibly enough avoiding crossing what are now arable fields (though were sheep pasture when the bridleways were used for local communication). The slight conundrum is that at the time of writing the latest available map (1993) does not show the diversions. You meet the end of an unfenced farm lane which runs north-west to the road to the 247m spot height. Do not follow this farm lane to the road, but turn left immediately off it to follow the hedge along on your left so that you have made a U-turn. You are now in Fair Field, a flat field on top of the downs with the farm lane on its northern side. You are heading south down the eastern side with a hedge on your left. Turn right when you meet the end of the field so that you are heading west, towards the copse by the road (at GR 520025). Turn left through a gate to head exactly due south across the flat plateau of Toller Down with Westcombe Coppice visible to your left; you have a hedge on your right for two fields. The almost intimate landscape around Kingcombe seems far away now as you make your way across the chalk uplands. This is Hardy's "featureless convexity of chalk and soil" described in *Far from the Madding Crowd*.

The descent to Toller Whelme is across grassy fields becoming ever steeper; the track shown heading north from the hamlet is shorter than the map shows, going hardly any further up the hill than the cottage. Turn right

Toller Whelme

on the road with some recently felled woodland on your left and follow it past the fine house on your right. The road bends to the right (take a few minutes to visit the church) and a track turns left up the hill, a green lane between high hedges waymarked as being part of the Wessex Ridgeway. Looking up this you see a gate in the high hedge; go through this and make your way diagonally up the hill and over the spur, through two gates to bring you to the field behind Pipsford Farm. There is no waymarking in this stretch and it appears that the footpath has been diverted to the right from the arrow-straight line due south that the map shows. You descend steeply to the gate by the farm and turn left on the tarred farm lane and then immediately right, off it to descend on a stony track to cross the River Hooke at its highest point on this walk.

The source itself is above Toller Whelme, a hydraulic ram now marking the exact spot. In former times the River Hooke was known as the Toller, although I have been unable to find out the date of the change. The name "Toller Whelme" takes its second element from the Anglo Saxon aiwelm - a source.

Over the river you head steeply up the hillside, following a line of electricity poles just to your right. You see a gateway leading onto the road to the left of a long line of high nut bushes; go through this and turn left on the road to head down the hill to the turning on the left to "Toller Whelme only".

Around 150 yards after this, at the beginning of the wood on your right you turn left through a farm gate and follow the grass field almost parallel to the road you have just left to go through a rickety stile in an overgrown hedge; a small wood lies a few yards to your left.

Follow the edge of the wood along to a stile at the corner leading to a field between two woods. Make your way down this to the road just above Hooke Court School and turn left onto the road. Retrace your steps along the road and turn left at the end of the ornamental pond on your left along the entrance to Hooke Springs. Keep the white-painted farmhouse to your left and turn immediately right off the drive along a grassy track, fording a tiny stream as you pass some netted-over fishponds downstream to your right. You head up a narrow, hedged old track, extremely wet and overgrown with bittercress to reach the Rampisham Hill road and cross over on a similar track on the far side (GR 537005).

*The bridleway is an old track between hedges which heads over Rampisham Down. The hedge on your left finishes so that you are walking on a lane below the level of the field to your left. You find yourself looking across a gully with the transmission masts above you to your left; go through a gate, where the sunken lane finishes and bear left across the field to the prominent gate in the far left corner. As you head along the track with the aerials to your left, the track improves towards the road. Turn right on the public road (GR 549007) to head down the hill for 100 yards to a waymarked gate on your left. You find yourself looking south-east down a long gully, the bridleway along its bottom marked by farm gates. You enter the wood and continue through it and exit in a small field with a sense of being in a hidden valley; on the far side of the field you see a gate partially hidden by a bramble brake; go through this to find yourself heading down to Lower Kingcombe on a hedged-in muddy track.

As usual the surface improves and becomes more used as you approach the road. You reach the road (GR 554993) to see a stile in an arch in the hedge on your left; go through this to follow the footpath south-east along the side of the farm, one field away to your right. At the bottom of the hill is a small pond in a horse-grazed field; cross over the stream that feeds it. Looking up the hill the route appears to be marked with a convenient horse jump which doubles as a stile through the fence. Beyond this is what may be termed a stepless stile - in fact it is a set of rails where a water pipe has been laid and the hedge replanted. Turn right here, down the gravel lane to the second bridleway sign to the left, pointing the way to Toller Porcorum. There has been some extensive relaying of old hedges here; for the middle stretch between Lower Kingcombe and Toller Porcorum you walk across two fields, the way marked by farm gates. You reach the village, walking through a farmyard. Turn left as you meet the public road in the village and follow it up to the Old Swan.

The Kingcombe Centre

In 1987 The Kingcombe Estate came onto the market and made considerable news in the national press. It had been in the possession of the Wallbridge family for generations and, located in a little-frequented enclave of the county, time had in many senses passed it by. Most remarkable was the state of the land; not a hedge had been grubbed nor a meadow re-seeded or sprayed. The Kingcombe Centre, under its director Nigel Spring, is effectively preserving this wealth in such a way that it is economically viable. There are courses here on a wide variety of countryside-related subjects, some of which cater for the disabled. It is an excellent place to come and learn more about almost any aspect of Dorset; lately these courses have attracted the interest of BBC Radio 4. The courses are residential and are run throughout the year and a brochure is available with details of them. The address can be found at the back of the book.

Thomas Hardy and the Hooke Valley

It is a happy coincidence that the area of the opening of *Far from the Madding Crowd* should be a part of Dorset that has changed less than any other since Hardy's day; it can be placed very accurately around the upper reaches of the Hooke Valley. The strongest claim to be the inspiration for "Norcombe", where the novel opens with Gabriel Oak as a leasehold farmer, is made by the village of Hooke. A key to this is the name of Westcombe Coppice, which Hardy would naturally alter to "Norcombe". This is one reason I highly recommend the northern loop of this figure-of-eight walk.

The blow to Gabriel Oak that causes him to lose his status as a farmer in his own right and move as a hired hand to Weatherbury is that of his dog driving his sheep over a drop. The opening scene of the excellent film of *c.*1970 (with Alan Bates, Peter Finch and Julie Christie) shows this taking place over the cliffs at Durdle Door, adding a touch of dramatic scenery to the event. In fact Hardy describes in minutest detail a deep chalk pit on the downs; several such on the slopes east of Hooke suggest themselves as the models for this.

39) Bronkham Hill, Corton and the Hardy Monument

Distance: 10 miles
Start: Upwey church
Map: sheet 194, GR 660853

I have a great love of ridge walking - this is one reason why I enjoy the Carpathians so much, with their mile upon mile of high ridges around 6000 feet high. This walk takes you to an altitude of one-tenth of this but the views from its two ridges are quite superb, both out to sea, across the Isle of

Portland and inland across the Frome Valley. The walk lies along two fine parallel ridges and across the uninhabited valley between. The first half takes you along one of the best sections of the inland route of the Dorset Coast Path and past some notable prehistoric sites. The walk starts by the cafe at the Wishing Well and passes no other habitation on its way bar isolated farms. It could easily and pleasantly be extended by a mile to visit the pub in Portesham.

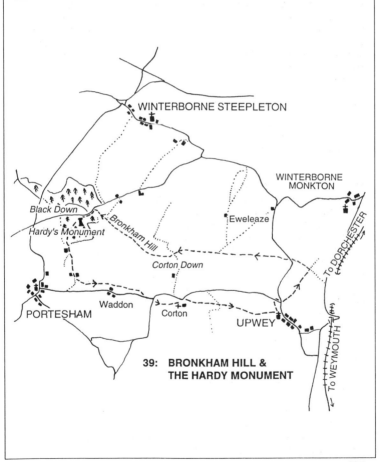

39: BRONKHAM HILL & THE HARDY MONUMENT

To reach the start, leave Weymouth on the A354 and turn left in Broadway on the B3151, signposted to Martinstown. A mile from the turn off the main road brings you through the narrow main street of Upwey to the Wishing Well. Bear left off the road here and drive up the dead-end lane past the church to park your car in the car park on its north side.

Turn left out of the car park and make your way up the shady lane which soon becomes a private drive. Turn left off this lane to follow the stream up the valley through the trees; you cross it twice and end up on its right-hand side as you look upstream. Turn left for a few yards on the tarred drive to a cottage, then left at the top of the rise, onto the public road. After 400 yards you reach the main road, with a row of council-type houses stretching up the road on your left. Cross over the road here and follow the blue bridleway sign pointing the way across a field of grazing. The path is not distinct on the ground; nevertheless it is easy to follow as it takes you up the bottom of an obvious dry gully, through a gateway in a dry stone wall. At the top of the gully you reach a T-junction of tracks (GR 667864); turn left here to follow the chalky track north-west to recross the main road over the downs to Martinstown. Ahead of you is the British Telecom transmission mast; you are now walking along the inland route of the Dorset Coast Path.

Making your way uphill, head west along the main ridge of the downs. There is an extra delight about walking along a ridge, be it ever so gentle as this one is. Your eye is taken beyond your immediate environment to distant views - in this case across the Frome Valley to the chalk downs to its north and left across Lyme Bay, the Fleet and the Isle of Portland. This is easy walking along a grassy track with the arable fields stretching away on either side.

At one point on the left you pass a tumulus sadly being ploughed out.

It is a common fallacy to consider that the countryside was a static entity until one's own lifetime when it started to be desecrated. A read of Barbara Kerr's excellent Social History of Dorset will dispel that myth. However, the rapid rural development of the latter half of the twentieth century has certainly affected the landscape you see from this ridge more than the previous several centuries, with its ploughing up of time-honoured chalk grassland, erection of regiments of pylons, widespread use of herbicides and insecticides and decimation of the population of those actually involved in working the land.

Ahead is the gorsy slope of Bronkham Hill and the dumpy pillar of Hardy's Monument, growing ever nearer. After 3 miles of striding along the ridge - easy walking punctuated with the occasional gate - you arrive at the road in the trees just before the monument, at Smitten Corner. Turn left on the road for a few hundred yards to bring you up to the car park by the monument.

The hill-top of Black Down was a well known viewpoint before the monument was built. Given exceptional conditions you can see Hameldown

Tor on Dartmoor (see my *Two Moors Way*, published by Cicerone Press). I have proved the intervisibility of the two points by seeing Hardy's Monument from Hameldown on a clear day in September, admittedly through Zeiss binoculars.

What should perhaps be explained to visitors to the county is that the monument has little to do with Thomas Hardy. It was erected in 1844 (when T.H. was four) to commemorate Admiral Lord Nelson's friend Admiral Sir Thomas Hardy. The village of Portesham which you are about to walk past on the ridge was Admiral Hardy's home. There is a connection of a sort with the writer because he claimed kinship with the admiral as part of his efforts to prove that he was descended from the kind of people whom he considered to be more elevated than his real ancestors. There is a fine passage in The Trumpet Major *when Bob Loveday, stricken with guilt at his lack of effort in the war to prevent an invasion by Napoleon, takes an evening walk over to Portesham from "Overcombe" and asks for a posting on board HMS* Victory *from Admiral Hardy. He is granted his wish and Bob sails to take part in the momentous victory of Trafalgar. Now that walk, to Thomas Hardy was an unremarkable evening walk of 7 miles there and 7 miles back, assuming that "Overcombe" be based upon Sutton Poyntz.*

From the gravel area around the monument look south-west, across the patch of heath in front of the conifer plantation. A path heads around some gravel diggings and, well signed, takes you down an obvious small gully into the trees. The gully deepens and leads to some beech trees by a small clearing well supplied with bluebells in spring. On your left is Benecke Wood. You exit from the trees by a fine stone barn with a modern roof of asbestos (Black Down Barn, GR 609869).

Tithe barns are a well known feature of the English countryside and it is tempting to think of all such well built barns with large, high and wide doors opposite each other - giving a slightly cruciform plan to the building - as being tithe barns. What are perhaps less well known, or at least not covered in school history, are threshing barns,· with large doors to admit the entry of waggons piled high with wheat straw. Such doors were positioned opposite each other and in the direction of the prevailing wind so as to give maximum airflow to the threshers working inside with their flails.

From Black Down Barn head up the well used farm track due south up the hill; keep left at the fork half way up to bring you to Portesham Farm. Here the map is a little at variance with what you find on the ground. There is no sign of a path heading south-east from the farm; walk 200 yards along the lane with a stone wall on your left and turn left through the first gate after the farm. The path takes you along the escarpment with a stone wall on your left. To your right is the predominantly pastoral landscape drained by the tributaries of the short River Wey. You can see the traffic moving fast along the busy B3151 Weymouth-Bridport road.

A mile of walking along this abrupt escarpment takes you across the private track snaking over the hill from Waddon House to the farm buildings at Bench. Four hundred yards after this you come to a scruffy overgrown hedge running down the hillside on your right. If you go as far as a water tank surrounded by a breeze-block wall you have gone too far. Just to the east of where the hedge meets the road is a stile; cross this and walk east along the road to the T-junction where you cross the road and go over a fine old stone stile into the field at the bottom of Corton Hill. Keep the fence to your right and make your way along the bottom of the hill to bring you to Corton Farm and its chapel.

This is situated just below a notch in the ridge; corf in Anglo-Saxon meant a cutting; the word also gave rise to Coryates which you have just passed and notably to Corfe in Purbeck which has now become known as Corfe Castle. Corton is first mentioned in Domesday as Corfetone; it was then a small village which has now declined to a single farm. The farmhouse itself is very fine and the chapel is well worth a visit; there is a wealth of information on its history inside.

From Corton walk along the farm drive and then turn sharp left to head steeply back up the hill, through the gap and immediately right to resume your ridge-top walking, this time along Friar Waddon Hill. After a mile and a half the path bears to the left, off the top of the ridge to head for the strip of wood running up behind Upwey church. The alignment of the path is somewhat obscured by the blue shading of "Mill" on the map; in fact it goes into the wood by a stile and goes down the middle of the wood, past the top of the churchyard and around the back of some cottages to reach the road through Upwey. Turn left to reach your car.

ACCOMMODATION

A full list of accommodation is available from tourist information centres in the county. The list below is not comprehensive; it does not attempt to be a list of all accommodation in the area of the walks. I have tended to include bed and breakfast establishments that are on the walk itself or within easy walking distance of it. I have only given grid references for establishments where they are outlying from a village. Inclusion here does not imply any recommendation by the author, unless mentioned in the text. Establishments are listed below in the same order as the walks. I have not included hotels or guest houses in the resorts of Weymouth or Swanage or, indeed, in the Bournemouth-Poole conurbation as these are not primarily catering for walkers. However, a holiday in either of the former could be combined with many of the walks in this book, using a car.

CHAPTER THREE: WALKS IN EAST DORSET

1) The Forests and Downs of Cranborne Chase

The Barleycorn House, Deanland, Sixpenny Handley, Salisbury, Dorset
    SP5 5PD (01725 552583)

2) Hambledon Hill, Hod Hill and Blandford Forest

Mr and Mrs D.Wright, Gold Hill Farm, Child Okeford, Blandford Forum,
    Dorset DT11 8HB (01258 860293)
Mrs J.Langley, Bartley House, Upper Street, Child Okeford, Blandford
    Forum, Dorset DT11 8EF (01258 860420)
Mrs S.Wright, Lattermere, Frog Lane, Iwerne Courtney, Blandford Forum, Dorset DT11
    8QL (01258 860115)
Mrs J.Moss, 4 Old Mill Cottages, Iwerne Courtney, Blandford Forum, Dorset DT11
    (01258 861049)
Mrs S.Elley, 6 Courtney Close, Iwerne Courtney, Blandford Forum, Dorset DT11 8RD
    (01258 860056)
Mr and Mrs J.Tory, Home Farm, Bryanston, Blandford Forum, Dorset DT11 0PR (01258
    452919)
    A mile of pleasant walking along footpaths and farm tracks brings you to Durweston
    and the Hambledon Hill walk.
Mrs P.Munro, Sutcombe Knap, The Lane, Durweston, Blandford Forum., Dorset
    (01258 450600)
Miss S.Portman, Portman Lodge, Durweston, Blandford Forum, Dorset DT11 0QA
    (01258 452168)

3) Bokerley Ditch and Martin Down

The Barleycorn House, Deanland, Sixpenny Handley, Salisbury, Dorset SP5 5PD
    (01725 552583)

4) Compton and Fontmell Downs and Melbury Hill

The Old Forge, Fanners Yard, Chapel Hill, Compton Abbas, Shaftesbury, Dorset SP7
    0NQ (01747 811881)
Pipers Mill, Fontmell Magna, Shaftesbury, Dorset SP7 0JP (01747 811729)
Hurdles Farm (Mrs Hillary Ballard), Fontmell Magna, Shaftesbury, Dorset SP7 0JP
    (01747 811028)

Melbury Mill (Mrs Bradley-Watson), Melbury Abbas, Shaftesbury, Dorset SP7 0DB
(01747 52163)

5) The Stour Valley and Forest Trail, Ferndown

The Coach House Inn, 579 Wimborne Road East, Ferndown, Dorset BH22 9NW
(01202 861222)
Plovers Barrow, 325 Ringwood Road, Ferndown, Dorset BH22 9AD
(01202 875888)
Cirendel, 155 Golf Links Road, Ferndown, Dorset BH22 8BX
(01202 875356)

6) The Woods and Lanes of the Crane Valley

The Fleur de Lys, 5 Wimborne Street, Cranborne, Dorset BH21 5PP
(01725 517282)
La Fosse Restaurant, The Square, Cranborne, Dorset BH21 5PR
(01725 517604)
Clematis, (Hilary Montgomery), Edmondsham, Cranborne, Dorset BH21 5RJ (01202
822 954)

CHAPTER FOUR: BETWEEN THE STOUR AND THE FROME

7) The Hinterland of Sherborne: In Raleigh's Domain

Pinford Farm, Milborne Port, Sherborne, Dorset DT9 5AB (01963 250213) (GR 664173)
Pinford Farm is far from the road; there can be nothing better than enjoying this walk
using Pinford as a base.

8) Milton Abbas, Hilton and the Downs

Wyvern House (Mr and Mrs Ford), Milton Abbas, Blandford Forum, Dorset DT11 0BL
(01258 880089)
Dunbury House, Milton Abbas, Blandford Forum, Dorset (01258 880445)

9) The Vale of the Stour

Plumber Manor Hotel, Sturminster Newton, Dorset DT10 (01258 72507) (GR 772118)
A nationally known luxury hotel - but tastefully so. Spoil yourself!
Ann Thorne, Etheridge Farm, Darknoll Lane, Okeford Fitzpaine, Blandford Forum,
Dorset DT11 0RP (01258 880445)
Pond View (Mr and Mrs Harvey), Fiddleford, Sturminster Newton, Dorset DT10 2BX
(01258 473326)

10) Trent and the Comptons

I suggest you find accommodation in Sherborne for this, of which there is a great supply,
easily booked through the tourist office (see useful addresses).

11) Buckland Newton and Dogbury Gate and Minterne Hill

Holyleas House, Buckland Newton, Dorchester, Dorset DT2 7DP
(01300 345214)
Rew Cottage, Buckland Newton, Dorchester, Dorset DT2 7DN
(01300 345467)
White Horse Farm, Middlemarsh, Sherborne, Dorset DT9 5QN
(01963 210222) - just over a mile's walk from Clinger Farm via Lyons Gate and
Grange Woods.

Almshouse Farm, Hermitage, Sherborne, Dorset DT9 6HA (01963 210296) - a mile's walk north of Dogbury Gate.

12) Plush and the Dorset Gap

The Poachers Inn, Piddletrenthide, Dorchester, Dorset DT2 7QX
(01300 348358)
The Old Bakehouse Hotel, Piddletrenthide, Dorchester, Dorset DT2 7QR (01300 348305)
The European Inn, Piddletrenthide, Dorchester, Dorset DT2 7QT
(01300 348308)

13) Melcombe Bingham and the Dorset Gap and 14) Rawlsbury Camp and Bulbarrow

The Fox Inn (Gary and Kathryn Witheyman), Ansty, Dorchester, Dorset
DT2 7PN (01258 880328, fax 881097)
Badgers Set (Lesley Dowsett), Cross Lanes. Melcombe Bingham, Dorchester, Dorset DT2 7NY (01258 880697)

15) Giant Hill and the Source of the Cerne

Cerne Park Farm, Cerne Abbas, Dorchester, Dorset DT2 7JT
(01300 341379)
Forge Cottage, Duck Street, Cerne Abbas, Dorchester, Dorset DT2 7LA (01300 341601)

16) Sandford Orcas to Cadbury Castle

The Queens Arms, Corton Denham, Sherborne, Dorset DT9 4LR
(01963 220317)
Applecroft, Corton Denham, Sherborne, Dorset DT9 4LS (01963 220476)
Wheatsheaf House, Corton Denham, Sherborne, Dorset DT9 4LQ
(01963 220207)
Corton Ash, Corton Denham, Sherborne, Dorset DT9 4LS (01963 220450)
The Alders, Sandford Orcas, Sherborne, Dorset DT9 4SB (01963 220666)
Ashclose Farm, Charlton Horethorne, Sherborne, Dorset DT9 4PG
(01963 220360)

17) Between the Cale and the Stour

The Ship Inn (Mr & Mrs Shanks and Mr A Hurst), West Stour, Gillingham, Dorset SP8 5RP (01747 838640)
Mrs J.Denning, Manor Farm, Fifehead Magdalen, Gillingham, Dorset
SP8 5RR (01258 820717)
Christina Trim, Stour Cross Farm, West Stour, Gillingham, Dorset SP8 5SE (01747 838183)
Kington Manor Farm, Church Hill, Kington Magna, Gillingham, Dorset
SP8 5EG (01747 838371)
Self-catering cottage at Middle Farm, Fifehead Magdalen, Gillingham, Dorset SP8 5RR (01258 820220). Highly recommended as a base for walking - dogs welcome. Contact Mrs Trevor

18) Tolpuddle, Dewlish and the Downs

Park Pale, Southover, Tolpuddle, Dorchester, Dorset DT2 7HG
(01305 848524)

201

CHAPTER FIVE: PURBECK AND SOUTH DORSET

19) Chapman's Pool, Kimmeridge and Swyre Head

Kimmeridge Farmhouse, Kimmeridge, Wareham, Dorset (01929 480990)

20) Dancing Ledge and St Aldhelm's Head

French Grass House, Kingston Road, Worth Matravers, Dorset.
  (01929 439443)

21) Corfe and the Purbeck Hills

Mortons House Hotel, Corfe Castle, Wareham, Dorset (01929 480988)
Bradle Farmhouse, Church Knowle, Corfe Castle, Wareham, Dorset
  (01929 480712)

22) Ballard Down and Godlingston Heath

Bankes Arms Hotel, Manor Road, Studland, Dorset (01929 44225)
Fairfields Hotel, Studland, Dorset (01929 44224)
Knoll House Hotel, Studland, Dorset (01929 44251)
Manor House Hotel, Studland, Dorset (01929 44288)
Studholme Hotel, Ferry Road, Studland, Dorset (01929 44271)
Purbeck Down, Glebe Estate, Studland, Dorset (01929 44257)

23) Durdle Door and Bat's Head

Cromwell House Hotel, Lulworth Cove, Wareham, Dorset
  (01929 41253/41332)
Lulworth Cove Hotel, Lulworth Cove, Wareham, Dorset (01929 41333)
The Old Barn, Lulworth Cove, Wareham, Dorset (01929 41305)
Shirley Hotel, Lulworth Cove, Wareham, Dorset (01929 41358)

24) The Land of the Trumpet Major

Dingle Dell, Osmington, Weymouth, Dorset DT3 6EW (01305 832378)
Rosedale, Osmington, Weymouth, Dorset DT3 6EW (01305 832056)
Selwyns, Puddledock Lane, Sutton Poyntz, Weymouth, Dorset DT3 6LZ (01305
  832239)

25) Portland Bill

The Old Hifh Lighthouse, Portland, Dorset DT5 2JT (01305 822 300)

CHAPTER SIX: WEST DORSET

26) Golden Cap, Stonebarrow and Chardown Hill
  See 28 below

27) Short Walks on the Golden Cap Estate
  See 28 below

28) Thorncombe Beacon, Quarry Hill and Eype Down

Chideock House Hotel, Chideock, Bridport, Dorset DT6 6HN (01297 89242)
Doghouse Farm, Chideock, Bridport, Dorset DT6 6HY (01297 89208)
Fernhill Hotel, Charmouth, Dorset DT6 6BX (01297 560492)
Newlands Hotel, Stonebarrow Lane, Charmouth, Dorset DT6 6RA
  (01297 560212)

Hensleigh Hotel, Lower Sea Lane, Charmouth, Dorset DT6 6LW
(01297 560830)
Eype's Mouth Hotel, Eype, Bridport, Dorset DT6 6AL (01308 423300)

29) The Lyme Regis Undercliff Forest and 30) The Lim Valley

Buena Vista Hotel, Pound Street, Lyme Regis, Dorset DT7 3HX
(01297 442494)
Springfield, Woodmead Road, Lyme Regis, Dorset DT7 3LJ (01297 443409)
Southernhaye, Pound Street, Lyme Regis, Dorset DT7 3HZ (01297 442077)
Quambi, Charmouth Road, Lyme Regis, Dorset DT7 3DP (01297 443117)
The White House, 47 Silver Street, Lyme Regis, Dorset DT7 3HR
(01297 443420)

31) Marshwood Vale and Hardown Hill

Cardsmill Farmhouse, Whitchurch Canonicorum, Bridport, Dorset DT6 6RP
(01297 89375)

32) Beaminster, Netherbury and Gerrard's Hill

Kitwhistle Farm, Beaminster Down, Beaminster, Dorset DT8 3SG
(GR 005033) (01308 862458)
Higher Langdon Farm, Beaminster, Dorset DT8 3NN (01308 862537)
The Manor House, Beaminster, Dorset DT8 3AE (01308 862311)
The Old Vicarage, 1 Clay Lane, Beaminster, Dorset DT8 3BU
(01308 863200)
Jenny Wrens, 1 Hogshill Street, Beaminster, Dorset DT8 3AE
(01308 862814)
Grey Cottage, The Green, Beaminster, Dorset DT8 3SD (01308 862284)
Daniels House, 29 Hogshill Street, Beaminster, Dorset DT8 3AG
(01308 862635)
Hill Farm, South Perrott, Beaminster, Dorset DT8 3HS (01935 891224)

33) Pilsdon Pen and Lewesdon Hill

Burstock Grange, Broadwindsor, Beaminster, Dorset DT8 3LL
(01308 868527)
Hursey Farm, Broadwindsor, Beaminster, Dorset DT8 3LN (01308 868045)

34) The Bride Valley and the Downs

Gorwell Farm, Abbotsbury, Weymouth, Dorset DT3 4JX (GR 575871) (01305 871401)

35) Abbotsbury and Puncknowle

Swan Lodge, Abbotsbury, Weymouth, Dorset DT3 4JL (01305 871249)
Linton Cottage, Abbotsbury, Weymouth, Dorset DT3 4JL (01305 871339)
The Crown Inn, Puncknowle, Dorchester, Dorset DT2 9BN (01308 897711)
Burwell Cottage, Puncknowle, Dorchester, Dorset DT2 9BN (01308 897716) (perfect
old self-catering cottage adjacent to the Crown, belonging to author's aunt - an
ideal walking base)
The Manor Hotel, West Bexington, Dorchester, Dorset DT2 9DF
(01308 897616)
Mod-na-Mor, Beach Road, West Bexington, Dorchester, Dorset DT2 9DG (01308
898181)

Chesil Coppice, West Bexington, Dorchester, Dorset DT2 9DD
(01308 897351)

36) Evershot and the Melburys

The Acorn Inn Hotel, Evershot, Dorchester, Dorset DT2 0JW (01935 83228)
Rectory House Hotel, Evershot, Dorchester, Dorset DT2 0JW
(01935 83273)
Summer Lodge Hotel, Evershot, Dorchester, Dorset DT2 0JR
(01935 83424)
Oak House, Melbury Osmond, Dorchester, Dorset DT2 0ND (01935 83468)
Frampton Farm, Leigh, Sherborne, Dorset DT9 6HJ (01935 872269)
Huntsbridge Farm, Leigh, Sherborne, Dorset DT9 6JA (01935 872150)
(Leigh is 2 miles north-east of Melbury Bubb)
Sydney Farm, Higher Halstock, Yeovil, Somerset BA22 9QY (01935 891249)
Halstock Mill, Halstock, Yeovil, Somerset BA22 9SJ (01935 891278) - Halstock (GR
5408) is half a mile west of Clarkham Cross

37) Askerswell, Powerstock Common and Eggardon Hill

The Marquis of Lorne (pub), Nettlecombe, Bridport, Dorset DT6 3SY
(01308 485236)
Oakleigh House, Powerstock, Bridport, Dorset DT6 3TE (01308 485526)

38) Kingcombe and the Hooke Valley

Watermeadow House, Hooke, Beaminster, Dorset DT8 3PD (01308 862619)
Kitwhistle Farm, Beaminster Down, Beaminster, Dorset DT8 3SG
(GR 005033) (01308 862458)

39) Bronkham Hill, Corton and the Hardy Monument

Millmead Country House Hotel, Goose Hill, Portesham, Weymouth, Dorset (01305
871432)

Campsites in Dorset

Unlike other forms of accommodation, campsites are marked on the OS map. I
recommend this as the best way of finding a campsite in the location you want.
Freshwater Holiday Park, Burton Bradstock, Bridport, Dorset DT6 4PT (01308 897317,
fax 897336)
Wood Farm, Axminster Road, Charmouth, Dorset DT6 6BT (01297 60697/560697)
Golden Cap Holiday Park, Seatown, Chideock, Bridport, Dorset DT6 6JX (01308
422139)
Highlands End Farm, Eype, Bridport, Dorset DT6 6AR (01308 422139)
Eype House, Eype, Bridport, Dorset DT6 6AL (01308 424903)
Binghams Farm, Melplash, Bridport, Dorset DT6 3TT (01308 488234)
Westhayes Caravan Park, Rousdon, Lyme Regis, Dorset DT7 3RD
(01297 23456) (also takes tents)
Bagwell Farm, Chickerell, Weymouth, Dorset DT3 4EA (01305 782575)
The Ranch House, Osmington Mills, Weymouth, Dorset DT3 6HB
(01305 832311)
Pebble Bank Caravan Park, 90 Camp Road, Wyke Regis, Weymouth, Dorset DT4 9HF
(01305 774844) (also takes tents)
Sandyholme Holiday Park, Moreton Road, Owermoigne, Dorchester, Dorset (01305
852677)

Giants Head Campsite (GR 675029), Dorchester, Dorset DT2 7TR
(01300 341242)
The Inside Park, Middle Farm House, Blandford Forum, Dorset DT11 0HG (01258
453719, fax 454026)
Thorngrove Centre, Common Mead Lane, Gillingham, Dorset SP8 4RE (01747
822242; evenings and weekends 825384)
Shaftesbury Football Club, Coppice St, Shaftesbury, Dorset (01747 53990 -club;
daytime 824767 or 53648)
Beacon Hill Touring Park (GR 975944), Poole, Dorset (01202 631631)

USEFUL ADDRESSES AND TELEPHONE NUMBERS

Tourist Information Centres in Dorset
The following offices can send up-to-date information on accommodation in their local
area. Bed and breakfast can also be booked through them.

Christchurch	(01202 471780)
Bournemouth	(01202 789789)
Blandford Forum	(01258 454770)
Dorchester	(01305 267992)
Poole	(01202 673322)
Portland	(01305 823406)
Shaftesbury	(01747 53514)
Sherborne	(01935 815341)
Swanage	(01929 422885)
Wareham	(01929 552740)
Weymouth	(01305 772444)
Wimborne	(01202 886116)

Dorset Tourism, 20-22 Christchurch Road, Bournemouth, Dorset BH1 3NL (01202
221001/2 fax 01202 221200)

Rights of Way Section, Transport and Engineering Department, County Hall, Dorchester,
Dorset DT1 1XJ

Ramblers' Association (Dorset area secretary): Mr B.Panton, 5 Nicholas Gardens,
Ensbury Park, Bournemouth, Dorset BH10 4BA (01202 526954)

The Kingcombe Centre, Lower Kingcombe, Toller Porcorum, Dorchester, Dorset DT2
0EQ (01300 320684)

BIBLIOGRAPHY

The Making of the English Landscape: Dorset, Christopher Taylor (Hodder & Stoughton
1970). More than worth the hunt in libraries and second hand bookshops, this is
a learned and highly readable discourse on man's impact on the post glacial
landscape of the county.

The Faces of Britain: English Downland, H.J.Massingham (Batsford 1936) One of those
myriad excellent books which are researched at great length, written, published
and never re-issued, whilst mindless hyped pulp goes on and on. This has an

excellent chapter on Dorset and is an informative and enjoyable discourse on England's chalk country.

The Making of the English Landscape, Professor W.G.Hoskins (Hodder & Stoughton 1955, also Penguin 1985).

The Place-Names of Dorset (English Place Name Society/Cambridge University Press 1977, School of English Studies, The University of Nottingham). Published in several volumes.

Dorset Place Names - their origins and meanings, A.D.Mills (Roy Gasson Associates, 1968, 18 Ashdene Close, Wimborne, BH21 1TQ). An endlessly fascinating reference work - a distillation of above.

The Concise Oxford Dictionary of English Place Names, Eilert Ekwall (OUP).

Bound to the Soil - A Social History of Dorset 1750-1918, Barbara Kerr (John Baker 1968). Examines selected parishes in the county in great detail. To put the Tolpuddle Martyrs into perspective I very much recommend her chapter on the Blackmore Vale and agricultural riots of 1830.

Old Dorset, M.B.Weinstock (David & Charles 1967). A highly readable discourse on random aspects of the county's history from the middle of the eighteenth century onwards.

Wildlife Walks of Britain, Valerie Russell (Grafton). This details two such in the county, both on Purbeck, at Studland and Kimmeridge. There is a lot of good information as to what can be discovered at these sites.

The Hardy Guides, Harmann Lea (Penguin 1986 - two volumes). Lea was a pioneering photographer and the touring companion of Hardy. This is a posthumous gathering of his writings and photographs.

Thomas Hardy's England, Jo Draper, edited and introduced by John Fowles (Jonathan Cape 1984). Fine text remarkably illustrated with Lea's original photographs taken between 1880 and 1910, using live models evoking the early nineteenth century.

Hardy's Wessex Location, F.P.Pitfield (Dorset Publishing Company). There seems to be a sizeable industry in producing books on Hardy's locations; I have included this one because it includes some worthwhile recent research and is laid out in such a way as to appeal to the idle browser as much as to the intense expert.

The Landscape of Thomas Hardy, Denys Kay Robinson (Webb and Bower, 9 Colleton Crescent, Exeter EX2 4BY). With informative, well researched text, sketch maps and fine photographs by Simon McBride, this succeeds both as a reference book and a coffee-table book.

Dorset from the Air, Christopher Chaplin (The Dovecot Press, Wimborne). Informative and attractive.

Dorset, Frank R.Heath (Methuen 1905 & 1908). Part of "The Little Guides" series - fascinating as a guide to the county at the time.

The Dorset Village Book, Harry Ashley (Countryside Books, first published 1984 and several times since).

A Brief History of Dorset, Cecil N.Cullingford (Phillimore 1980). Informative, well illustrated and highly readable - recommended.

Dorset - City and County History Series, J.H.Bettey (David & Charles).

Unknown Dorset, Donald Maxwell (Bodley Head 1927). The author has written "unknown" counties. It is a pleasant portrait of the county between the wars.

Dorset - "The King's England" series, Arthur Mee (Hodder and Stoughton 1939). A good guidebook of its day.

Hidden Dorset, various contributors (Dorset Federation of Women's Institutes and Countryside Books). A distillation of long memories county-wide - a delight.

Dorset Curiosities, George Osborn (Dovecot Press). Eccentric and fascinating.

Dorset Villages, Roland Gant (Robert Hale 1980). A personal view, well researched and written.

Wessex Has Their Bones, Douglas Greenwood (Gasson Associates, 18 Ashdene Close, Wimborne BH21 1TQ). A necrophile's Who's Who to the county - it contains details of the resting places of a great number of notables. It is well worth checking to see if your walk takes you past any.

Literary Dorset, Rodney Legg (Dorset Publishing Company, North Street, Wincanton, Somerset BA9 9AT). A miniature encyclopedia of authors and locations from a prolific and popular local author.

The Dorset and Somerset Rebellion, K.Merle Chatsfield (Dorset Publishing Company). A fine pocket-sized history of local events of the ill-fated 1685 Monmouth rebellion against the unpopular James II.

A Dorset Camera, David Burnett (Dovecot Press). My walks take you past a number of spots shown, before 1914; this is a fascinating historical document and contains some superb photographs.

The Wild Flowers of Dorset, Stuart Roberts - no relation (Dovecot Press). Well researched and presented.

The Stour Valley Path, Edward R.Griffiths (Green Fields Books, 13 Dalewood Avenue, Bear Cross, Bournemouth BH11 9NR). Who can fail to like a guidebook that introduces itself by claiming that it "evokes the spirit of English Arcadia"?
In the years before writing this book I have learnt a great deal about the county where I grew up from the pen of Ralph Wightman, any of whose books or articles I recommend.

Moonfleet, J.Meade Falkner. A rattling good tale, perhaps too much used as a school text.

The French Lieutenant's Woman, John Fowles. This is a superb novel which can scarcely be recommended too highly. It was written and largely set in Lyme Regis. The film (starring Jeremy Irons and Merryl Streep) was largely shot in the town as well.

All of Thomas Hardy's major works are continually in print in various editions. Unbeatable value for money are the Wordsworth Classics editions, currently 99 pence a copy. These are reprints of old editions. If you want to enjoy Hardy on video, in my opinion the best film of his novels is *Far From the Madding Crowd,* circa 1969, starring Julie Christie, Alan Bates and Peter Finch. It is quite excellent. Also available are Roman Polanski's *Tess* (with Natassia Kinski) and the serial production of *Jude the Obscure* (with Robert Powell).

* * *

Printed by CARNMOR PRINT & DESIGN
95-97 LONDON ROAD, PRESTON, LANCASHIRE, UK.